The Rose Bible

THE ROSE BIBLE

Rayford Clayton Reddell

PHOTOGRAPHS BY *Robert Galyean*

CHRONICLE BOOKS

SAN FRANCISCO

ACKNOWLEDGMENTS

This book is dedicated to Bob Galyean, not simply because of his splendid photographs, but because I never would have written it without him. The rose and fragrance madness at Garden Valley Ranch has grown beyond my imagination; thankfully not beyond his.

I also owe thanks to the following:

Martha Stewart, for writing such a fine foreword and for her staunch support.

Tom Carruth, that walking computer software package of rose lineage.

My rosebuddies listed in Chapter 15, especially Dan Bifano, who acts like he's my agent.

To the excellent advice from gifted rosarians: Keith Zary, Miriam Wilkins, Dennison Morey, and Tommy Cairns.

To those generous gardeners who let us photograph their wonderful roses—Kay Woods, Sally Jordan, Denise Hale, John Dallas, Katie Trefethen, Peter Newton, and, most of all, Gerd Perkins for allowing us to photograph at her spectacular Plumpton Place in East Sussex, England.

To Bill Radler for the photographs of winter protection of rosebushes.

To the gardeners at Sissinghurst, St. Albans, Mottisfont, and Castle Howard in England; Bois de Bologne and Rosarie de l'Hay just outside Paris; Spain's Park Retiro and Generalife in the Alhambra; the Edinburgh botanical gardens; Washington Park in Portland; the Huntington Gardens in Pasadena; and the majestic Filoli gardens in Woodside, California.

To the magnificent staff at Garden Valley Ranch.

Printed in Hong Kong

Distributed in Canada by Raincoast Books
8680 Cambie Street
Vancouver, British Columbia V6P 6M9

10 9 8 7 6 5 4 3 2 1

Chronicle Books
85 Second Street
San Francisco, California 94105

www.chroniclebooks.com

Interior design by John Fontana
Cover design by Pamela Geismar

Library of Congress Cataloging-in-Publication Data:
Reddell, Rayford Clayton.
The rose bible / by Rayford C. Reddell : photography by Robert
    Galyean.
    p.   cm.
    Originally published: 1st ed. New York : Harmony Books,
c1994.
    Includes index.
    ISBN 0-8118-2159-5
    1. Rose Culture. 2. Roses. I. Title.
    SB411.R395   1998
    635.9'337347—dc21   98-6832
                             CIP

CONTENTS

FOREWORD

About twenty-two years ago, I received a most beautiful Mother's Day present from my husband and young daughter—twelve Hybrid Tea rosebushes. Planted in my very first rose garden, with santolina edges and corners of English boxwood, this simple rectangular piece of ground was transformed within a month into the most fragrant and beautiful spot in my two-acre garden. I started to love roses, not only for their beauty and fragrance, but also because of their growing habits and ease with which they seemed to flourish in my Connecticut landscape. And I still had not even heard about "Old" roses, Shrub roses, Bourbons, Centifolias, and Hybrid Perpetuals.

Within the next ten years I learned much more about the species, cultivars, and varieties of the immense rose genus, and I formulated within my own personal experience a group of favorites, which I planted in profusion in my Westport garden. I constructed trellises like those found at Monet's garden in Giverny and covered them with beautiful, prolific climbers like 'Alchymist' and 'Paul Lede' and 'Shot Silk' and 'Félicité et Perpétue'. I learned how to care for each bush, shrub, and climber, and waited patiently for the profusion of blooms each June, and for the second flowering late in the summer.

I started noticing rose gardens everywhere and ruthlessly critiqued mine against them. I laughed at my attempts at rose gardening after I witnessed the famous English gardens—Mottisfont Abbey, Hidcote, and Upton House to name a few. After some trips to California, I wondered how I ever fancied myself a rose gardener when what I witnessed there was so superior to what I was able to grow in Connecticut.

More studying and experimenting resulted in modest success. The climbers started to really climb after some serious doses of fish emulsion, manure, and compost. Winter wrappings secured a higher percentage of healthy bushes after severe winters, and spring doses of Epsom salts created better foliage and more blooms.

Encouraged, I planned my ultimate rose garden in East Hampton, a one-acre architecturally structured garden of trellises, tuteurs, arches, and pillars in which more than six hundred different types of Old varieties were planted. Most thrived and grew well and rather quickly. Compared to my attempts in Connecticut, the East Hampton roses seemed healthier, faster growing, and more secure.

My travels continue to take me abroad, often to gaze upon rose gardens of great beauty and inspiration. On a trip two years ago to California, to a small town called Petaluma, friends took me to the fabled home and gardens of Ray Reddell. I had heard much about his roses, many professionally grown for the cut-flower market. I had seen arrangements and wedding bouquets created from his glorious blooms and did not dare contemplate the gardens from which they came, being faint with envy. Nothing prepared me for the utter profusion of blooms in Petaluma, the size of the bushes, the thickness of the canes, the size of the flowers, and the perfume of the place. I fell in love with roses all over again, vowing to become a better grower myself, a better student of all the amazing roses of the world. I ferreted out every book I could find that would help me with the task of growing roses like Ray's.

Now I have my own Ray Reddell book, full of his inspired wisdom and knowledge. His dedication toward fine rose growing, and his insistence that most of us can grow and nurture beautiful roses, is invaluable encouragement to all of us. Thank you so very much, Ray.

Martha Stewart

PREFACE

When I wrote *Growing Good Roses*, I declared open love for Modern Roses. Not only was I hopelessly smitten by roses that bloomed repeatedly from Mother's Day to Halloween, I became so rose-struck that I wasn't satisfied until I went commercial and began growing roses for the sale of their irresistible blossoms.

Once I had my rose ranch with 4,000 bushes blooming their heads off for more than half the year, I decided to find out for myself why everyone fussed so over Old garden roses. Although I didn't hold great expectations for their marketability as cut flowers, I planted 40 shrubs of Old Roses that enthusiasts agreed were picks of the litter.

Just as I predicted, my Old Roses proved a flop at the flower market. First, their stems were short compared with the 3-footers I cut from my Modern varieties. Then, their blooms came all at once, making it impossible to plan around their flushes.

Still, I noticed certain enviable characteristics. Because I had been assured that these varieties needed no pampering, I gave them none. I fed them only with leftover fertilizers, and I didn't spray them with those chemicals I dared not withhold from my Modern Roses. In spite of my neglect, my Old Roses didn't just grow, they flourished, and each successive season brought more blossoms than I had imagined possible.

One day, a fine gardener whose opinions I respect stopped by for lunch. "You know, Ray," she said, "you've simply developed tunnel vision where roses are concerned. If a bush doesn't bloom all summer, you don't think it's worth the dirt it's planted in." Although her frank words startled me, I snapped to attention when she asked what it would take to get my precious wisteria, lilacs, bearded irises, or daphne away from me.

"Oh, something like the marines," I answered truthfully.

"Well, there you are," she said, smiling smugly over her round-one victory, "you simply have to stop comparing Old Roses with their Modern upstarts, and begin treasuring them the way you do other one-time bloomers."

She had a point. "Still," I said, "they won't sell at the flower market."

"Oh, to hell with the flower market," she retorted. "Try landscaping a few dowagers in that fragrant garden of yours and see how unwillingly you'd turn loose of them after two years."

As you've guessed, she was proved correct, I wrong. I couldn't dig holes fast enough to accommodate 100 new (to me) Old Roses. Next, of course, I realized that my quest had only just begun. As soon as I came to admire the parents of my beloved Modern Roses, I yearned to cultivate their grandparents.

Now I grow roses from the entire genus—from species roses that flourished long before man to roses yet to bloom. Undoubtedly, some rosarians will surely criticize how I've traced the development of the genus *Rosa*. "Too simplified," I can already hear my peers saying, "it just wasn't that easy." My response: Neither must it be complicated; in fact, as I see it, the evolution of the genus *Rosa* is simple.

First, there were species roses. Then the Renaissance came along and hybrids emerged. Next, free-flowering varieties from the Orient reached Europe, and eventually nineteenth-century breeders developed the Modern Rose. If you grasp this four-step evolution, the rest is easy—roses that no one is certain where to rightfully place in history fall into order.

Although no disclaimers are required for this history lesson, I offer certain caveats where rose culture is concerned. For instance, no rosarian is an expert on the behavior of rose varieties the world over, only on those where he or she gardens.

My roses and I reside in a temperate climate, Zone 9 according to the USDA. In weather terms, that means that winter temperatures rarely dip below 20 degrees F.; practically speaking, it means that I can grow any rose I like without fear of losing it to winter. Because my zonal microclimate also dictates that summers aren't scorchers, the roses that perform best for me are Modern varieties with fewer than 40 petals and Heirloom Roses that don't mind maturing their petal-packed blossoms slowly.

Roses that grow well in Petaluma, California, behave as though they were hybridized just for us. Those that don't— well, we make do, assuming the variety appeals so strongly that we'll put up with it even though we've witnessed its true glories elsewhere. In New Zealand, for example, I've seen 'Dainty Bess', the fabulous five-petaled Hybrid Tea, that made me cringe with envy. In the next bed, however, I saw blossoms from the majestic 'Queen Elizabeth' rose that were a joke compared with mine. At David Austin's garden in Albrighton, England, I spotted English Roses that made me eat my heart out, but I also found Modern Roses that looked diminutive next to mine. I ask friends in Santa Barbara, California, not to call each April to tell me about their magnificent first flush of roses— I have another month to go (rosebuddies in Wisconsin have yet another six weeks). Then there are the gardens I visit in chilly Vermont where no rose varieties younger than 300 years old are grown—anything more modern freezes to the ground.

To help readers growing roses where climate variances such as these occur, I've solicited the help of fine rosarians from growing areas markedly different from my own—deep freeze, Deep South, boggy Florida, arid Arizona, southern California. Their collective advice is offered in chapter 15 and should be taken into account if you grow roses in climates similar to theirs.

Even more important, you must learn what's happening with roses as close to your home as possible. In rosedom, nothing beats local talent. In fact, rely on no source other than one published by your local rose society for how tall certain rosebushes grow or how bountifully they bloom. What shines in Portland, Oregon, may sulk in Portland, Maine, and vice versa.

Finally, this book makes no claim to mentioning more than a small portion of roses already recorded. Current rose references list more than 16,000 entries. Not all of these are in commerce, of course, and an even larger number aren't worth considering for one reason or another.

Readers will note that certain roses are pictured but not described in the text. That is because these varieties are either unproved, not readily commercially available, or deserving of no more verbiage than their caption affords.

My hope, obviously, is that roses will be grown by everyone—those who refuse to pamper them and those who can't pamper them enough; rosarians single-minded in their devotion to the Moderns and those addicted to Heirlooms; people who love blossoms the size of cabbages and those who admire only microminis; gardeners hooked on every color but blue and gardeners devoted solely to the "red, red rose." There's a rose for everyone.

ONE

Evolution of the Species: B.C. to the Renaissance

Argument still rages over the historical progression of the genus *Rosa*. Archaeologists disagree about the age of the genus, although fossil evidence in Colorado and Oregon suggests that roses flourished at least 32 million years ago.

Botanists quarrel over how many species of roses ever existed, but they agree that today there are surely between 100 and 200 species, depending on how many characteristics are required to separate one species from another. Plantsmen quibble over when and where roses first appeared in gardens, although most concur that cultivation probably began in China some 5,000 years ago. In spite of such petty arguments, devotees of rose lore agree that deciduous roses of bushy, trailing, or climbing habits grew throughout the Northern Hemisphere long before *Homo sapiens* existed. No one, of course, is certain how roses developed in the first place, but it's easy to imagine that even the earliest of species were so pleasant that people moved them into areas where they hadn't existed before, thereby setting the stage for natural mutations.

Early rose species blossomed with single flowers of five (rarely four) petals. Because these "single" blossoms were

R. EGLANTERIA, *also known as the sweetbrier rose, is a beauty among species roses. Mature plants are majestic, showered with pretty pink blossoms, and swathed in tough foliage that smells precisely like green apples.*

brightly colored and scented, they attracted insects to their readily accessible, fertile pollen. These wild roses further ensured their endurance by developing prickly thorns to protect themselves from predators.

Although it's difficult to imagine that even the earliest of roses weren't appreciated for their beauty and fragrance, it seems that their edible and medicinal properties were once valued more than aesthetics. Blossoms were sweet to taste, tender young shoots were deliciously nutty, and hips (the rose's fleshy fruit) were nourishing.

These early wild roses weren't named, of course; that was not to occur until Carolus Linnaeus and his followers began making sense of prehistoric botanical mishmash. Keep this in mind when you read that a rose thought to have existed in, say, China or the Himalayas some 3,000 years ago made its official debut in the late eighteenth century. The date of introduction is simply the first time that botanists agreed on suitable nomenclature.

The ancient roses are conveniently divided into four groups by their place of origin—Europe, America, the Middle East, and Oriental Asia. The 24 roses I discuss from these four groups hardly exhaust the formidable list of known species. They

R. **HELENAE,** *technically a "near species," produces scads of fragrant white flowers in weighty sprays, followed by a hefty crop of scarlet oblong hips. As seen here, R. Helenae makes a smashing companion for* Clematis x Durandii.

are, however, those roses that experts agree laid the foundation for all that followed.

EUROPEAN SPECIES

R. ARVENSIS, commonly known as the field rose, undoubtedly laid the footwork for many creepers that followed. Bushes have thin, dark wood that hovers close to the ground or rambles over supports to 20 feet. Blossoms are pure white and medium-sized and have ample, flashy, golden anthers.

R. CANINA, or the dog rose, is the most common wild rose native to Europe. Although it's usually restricted to fields and orchards because of its gangly growth to 10 feet, bushes produce lovely, sweetly scented foliage, along with flowers that are typically pale pink but sometimes white. Orange-red hips that shower the plants in the fall are treasured as a rich source of vitamin C and also for making flavorful wine. Until the early 1900s, *R. canina* was a favored choice for rootstock, onto which hybrids were budded.

R. EGLANTERIA, the sweet briar or eglantine rose, is similar in appearance to *R. canina* in that its blossoms are single and blush pink, but it's treasured for its scented foliage (thought to smell like green apples), which is actually more strongly perfumed than its blossoms. Left to their own devices, bushes can grow to 15 feet and produce scads of hips in the fall that persist well into winter. If confined to a garden, plants should be pruned to encourage new growth, since

perfume is concentrated in young tips.

R. PIMPINELLIFOLIA, the burnet or Scotch briar rose, is an easily grown species, for it will thrive in most soils, particularly sandy ones. Blossoms that appear in spring are creamy white with pronounced stamens. Foliage is small; stems have closely set, prickly thorns; and hips are currantlike and almost black. This species boasts a host of hybrids, many of which are perpetual flowering.

R. VILLOSA, native throughout Europe and also known as the apple rose, develops into a manageable bush with grayish, downy foliage that many admirers believe smells like ripe apples. Clear pink, fragrant flowers are secondary to large, apple-shaped, crimson hips that are symmetrically covered with bristles.

AMERICAN SPECIES

These seven natives to America flower later in summer than do their European cousins, and with less variation in color. They have, however, an enviable trait in that their foliage turns various autumnal shades each fall—yellow, orange, scarlet, or burgundy.

R. BLANDA has a host of nicknames —Hudson Bay rose, Labrador rose, meadow rose, and smooth rose. In many ways, this species is similar to the European *R. canina*, except that it is less vigorous (growing usually to only 5 feet), its blossoms are darker pink, and hips are pear-shaped rather than globular.

R. CAROLINA, like *R. blanda*, is relatively thornless. Bushes are as wide as they

are tall, usually to 3 feet, and are covered in summer with single, soft pink, lightly fragrant blossoms. *R. carolina* has a splendid natural hybrid, *R. carolina plena*, which, although shorter than its predecessor, produces charming, clear pink flowers that are double rather than five-petaled.

R. FOLIOLOSA is virtually thornless. Although it is tolerant of wet growing areas, it differs from similar American species in that its foliage is curiously elongated and its flowers have petals of unequal size.

R. NITIDA makes a short shrub with thin stems and dainty foliage that turns crimson in fall. Flowers are deep pink, single, and small (but plentiful), and hips are tiny, oval, and covered with bristles. *R. nitida* is widely distributed over Canada and the United States.

R. PALUSTRIS is surely in the ancestry of the majority of rose hybrids that tolerate soggy growing conditions. Also known as the swamp rose, *R. palustris* will thrive even in a bog, producing ample mid- to dark green foliage on an upright 4-foot bush. Blossoms are single and dark pink and appear intermittently throughout summer. After flowering, oval hips form at the tips of reddish stems.

R. SETIGERA, or the prairie rose, grows wider than it does tall. Although bushes may reach 5 feet in height, their arching, languid branches stretch to more than 6 feet. Flowers that appear in clusters are single, deep pink, and followed by small, red, globular hips.

R. VIRGINIANA makes an upright 5-foot

R. CALIFORNICA *is known as a "variable" species rose because what's a species in one part of the world is considered an "improved strain" elsewhere. Mid- to light pink, 1½-inch, five-petaled flowers are formed in large clusters. Because its moderate growth is easily trained, R. californica makes a fine companion for small trees.*

R. GLAUCA *is often grown for its foliage alone, which takes on distinct reddish overtones as each season progresses. The flowers are special, too, particularly when the five fresh petals glow pink except for a white halo around crisp yellow stamens.*

R. CAROLINA GRANDIFLORA, *another "near species," blossoms with particularly cheerful two-inch bright pink flowers. Foliage is not only lush, but leaves are also noticeably larger than those of true species roses.*

bush fully clothed in light green, glossy leaves. Blossoms are single, clear pink, and fragrant and have bright yellow stamens. Fruits are orange, round, and fat and persist on plants well into winter.

MIDDLE EASTERN SPECIES

The contribution of roses native to no other area is as easy to pinpoint as that of roses from the Middle East: color—specifically, yellow. Wild roses from Afghanistan and Southwest Asia blossomed in colors from pale yellow to sulphur, hues that would later figure heavily into hy-

bridizers' pollinating palettes. Yet the gift of yellow to rosedom was a mixed blessing, for the accompanying characteristics of these roses were thoroughly undesirable. First, wild yellow roses were puny in comparison with the vigor of their pink and white cousins. Second, whereas yellow species roses almost always smelled, they didn't always smell good. Finally, these roses were the first to be plagued with the persistent rose affliction we now call blackspot. Still, they *are* yellow.

R. ECAE, native to Afghanistan, makes a small, quite thorny shrub with reddish brown wood and fernlike foliage. Blos-

soms look like buttercups and have pronounced stamens protruding above their rich yellow petals. *R. ecae* is "tender," meaning that it appreciates warm, sheltered growing conditions.

R. FOETIDA, the Austrian briar rose, makes a handsome bush that reaches 8-foot heights, with bright green foliage, chestnut brown stems, and black thorns. Blooms are large and golden yellow with prominent stamens, which are also yellow. *R. foetida* developed a sport (a spontaneous mutation) that has become even more famous than its parent: *R. foetida bicolor,* ubiquitously known as 'Austrian

Copper'. Bushes of 'Austrian Copper' are known for their habit of reverting to the original color of their predecessor, meaning that blossoms of both yellow and eye-blinking copper-orange simultaneously appear on one bush.

R. HEMISPHAERICA, native to Southwest Asia and commonly known as the sulphur rose, is not only richly yellow, its blooms have the added distinction of being double. Bushes grow to be 6 feet tall and are smothered in grayish green foliage. As its common name implies, *R. hemisphaerica* is rather unpleasantly perfumed.

ORIENTAL ASIAN SPECIES

While roses mentioned so far had desirable growth habits or pleasantly colored blossoms, those from Oriental Asia, particularly China, were vital for their ability to bloom repeatedly—a characteristic we now take for granted. The word for this trait is "remontant," which I used to resist because it sounds stiff. But, having tired of restriction to phrases such as "repeat-bloomer" or "recurrent flowering," now "remontant" seems less horticulturally precise. Besides, it captures the trait in a single word.

Because plantsmen weren't always allowed to roam the countryside at will, by the time would-be hybridizers were allowed to take cuttings during the late eighteenth century, many roses had developed natural mutations so similar to the original species that it became impossible in several cases to be certain which

came first. It doesn't matter, of course, except for setting the record straight.

R. BANKSIAE NORMALIS, ironically the last of the four Banksian roses to be introduced to the horticultural world, is considered to be the true species. Two natural mutations, however, are held in higher esteem: *R. banksiae banksiae* and *R. banksiae lutea.*

All Banksian roses have virtually identical mammoth growth habits, with blossoms that smell unmistakably of violets; they differ only in their flowers. *R. banksiae normalis* has quaintly shaped, single white flowers; *R. banksiae lutescens*, single yellow blossoms; *R. banksiae banksiae*, also known as the Lady Banks rose, blossoms with double white clusters; and *R. banksiae lutea*, also double, has butter yellow blooms. Banksias have but one flush of bloom, spectacular in all cases.

R. BRACTEATA is also known as the Macartney rose because Lord Macartney brought it back from a diplomatic visit to China in 1793. Early in the nineteenth century, the species was introduced to America, where it behaved as though it were native there, too, particularly in the southeastern states. Bushes that get to be 8 feet tall and just as wide are most easily grown as climbers. Flowering commences in June and continues intermittently until November. Branches are covered with vicious thorns, but blossoms are remarkably delicate, single, pure white, and fragrant. An early hybrid, *R. bracteata* 'Mermaid', introduced in 1918, has become even more famous, since it, too,

develops into a fountainous plant. Blossoms that shower the bushes throughout summer are fragrant, single, and lemon yellow. Foliage is large, dark green, and practically evergreen.

R. CHINENSIS, the original China or Bengal rose, is shrouded in mystery and conjecture. In fact, there is considerable doubt whether it even exists any longer. Records of early plantsmen give few clues to precise characteristics of the original species, other than that it was said to have been erratic both in growth habits and in color, varying from 4 to 20 feet and from white to red. Although reports of such discrepancies give one pause, it must be remembered that roses from China are notorious for their variable qualities. In any case, experts agree that this chameleonlike species was surely the parent of the vast hybrids introduced from China by the early eighteenth century.

R. LAEVIGATA is similar to *R. bracteata*, except that it blossoms only in spring. Like its cousin, *R. laevigata* has pronounced hooked thorns and flowers that are single, large, and white with lovely golden stamens. Although *R. laevigata* decidedly began its life in China, many people mistakenly believe that it is native to the southern United States, where it is known as the Cherokee rose, because it so deliberately established itself there when introduced in the late eighteenth century.

R. MOSCHATA, the original Musk rose, came dangerously close to extinction. Although it was known that the true Musk rose bloomed in autumn, plantsmen

R. PENDULINA *is obviously so named because of its pendulous hips. When young, hips are dark orange; as they mature, they turn scarlet. Flowers, although predictably pink, are formed in abundant large clusters. R. pendulina has several, virtually indistinguishable, hybrid forms.*

R. SPINOSISSIMA, *in its true species form, produces scads of creamy white flowers with glowing yellow centers. Garden forms are available that blossom with white, yellow, pink, or purple flowers. In all cases, the show is splendid.*

R. PALUSTRIS *is better known as the swamp rose because it actually prefers moist bog to well-drained soil. It also blooms over an extended period compared with that of most species.*

R. FOETIDA *helped bring yellow to rosedom, but it was a mixed blessing—with it came blackspot. If R. foetida's color isn't flashy enough for you, have a look at its bicolored sport, Austrian Copper.*

R. BANKSIAE LUTEA *is a natural mutation of the true species,* R. banksiae normalis, *but it's held in greater esteem because of its lovely color and rambunctious growth. The faint violet perfume is another plus.*

R. MOYESII, *a species rose native to western China, is commercially available in a number of "strains," which are color variations among forms. Whatever their color, all family members produce superb foliage and splendid flagon-shaped hips.*

latched on to natural mutations of the original species and purported them to be *R. moschata*. These pretenders had a lot going for them—besides developing into mammoth bushes, they blossomed with lovely creamy white flowers that smelled deliciously of musk. But their blossoms were long gone by autumn, thereby exposing their pretense. Thanks to Graham Stuart Thomas, the British horticulturist who has set the record straight on many species, the confusion ended in 1963 when he discovered a plant of the true *R. moschata*. Cuttings have since been spread around the world.

In contrast to later hybrids, *R. moschata* is a relatively short climber (to 10 feet) with grayish green, oval foliage and hooked thorns. Flowers, which commence in late summer and continue blooming into fall, are produced in widely spaced clusters that begin life creamy beige but turn white before dropping. If hips are produced at all, they are small and oval.

R. MOYESII has blood red, single flowers and handsome dark green foliage—a striking combination, especially among species roses. Still, the reason this ancient variety is so treasured has nothing to do with color, but rather with the dramatic

fruits that follow flowering. Although the orange hips of *R. moyesii* aren't large, they're reliably produced each year, abundant, pendulous, and shaped like flagons. If you decide to plant this rose, after allowing for a bush that will grow to 10-foot heights with arching branches more than 6 feet long, try to obtain cuttings. Seedlings are often sterile, never producing the famous dramatic hips.

R. MULTIFLORA has been praised as an ideal impenetrable hedge ever since its discovery in eastern Asia during the early nineteenth century. Although its summer flush of bloom is over soon after it begins,

This particular strain of the moyessi *clan,* **R. MOYESSI SUPERBA,** *produces deep rose flowers that fade to mid-pink as they age. The* moyesii *roses, famous for their fertility, are the great-great-grandparents of many modern roses.*

R. SPINOSISSIMA *sometimes produces black hips, but many are dark red; all are globular and are carried along the entire length of spindly but strong stems. Branches of hips are favored holiday decor, and fruit lasts well whether or not stems are in water.*

R. ROXBURGHII *got its nickname of chestnut rose because its prickly buds look like a chestnut burr. The chestnut rose is native to eastern Asia and has one long season of bloom from late spring through mid-summer, followed by a fine crop of hips.*

R. multiflora is as floriferous as any rose, species, or hybrid. Sweetly perfumed blossoms, which are produced on wood grown the previous year, are small and white and appear in clusters, sometimes with more than 100 flowers in a single cluster. When the bush is in full bloom, the abundant flowers entirely conceal light green foliage. Although the bush produces wood that is smooth, its leaves are covered with fine hairs on both sides. Because of its massive root system, *R. multiflora* has long been treasured as understock, onto which other roses are easily budded.

R. RUGOSA is native to China, Japan, and Korea. Records, including drawings, document that *R. rugosa* was cultivated in northern Chinese gardens more than 1,000 years ago. Plants develop into vigorous, hardy shrubs up to 8 feet in height and almost as wide. Blossoms range in color from deep pink to purplish red and continue throughout summer, well into fall. Unlike the yellow stamens customarily found in most species, the stamens of *R. rugosa* are creamy. Foliage is also unmistakable—apple green, corrugated, and tough as leather (virtually impenetrable to blackspot and mildew). Blooms are followed by large, red, tomato-shaped hips of unequal size, reputed to be richer in vitamin C than those of any other rose.

R. WICHURAIANA, an ancient native of China, wasn't introduced to the world at large until 1860. The American firm of Jackson & Perkins welcomed it with open arms and quickly scrambled its pollen to hybridize some of the world's favorite Ramblers, beginning with 'Dorothy Perkins' in 1900. The species is almost evergreen and forms a dense climber or procumbent shrub. Foliage is dark green and glossy, while flowers are single and white and appear in profusion during midsummer. Hips are oval and dark red.

Antique Roses:
The Renaissance to 1799

Roses continued to prosper during ancient times even though flori-culture was considered a trivial pursuit. It seemingly never dawned on anyone (if such a person with time on his hands actually existed) that variations in

early roses might occur if their hips were harvested and the seeds within replanted. Then came the Renaissance, and with it an intense desire for beauty everywhere, even in the garden. Spare time could now be justified for exploring new plant forms, and long-confined secrets of the rose were at last unleashed.

In Gerard's *Herbal,* for example, published in 1597, a mere 14 roses are discussed. Already by 1629, the English botanist John Parkinson mentioned 24 roses in his *Paradisi in Sole Paradisus Terrestris.* When the Dutch and French tried their

hand at breeding, all hell broke loose. By the end of the eighteenth century, there were more than 1,000 varieties of roses. Finally, in the mid-nineteenth century, the true rose revolution began as plantsmen created the modern era of rose hybrids.

For now, we'll stick to the Antiques.

'MARIE LOUISE' produces incandescent pink flowers so large that they weigh down the tips of the stems that carry them. No matter; you'll gladly lift their nodding heads to enjoy their sumptuous perfume. Petals swirl through several patterns before they finally quarter themselves.

'BELLE DE CRÉCY' *is a beloved Gallica packed with perfume. Its petals undergo a wondrous change—from cerise to violet to mauve. The stems on which blooms appear are practically thornless.*

'DUCHESSE DE MONTEBELLO', *in most gardens, is the first Gallica to bloom. Fully petaled blossoms mature into fragrant, open cups. Many rosarians believe that the Duchesse should be classified as a Hybrid China. Personally, I don't care, as long as I can grow her.*

'CAMAIEUX' *is the queen of striped roses. Not only are her creamy white petals madly splashed crimson, then purple, then lilac, but they never lose fragrance as they age. The bushes on which blooms appear are winning, too.*

The roses labeled Antique are those that established themselves as classes prior to the end of the eighteenth century: Gallicas, Damasks, Albas, Centifolias, and Mosses. Although each family distinguishes itself from others, all members share certain similarities.

First, Antique Roses have only one period of bloom—a characteristic some people consider disadvantageous. Keep in mind, however, that many of these roses produce as many flowers in a single blooming season as do their repeat-blooming grandchildren throughout the year; their blossoms are merely restricted to one flush.

Second, roses from these families mature into shrubs rather than bushes. Although there is considerable variation even within classes, the average shrub gets to be 5 feet tall and about half as wide.

Third, Antique Roses are revered for their mature blooms rather than for their buds. In spite of the fact that the buds of many of these fine Old Roses are charming, they more often look cuppy rather than elegant. During bud development, petals appear curiously twisted or trapped against their neighbors, causing one to fret that nothing spectacular will ever occur. In fact, however, it is the incredible array of forms that mature blossoms assume that make Antique Roses so fascinating. They may, of course, remain cupped, but more often blossoms flatten into complex patterns as they swirl or quarter their petals. Some continue to grow by reflexing into a dome. Others conclude by revealing clusters of stamens or button eyes in their centers. However they finish their outrageous show, blossoms of Antique Roses are delightful to watch mature.

Compared with Modern Roses, members of these families bloom in restricted colors. Pink, of course, is the most common color in all rosedom, and more varieties in these families are pink than any other color. Several, however, are white, mauve, maroon, or purple. Yellows are few, as are true reds.

Finally, Antique Roses are much less finicky than their Modern offspring. Not only are they comparatively disease resistant (except for inevitable mildew), roses in these families aren't fussy about the soil in which they grow. In fact, many experts recommend no additives while planting, insisting instead that shrubs acclimate themselves to the soil in which their roots are buried. These same "grow-or-die" gardeners endorse no fertilizers or chemical sprays.

The five families of Antique Roses are presented here as they occurred historically, not by their assumed importance.

GALLICAS

The Gallicas are the oldest of all Antique garden roses; they are also the most highly developed (only about 50 hybrids are now in general cultivation, but there once were more than 900 named varieties). Besides the development of their own prodigious family, Gallicas figure prominently in the ancestry of the other four classes of Antique Roses. Early records and paintings prove that the Greeks and Romans were fond of Gallica roses long before the French gave the family its name.

Although there are a few soft pinks, most Gallicas blossom in strong colors— deep pink, purple, violet, and mauve, with crimson shadings in between. Many varieties are dramatically striped or mottled; almost all are fragrant.

Two dozen Gallicas seem to have best stood the test of time:

ALAIN BLANCHARD is officially classified as semidouble, but fully open blooms appear single. Fragrant, purplish crimson petals encircling prominent golden stamens take on a pronounced mottled look as they age. Bushes are thorny, are well clothed in mid-green foliage, and grow to 4-foot heights with about as much girth.

ANAÏS SÉGALES is not only free flowering, but its sweetly scented blooms are exquisitely formed, almost as though each one were hand-groomed. Blossoms start out reddish mauve but end up lilac-pink with a dead-center green button eye. Bushes are low growing, with arching canes and small, light green foliage.

ANTONIA D'ORMOIS is faithfully included in collections of Gallica roses because it is the last member of the family to bloom. Blush pink blossoms fading to white on their petals' edges are fully double and nicely perfumed.

'**HIPPOLYTE**' *produces violet-colored blossoms on nodding, thick, almost thornless stems. Foliage is particularly smooth for a Gallica, while bushes are notably vigorous (to 6 feet) and smothered in small, dark green foliage that has no time for disease. Fat, compact buds mature into buxom blossoms.*

'**TUSCANY**' *has vivid maroon to crimson petals and golden stamens. Its foliage, as you see, is no stranger to blackspot. 'Tuscany Superb', developed later, is an improvement in every way.*

'**OFFICINALIS**', *while known as the apothecary's rose, was praised more highly for its medicinal qualities than for its contribution to the garden. Now, 'Officinalis' is back in the landscape, where, properly cultivated, it often serves as a ground cover.*

If flower perfection appeals to you, by all means consider **'ANAÏS SÉGALES'**; *mature blossoms actually appear to be handcrafted. If color change is your thing, 'Ségales' also fills the bill—from reddish mauve to lilac-pink.*

'ALAIN BLANCHARD' *is a rose of choice for those gardeners who like petals with a mottled look. Purplish crimson petals may be uniform in color at first, but they take on pronounced mottling as they age. They're fragrant from start to finish.*

'GEORGES VIBERT' *reminds many people of a carnation because each of its flowers is about the same size and shape of a carnation, and also similarly striped. But 'Vibert' is a rose all right, and a particularly thorny one at that.*

ASSEMBLAGE DES BEAUTÉS freely flowers with intensely fragrant blossoms of cherry red, crammed full of petals. As blooms age, they take on a purple cast and reflex into a ball just before they reveal a tiny, green, button-eyed center. Foliage is small and bright green and smothers a relatively thornless bush.

BELLE DE CRÉCY is a classic Gallica rose not only because of its powerful fragrance, abundant bloom, and practically thornless stems but moreover for the ability of its blossoms to change colors. Blooms start out cerise pink, then turn Parma violet, and end up grayish mauve.

BELLE ISIS was always a famous member of the Gallica clan, but it became even more renowned when it sired 'Constance Spry', the forerunner of David Austin's English Rose. 'Belle Isis' grows into a tidy upright shrub smothered in gray-green foliage. Its strongly perfumed, flesh pink blossoms open flat but are fully double.

CAMAIEUX is considered to be one of the finest striped roses in all of rosedom. Against a background of creamy white, stripes appear on petals that are first crimson, then purple, and finally lilac, fragrant all the while. Bushes get to be about 3 feet by 3 feet and cover themselves in gray-green foliage.

CARDINAL DE RICHELIEU is one of the darkest of all roses. Although buds start out deep pink, they mature to deep purple. Individual, strongly fragrant blossoms, which are actually rather small, seem larger because petals reflex into a ball. Unlike most Gallicas, the Cardinal responds well to severe pruning.

CHARLES DE MILLS produces the largest and most spectacular blossoms of all the Gallicas. When fully opened, with quartered petalage surrounding a dark green eye, blooms look as though their maroon-to-purple petals have been trimmed with scissors into perfect symmetry. Alas, fragrance is only mild, but the bush makes up for this oversight with astounding vigor.

CRAMOISI PICOTÉ is an oddity among Gallica roses in that its blossoms look like pompon chrysanthemums and have little noticeable fragrance. The bush, however, is vigorous and has attractive dark green foliage and thornless stems. Blooms start out crimson but turn deep pink as they mature.

D'AGUESSEAU is the most brightly colored member of the Gallica family, with fiery crimson petals that fade to cerise pink along their edges. When fully open, petals form quarters around a dark green, button eye, which is visible only when blossoms reach full maturity.

DUC DE GUICHE is considered a "heavy" among Gallicas because its blooms are crammed with petals that at first open into a cup shape, then reflex into massive blossoms. Color is majestic, too—wine-magenta with purple shadings. To cap it off, fragrance is lusty.

DUCHESSE D'ANGOULÊME is a charming little Gallica, especially because of the way its sweetly scented, saucer-shaped blossoms seem suspended from the tips of the bush's arching branches. Petals are so clear a pink that they appear translucent, hence the nickname wax rose.

DUCHESSE DE MONTEBELLO is praised among Gallicas for many reasons, not the least of which is its tendency to be the first of the family to bloom. Blos-soms are soft pink, fully double, and fragrant and form open cups when mature. Foliage is a particularly pleasant shade of gray-green.

EMPRESS JOSEPHINE is a must among collections of Gallica roses, if not so much for the rose itself, then certainly in tribute to its namesake. The sole problem with 'Empress Josephine' is its modest (if present at all) fragrance. Otherwise, blossoms are showy—double, heavily textured, wavy, and colored deep rose with lavender veining. Although bushes tend to sprawl, they remain dense and cloaked with abundant foliage.

GEORGES VIBERT is reminiscent of a carnation on three counts—its similar size, shape, and regular striping. The basic color of the quilled petals is blush pink, but there is a striped overlay of carmine-to-purple (the depth of coloring depends on the weather). Foliage is dark green, and stems are unusually thorny for a Gallica.

GLOIRE DE FRANCE makes a low-growing, spreading shrub, with profuse, double, medium-sized blossoms. Petals are reflexed and lilac-pink, fading at their edges as they mature (most noticeably during hot weather).

HIPPOLYTE produces some of the most exquisitely formed blossoms of all Gallicas; they are mauve-violet, flat at first, then reflexed into a ball. The bush is vigorous (to 5 feet), smothered in small, dark green leaves, and almost thornless.

OFFICINALIS is both the oldest and the most famous of the Gallica roses, except, perhaps, for its sport, 'Rosa Mundi' (see entry in chapter 7). 'Officinalis' is also steeped in history, with nicknames to prove it—the red rose of Lancaster, because it was the rose chosen by the House of Lancaster during the Wars of the Roses, and the apothecary rose, because during medieval times it was more highly praised for its medicinal qualities than for its beauty in the garden.

'Officinalis' is a fine rose indeed, liberally producing fragrant, semidouble, soft crimson blossoms with pronounced golden stamens. Bushes arch gracefully and are covered with dark green foliage. Grown on its own roots, 'Officinalis' serves garden duty as a ground cover, since it suckers and spreads freely. When budded onto rootstock, bushes remain a manageable size—to 4 feet tall and about as wide. As a final bonus, 'Officinalis' is a late bloomer, a desirable quality when other Gallicas have finished their show.

POMPON PANACHÉE is a little treasure—an upright bush that produces small, flat, double flowers on thin, wiry stems with tiny leaves. Petals have a cream background but are striped with dusty pink.

PRÉSIDENT DE SÈZE is a chameleon among Gallicas in that its madly varying colors are ever-changing, due largely to prevailing weather. Buds start out lilac, but before the heavily petaled blossoms reach maturity, they may include brown, cerise, gray, magenta, purple, violet, or white in their complicated color scheme. Blooms are pleasantly fragrant, foliage

is gray-green, and stems are thornier than those of most Gallicas.

SISSINGHURST CASTLE is perhaps more famous for where it was discovered and by whom than for its merits as a rose. Vita Sackville-West found the offbeat Gallica among the rubble when she and Harold Nicholson were restoring Sissinghurst. Although she was delighted with her "find," I seriously doubt that Vita would have paid the rose much attention had she simply discovered it at a nursery.

When 'Sissinghurst Castle' is "on," it is indeed lovely, with deep maroon, pleasantly scented petals surrounding prominently displayed, deep golden anthers. When the weather is "off," however, petals become muddled. Foliage is small but abundant, and stems are brittle but relatively thornless.

TRICOLORE DE FLANDRE is a famous member of the Gallica family, undoubtedly due to the dramatic striping of its fragrant blossoms—basically pink, but heavily striped with lilac, magenta, and purple. The bush is relatively short (to 3 feet), and foliage is smooth and dark.

TUSCANY SUPERB fairly pushed its predecessor 'Tuscany' off the market because it's truly an improvement. Whereas

---

'ROSE DE RESCHT' *was brought to England from Persia in the early 1940's, and has stumped rose antiquarians ever since. In America, it's marketed as a Damask; in England, as a Portland. The fuchsia-red, shaded-lilac petals are intensely fragrant wherever they grow.*

'CELSIANA' *is the quintessential Damask rose, with robustly fragrant dark blossoms that age to light pink. The petals of this wonder look as though they've been meticulously fashioned from scraps of antique silk.*

'LA VILLE DE BRUXELLES' *produces unusually large, hot pink flowers whose petals reflex at their outer edges to accentuate the button-eyed center of mature blossoms. Fragrance is everything you'd want it to be, as is overall vigor.*

'MADAME ZÖETMANS' *is a regal lady — elegantly colored creamy white, abundantly petaled, and richly fragrant. Blossoms arrange themselves in sprays that look so perfect you suspect that someone placed them by hand. Plants are well behaved and properly clothed in handsome foliage.*

'Tuscany' was praised for its glorious, dark red, velvety flowers with dramatically contrasting yellow stamens, 'Tuscany Superb' possesses these same attributes, plus larger flowers with heavier petalage and stronger perfume flourishing on a more vigorous bush with better foliage.

DAMASKS

Not as old as Gallicas, but plenty ancient, the original Damask rose is believed to be a natural hybrid between a Gallica rose and *R. phoenicea*, a wild sprawling species bearing small white flowers. It is also generally agreed that the Persians were the first people to cultivate Damask roses in their gardens and that Damasks reached Europe with the help of the Crusaders.

In general, Damask roses grow taller than Gallicas, often to 5 feet. Also, their overall form is looser and their bushes thornier than Gallicas.

As the very name suggests, Damask roses are usually powerfully fragrant. Although there are exceptions, blossoms of Damask roses are typically clear pink, with no purple-to-red shadings, and bushes are most often covered with gray-green, elongated foliage that is downy on the underside.

With the notable exception of *R. damascena bifera*, also known as 'Quatre Saisons', Damask roses bloom only once each summer. If hips are formed, like the foliage that surrounds them, they are normally long and thin.

It seems obvious that certain Damask roses are destined to survive the test of time:

BOTZARIS is clearly related to the Alba family of roses, to which it owes a debt for superb perfume and lovely coloring. Blossoms are beige-white, flat, and often neatly quartered; bushes are prickly and covered in pale green foliage.

CELSIANA, with its graceful bush covered in grayish green foliage and nodding blossoms, is considered to be an exemplary Damask rose. Strongly fragrant blossoms that lighten from dark to pale pink are comprised of petals that look as though they've been fashioned from crumpled silk.

GLOIRE DE GUILAN, although thought to be Antique, was discovered only in 1949—in Iran, where it was cultivated for attar of roses. Besides being outrageously fragrant, 'Gloire de Guilan' is distinguished also for its flat, quartered blossoms that are a particularly clear pink.

HEBE'S LIP is notable among Damask roses for the coloring of its semidouble blossoms—cream-tinged rose. Bushes are short but vigorous, are thorny, and carry ample fresh green foliage.

ISPAHAN, also known as 'Pompon des Princes', is a treasured member of the Damask family because its large, warm pink, lustily fragrant blossoms make fine, lasting cut flowers. Bushes bloom over an uncommonly extended period.

LA VILLE DE BRUXELLES is a sumptuous Damask because of its unusually large, divinely scented, rich pink blossoms with reflexing outer petals. Bushes are strong upright growers, and foliage is large and shapely.

MADAME HARDY is named for the wife of the head rose gardener to Empress Josephine. The Madame is also one of my picks for immortality among Damask roses (see entry in chapter 7). For now I'll mention only that few roses rival 'Madame Hardy' for perfection of flower.

MADAME ZÖETMANS has never had the popularity in the United States that it enjoys in Europe, but it certainly isn't for lack of fragrance. Blossoms are creamy white and double and contain a button eye. Madame was hybridized by Marest of France in 1830.

MARIE LOUISE was bred at Malmaison and introduced in 1813. 'Marie Louise' is a dramatic rose, with glowing pink, deeply fragrant, exceptionally large blossoms that are so heavy that they weigh down their stems. Petals reflex at first, then flatten and quarter.

OMAR KHAYYAM, as we know this rose today, was supposedly raised from seed gathered at Omar Khayyam's grave at Nashipur, Persia. Bushes are low growers and are covered in gray-green foliage and small prickles. Flowers are small, too, but light pink, double, quartered, and sweetly fragrant.

QUATRE SAISONS, as already mentioned, is the black sheep of the Damask family of roses. That's because, as its name suggests, it flowers repeatedly, often more than a mere four times each year. Blossoms are silky pink and heavily perfumed.

SAINT NICHOLAS produces a short bush that flowers profusely with deep pink, almost single blossoms that feature bright yellow stamens. Fragrance is weak for a Damask.

YORK AND LANCASTER probably didn't begin life as legend would have us believe, but it's a nice story anyway, claiming that members of the opposing families fighting the Wars of the Roses each took a bloom from a single bush—one red, one white. Actually, the darker-colored blooms of 'York and Lancaster' are pink, not red, but white flowers also appear. More frequently, however, the semidouble, fragrant blossoms are randomly splashed with both colors, no two alike.

ALBAS

Although the origin of many ancient roses is a matter of conjecture, there is little doubt how Albas came into being—Mother Nature hybridized the Damask rose (specifically *R. damascena bifera*) and the ubiquitous European species *R. canina* (dog rose). It is also generally agreed that Linnaeus, the father of botany, named the family. As the name suggests, Albas are usually white or off-white (never deeper than mid-pink). Nearly all are fragrant.

The Romans are credited with distributing the Alba roses throughout Europe. Romans grew Albas, it is thought, primarily for medicinal purposes, although it is clear that their beauty was appreciated, too, for their blossoms appear in paintings and etchings from the period.

Alba rosebushes grow taller than either of their predecessors. In fact, Albas were once called tree roses because they often reach heights of more than 6 feet. Not only do they tower, Albas are also

considered to be the hardiest and most easily grown of all roses, accepting even considerable shade.

These varieties of Alba roses deserve a permanent garden spot:

AMELIA, a short member of the Alba family, produces ample blossoms with petals that are sweetly fragrant, medium pink, and semidouble around golden yellow anthers. The parentage of 'Amelia' is unrecorded, but she was bred by Vibert in 1823.

BELLE AMOUR, discovered as a chance seedling growing on the wall of a convent in Normandy, produces a vigorous shrub and clusters of salmon-pink and myrrh-scented blossoms.

CELESTIAL is heavenly indeed, particularly the substance of its elegantly shaped petals and their sweet scent. Don't plant 'Celestial' unless you can afford the 5-foot by 5-foot space that a mature bush assumes. And don't try pruning bushes low or they'll spend the next season reaching the height at which they're comfortable before blossoming. Otherwise, 'Celestial' is a treasure.

FÉLICITÉ PARMENTIER is the favorite Alba of many rosarians, and for good reasons—bushes are tidy but upright, and

'MADAME PLANTIER' has flowers that resemble those of Noisettes, but the bush is pure Alba—to 6 feet all around. Plants literally shower themselves in clusters of creamy white blossoms that are long on fragrance. If requested and properly trained, plants of the Madame also obediently climb.

R. ALBA SEMI-PLENA *is also known as 'White Rose of York' because the York family supposedly adopted it as their symbol during the Wars of the Roses. Good choice—powerfully fragrant, soft white blossoms with fat, golden yellow, stamen-packed centers flower on an elegant tall shrub.*

'FÉLICITÉ PARMENTIER' *produces perfectly quartered blossoms that start out fresh pink, then fade to creamy white. Blooms are so tightly packed with petals that you can't imagine where you'd place a spare one. Stems are notably thorny, but plants are handsomely bushy.*

'MADAME LEGRAS DE ST. GERMAIN' *is a study in perfection. Not only are blossoms creamy white, they're also packed with petals and perfume. Leaves are pale green and bushes are vigorous growers, serving equally well as graceful sprawling shrubs or as modest climbers. Madame's wood is virtually thornless.*

cunningly quartered, scented blossoms are crammed with pink-fading-to-cream petals.

MADAME LEGRAS DE ST. GERMAIN is a must for people fond of rosebushes with few thorns. An even greater bonus of this fine rose is prolific flowering of creamy white, heavily petaled, scented blossoms that develop into perfect domes. With proper support, Madame makes a splendid climber to 15 feet.

MADAME PLANTIER is sometimes listed as a Noisette because its blossoms favor that family; its bush, however, is more of an Alba—to 6 feet all around, if con-

tented. Sprawling shrubs shower themselves in clusters of small, robustly fragrant, creamy white blossoms with a green button eye. Madame also does double duty as a climber.

MAIDEN'S BLUSH, as I confess in chapter 7, is my favorite member of the Alba family. Known in France as 'Cuisse de Nymphe' (literally, "nymph's thigh"), 'Maiden's Blush' makes a gracefully arching shrub with an abundance of bluish gray foliage. Blossoms with an uncompromising fragrance have reflexing, blush pink petals. The standard version of this variety is called 'Great Maiden's Blush';

there is also a small 'Maiden's Blush', which produces a shorter bush with smaller flowers but is otherwise identical to its predecessor.

POMPON BLANC PARFAIT is a slow-growing Alba thought by many gardeners to be worth the wait. Fat pink buds open to blush pink rosettes on short, thin stems. Fragrance is only slight, but blooms persist over an extended season and last well as cut flowers.

QUEEN OF DENMARK is regal indeed. Although buds start out cupped, they later mature into exquisitely formed, quartered blossoms that are rosy pink and

*'**Maiden's Blush**' is called 'Cuisse de Nymphe' in France because its color is said to resemble that of the thigh of an aroused nymph! The bushes on which these sensually colored flowers grow are large but graceful and amazingly tolerant of shade.*

*Don't plant '**Celestial**' unless you can accommodate a mature bush 5 feet in all directions. If you can, you won't be disappointed. As the name implies, 'Celestial' is heavenly, indeed. Blossoms not only have wondrously shaped petals, they're sweetly scented, too.*

*Some gardeners plant '**Belle Amour**' for the vigor of its bushes, others for the salmon-pink tones of its blooms, and yet others because blossoms are scented of myrrh—three perfectly sound reasons.*

sumptuously perfumed. Bushes are relatively short but a snap to grow.

R. alba Semi-plena was once widely cultivated in Bulgaria for making attar of roses. Powerfully fragrant, milky white blossoms with thick yellow centers flower on a bountiful, elegantly shaped, tall shrub with gray-green foliage. Long red hips form in fall.

CENTIFOLIAS

Because Herodotus and other historians writing before the birth of Christ mentioned roses with 60 to 100 petals (also called cabbage roses), early rosarians be-

lieved that reference was being made to *R. centifolia*, thought to be a species. Recent cytological studies by plant pathologists, however, prove beyond doubt that *R. centifolia* isn't a species at all, but rather a complicated hybrid of *R. canina*, *R. gallica*, *R. moschata*, and *R. phoenicea*.

Remember from the historical notes made at the beginning of this chapter that the Dutch were credited with enormous strides in the creation of roses—an extension of the enthusiasm sparked by the Renaissance. Although no one is yet certain how the original *R. centifolia* came into being, it is clear that the roses we now

call Centifolias were developed by the Dutch during the seventeenth century. By the eighteenth century, these clever hybridizers had managed to create more than 200 varieties, motivated, no doubt, by the plants' popularity among Dutch and Flemish artists, who used them extensively as floral subjects in their paintings.

The two words most often used to describe the open growth habits of Centifolia rosebushes are "lanky" and "lax"; the many-petaled blossoms are usually called globular. In spite of this rather crude garden terminology, Centifolias are anything but clumsy. Quite the contrary,

'CHAPEAU DE NAPOLÉON' *got its name from the fact that, while developing, blossoms are shaped like a three-cornered hat. Once open, blossoms are typical of the Centifolia family, only lighter pink. Fragrance is strong and so are bushes.*

'DE MEAUX' *is the perfect choice for gardeners who like Centifolia blossoms in diminutive sizes. Although the miniature flowers are less than an inch wide, they're exceptionally well shaped and sinfully fragrant.*

'PETITE DE HOLLANDE' *smothers its plants in little, light pink, sweetly fragrant blossoms. The foliage that covers plants is also appropriately small; glossy and disease resistant, too. 'Petite de Hollande' is a fine choice for growing into a standard (tree rose).*

they rank high among the Antique Roses considered to be graceful.

Blossoms of Centifolias mainly are pink, with several hybrids that include soft shades of crimson, purple, and mauve; a few are white. Almost all are powerfully fragrant and heavily petaled.

There has been considerable controversy recently over whether or not certain varieties classed as Centifolias really belong to that family, including 'Fantin-Latour', usually considered to be the epitome of the Centifolia clan. Rosarians fascinated with controversies such as these point out that some "Centifolias" are more likely first-generation crosses of one of the Chinese stud roses with a European variety. Proponents of the theory also believe that suspect roses should be labeled Hybrid Chinas. I'm sympathetic toward the thinking, but resistive to the reclassification.

If cabbage roses appeal to you, please consider the following:

CENTIFOLIA, which is known to have existed prior to 1600, is the prototype of the family, possessing large, heavily petaled, rich pink blossoms with classic Old Rose scent. Bushes are strong but graceful and covered with coarse foliage and plenty of thorns. 'Bullata', thought to be a sport of 'Centifolia', grows shorter than its parent and has smaller blossoms; it also has curious, oversized, crinkled foliage, hence its nickname, the lettuce-leaved rose. Rosarians have hypothesized that the blossoms of Bullata are inferior to those of Centifolia because its bushes spend too much energy producing foliage.

CHAPEAU DE NAPOLÉON, sometimes listed as a member of the Moss family of roses as 'Crested Moss', is so named because its odd oversized sepals compress buds into what looks like a three-cornered cocked hat. When petals finally force their way open, blossoms closely resemble those of 'Centifolia', except they are a lighter shade of pink. Fragrance is strong, and bushes that reach moderate heights are well foliated.

DE MEAUX is a perfect miniature Centifolia. Although the pompon flowers seldom exceed an inch in width, they're perfectly formed, warm pink, and richly fragrant. Bushes are short, twiggy, and covered in small, light green leaves. 'De Meaux' makes a terrific tree rose.

'De Meaux' has a white sport that is like its parent in every way except color, basically white with tinges of pink.

FANTIN-LATOUR, named for the beloved French artist whose paintings featured floral bouquets that almost always included roses, is my favorite Centifolia. Discussed in detail in chapter 7, 'Fantin-Latour' produces large, soft pink blossoms that are cupped at first, then flat, and always richly perfumed. Shrubs are vigorous but graceful growers.

IPSILANTE, considered by certain Old Rose enthusiasts to be a Gallica, is treasured not only for its large, fragrant, lilac-pink blossoms but also for its resistance to disease. Prickly bushes grow to medium heights.

*'**TOUR DE MALAKOFF**' is an exceptionally large Centifolia rose with equally distinguished loosely double, cupped, informal blossoms, which are shaded from crimson-purple to gray-violet. Because its growth habits are so lax, 'Tour de Malakoff' benefits from support, making it a satisfactory climber.*

JUNO produces globular pink buds that mature into notably fragrant, blush, flat blossoms with a button eye. Bushes are lax but graceful.

PAUL RICAULT is particularly generous with blossoms that enjoy a long season of bloom. The fragrant flowers are double and are packed with deep rose petals that roll back as they age. Bushes are reasonably vigorous.

PETITE DE HOLLANDE, another miniature Centifolia, differs from 'De Meaux' mostly in its lighter pink color. Otherwise, like its more famous sister, richly fragrant small blossoms shower a bushy mid-sized shrub clothed in appropriately sized foliage.

ROBERT LE DIABLE, although scented, is more famous for the unique color combination in its blossoms and because it is a reliable late bloomer. 'Robert le Diable' is a chameleon among roses, with petals of blossoms ranging in color from lilac-gray to mauve, purple, violet, and carmine. Not only do these bloom late in the season, but they occur on shrubs with a propensity toward lateral rather than upright growth.

SPONG is my least favorite of the miniature Centifolias because of its "bad finish," as rosarians say, which in the case of 'Spong' refers to holding on to its pink-fading-to-cream petals even after they've withered and died.

THE BISHOP obviously has a lot of Gallica in him, and his flowers are the main tip-off—rosette-shaped blossoms that eventually flatten entirely. Color is dramatic, with shades of magenta, violet, and gray, the amalgamation of which sometimes makes blooms appear blue. Fragrance is strong, and bushes are upright.

TOUR DE MALAKOFF makes the largest shrub of any Centifolia discussed here, so large that it appreciates support for its wide-spreading limbs. Free-flowering, scented, large blossoms are shades of purple, magenta, crimson, and violet.

MOSSES

The first Moss rose, believed to be a sport of a Centifolia rose, caused quite a stir in rosedom when it occurred sometime in the late seventeenth century. According to Dr. C.C. Hurst, that fine British geneticist who set straight the historical development of Antique shrub roses, the first reliable observance of a true Moss rose was in Carcassonne, France, in 1696. I can't imagine why it took longer than another 150 years for a Moss rose to catch on, but it wasn't until the latter half of the nineteenth century that the majority of Moss roses in commerce today were hybridized. They then enjoyed a 30-year rage, especially in Victorian England.

Moss roses are distinguished by conspicuous glandular mosslike growth on their stems, calyxes, sepals, and, in some cases, even leaflets. Degree of mossing differs widely among family members— sometimes heavy, other times light; sometimes prickly, other times soft.

Because Moss roses were developed from extensive breeding, they inherited traits from a multitude of ancestors. Blossoms, the majority of which are richly perfumed, range in color from white to maroon, and the shrubs on which they grow vary from miniatures to skyscrapers. Desirable varieties include:

ALFRED DE DALMAS, known equally well as 'Mousseline', is particularly floriferous, repeating its bloom all growing season. Buds have greenish brown moss, and the mid-sized open flowers are pale pink, cupped, and sweetly scented. Plants are bushy, with spoon-shaped foliage.

BLANCHE MOREAU is also a repeat-flowering Moss rose, but most seasons it has only two periods of bloom—early and late. Mossing is dark, but button-eyed flowers are pure white, double, and fragrant. Be forewarned that Blanche is highly prone to mildew.

CAPITAINE JOHN INGRAM is a masculine rose. Red-mossed buds open into deeply fragrant, maroon-purple–dusted-lilac blossoms with a button eye. Bushes are vigorous and spiny with thorns.

COMTESSE DE MURINAIS has a strict policy of offering only one flush of bloom each season, but it's a stunner. Shell pink buds encased in bright green moss mature into double, quartered, flat blossoms. Not only are the flowers fragrant, the moss is, too, releasing a balsamlike fragrance when fingered. Bushes grow tall enough to need support.

DEUIL DE PAUL FONTAINE produces fragrant, maroon-purple blossoms on a short, thorny plant. There are at least

'GLOIRE DES MOUSSEUX' *is the Moss rose for gardeners into size. Not only are blossoms huge, flat at maturity, and densely petaled, they're also soft pink and decadently fragrant. "Mossing" occurs mostly on the distinctively long sepals that support each bloom.*

'HENRI MARTIN' *isn't notably mossy, but its blossoms are as pure crimson as any Moss rose could be. Blooms are only lightly fragrant, but they're produced in abundance and followed by crops of red hips. Here, white nicotiana helps you realize just how vivid Monsieur Martin's color is.*

'SALET' *is the favorite Moss rose of gardeners who like lots of blossoms. Although its bush requires training, and even though mossing is only light, 'Salet' is treasured for its clear pink blossoms surrounded by bright green foliage. The sweet fragrance doesn't detract one bit.*

two flushes of bloom each season, often more.

GENERAL KLEBER grows as wide as he does tall—in most climates to 4 feet. Bright green moss is abundant, and blossoms are satiny pink with a button eye. Bushes are relatively thornless and massed in perky green foliage.

GLOIRE DES MOUSSEUX produces the largest blooms of all the Moss roses— clear pink, fully double, and quartered, with petals that reflex as they age. Fragrance is strong, and bushes have thick canes and pale green leaves.

HENRI MARTIN is famed for its color—

as pure crimson as you can imagine. Although mossing is sparse, dainty fragrant blossoms are abundant on a wiry-stemmed bush that sets red hips in the fall.

JAMES MITCHELL, although small of flower, has the agreeable habit of blooming early. Buds are heavily mossed but open into clear lilac-to-cerise-pink, fragrant blossoms. Shrubs are tidy.

JEANNE DE MONTFORT is a giant among Mosses, growing to heights suitable for a pillar rose. Brown moss develops on tight buds that ripen into perfumed, medium pink blossoms featuring bright yellow

stamens. Foliage is a distinguished shade of dark green.

LITTLE GEM is the Moss member for fanciers of miniature roses. Crimson, fragrant, pompon flowers occur over a long season on a shrub that's short, compact, and loaded with moss (even on stems).

LOUIS GIMARD produces a densely mossed bush and large, heavily petaled, fragrant blossoms blended of magenta and mauve. Shrubs are tall, slender, and clothed in red-veined, dark green foliage.

MME LOUIS LÉVÊQUE is only lightly mossed, but her finely textured blossoms

'MADAME DE LA ROCHE-LAMBERT' *produces tight, petal-packed crimson buds that mature by flattening their crimson-purple petals into platter-sized blossoms. Perfume is steady, as are blossoms that occur well into fall. Although she won't grow tall, this Madame forms a handsome, well-shaped shrub.*

'LITTLE GEM' *is a fine selection for gardeners who yearn for a Moss rose with miniature blossoms. Not only does flowering persist over an extended period, bushes are loaded with moss (even on stems).*

'MOUSSELINE', *commonly marketed as 'Alfred de Dalmas', is a particularly floriferous Moss rose. Buds with sparse greenish brown moss mature into sweetly fragrant, cupped, light pink blossoms. Bushes are smothered with spoon-shaped foliage.*

are large, soft pink, and intensely fragrant. Although buds and young blooms are shaped like cups, they eventually mature into buxom beauties. Second crops of bloom usually appear.

MARÉCHAL DAVOUST is a Moss rose treasured for its contribution to the landscape. Shrubs are shapely and arch with buds covered in greenish brown moss. Strongly scented blossoms range in color from purple to mauve, with petals reflexing around green button-eyed centers.

NUITS DE YOUNG is a Moss must for gardeners who like darkly colored roses. Buds are so purple that they look black, and blossoms handsomely frame a boss of golden stamens. Mossing is slight, foliage is small, and bushes are erect.

RÉNÉ D'ANJOU is not in general commerce these days, though I can't imagine why. Both foliage and moss are tinted bronze, and blossoms are fresh pink and deliciously scented. Shrubs may reach 4 feet but aren't particularly vigorous.

SALET is the most reliable of the repeat-blooming Moss roses. Purists complain that the bush is coarse in its growth but admit that it's upright and lightly mossed. Double blossoms are rose-pink and scented; foliage is bright green.

WILLIAM LOBB requires forethought before planting. Shrubs are so vigorous that they eventually demand support. Still, the blossoms are worth the trouble—sinfully fragrant and purple to gray with a lighter reverse to each petal.

THREE

The Rose Revolution: 1799 to 1867

As the eighteenth century drew to a close, an event occurred that forever altered the destiny of roses: the arrival in Europe of *R. chinensis*, the China rose. Roses from Oriental Asia possessed the enviable quality of repeat blooming.

Here, at last, was a way to get the glory of rose blooms throughout the summer. Naturally, nineteenth-century hybridizers couldn't wait to get their hands on pollen from these "remontant" strains. The very thought of roses blossoming half the year drove them to frenzied aspirations, and, once

they had solved the mystery of how to make this thrilling event happen, five whole new families developed that paved the way for the Modern Rose. But first, the setting of the stage where the revolution took place.

AN EMPRESS, A RIVAL, AND FOUR STUDS

In 1799, while Napoleon was off campaigning in Egypt, Empress Josephine Bonaparte purchased Malmaison, a château on 650 acres located 40 miles outside of Paris. Although

'SOUVENIR DE LA MALMAISON', named for Empress Josephine's château near Paris, is a sight to behold when the sun shines properly. Then, mature blossoms are studies in perfection; they're also delicate blush pink from start to finish and sweetly scented. Thanks to a climbing sport, this fine Bourbon grows well vertically, too.

the empress claimed she wanted to live there (rather than with her husband in his Parisian residence), her secret scheme was to have the first garden devoted to a single genus—*Rosa*. Josephine was passionate over roses, and she vowed that her roseraie was to house the best varieties of roses from every part of the world. To make her dream garden a reality, and because money was no object, the empress retained the services of three important men to further her cause.

First, Louis Berthault was commissioned to landscape the property. His design not only allowed for a commodious sunny location for the cultivation of roses, but also for a lake fed by cascading streams, a fine collection of trees, and a classic "Temple d'Amour" built on a rocky knoll with a commanding view.

Next, Josephine hired Claude Antoine Thory, the most famous botanist then in France, to assemble her massive collection of roses—several plants each of 167 Gallicas, 27 Centifolias, 9 Damasks, 8 Albas, and more than 20 species roses.

Finally, the empress appointed Pierre Joseph Redouté, the most famous botanical artist ever, to immortalize her roses in paintings. With a text by Thory, Redouté published 117 colored drawings of Josephine's collection in *Les Roses*.

Living just close enough nearby for gossip to spread with annoying regularity was Josephine's arch rival, the Comtesse de Bougainville, who also vowed to amass rare plants, particularly roses. The two ladies were determined to outdo each other, especially when they heard about the availability of four virile stud roses from China.

Two of these, 'Slater's Crimson China' and 'Parsons' Pink China', had reached Europe in 1792. Although talk of their supposed virility had preceded them, early hybridizing efforts were disappointing. We now know, of course, that this was because these roses had simply been crossed with existing European varieties, and the hybrids that resulted were nothing spectacular. Then it occurred to someone (probably Thory) to recross these unexceptional hybrids with the original Chinese varieties, and, at last, the remontant mystery unfolded.

In 1809 word reached France that a new stud rose had been discovered in the Orient. 'Hume's Blush China' was reputed to be of such promise that Empress Josephine and Comtesse de Bougainville resolved to get it to France posthaste, whether or not the Napoleonic Wars were also raging. Josephine, of course, held the upper hand, and she exercised her waning influence (Napoleon divorced her the following year, apparently because of her inability to produce an heir, though some say because her devotion to roses outweighed that to him) to gain diplomatic immunity for the ship delivering 'Hume's Blush China' to Malmaison.

Ten years later, the fourth Chinese stud rose arrived. Unfortunately, Josephine was dead, never to see the fruits of her labors or to revel in the lovely rose named after her, 'Empress Josephine', or the magnificent variety that bears the name of her château, 'Souvenir de la Malmaison'. Empress Josephine Bonaparte remains, however, the greatest benefactress of roses, ever.

Before the four studs were returned to pasture, they sired five new families of roses: Chinas, Portlands, Bourbons, Hybrid Perpetuals, and Teas.

CHINAS

If you ask botanists to explain why China roses look unlike all others, they'll tell you that Chinas are diploid, meaning that the cells within their woody growth have only two sets of chromosomes, whereas most roses are tetraploid, luxuriating in the abundant growth that their extra sets of chromosomes afford them.

If you ask a gardener to tell you how he spots a China rose (even without telltale blossoms to pinpoint identification), he'll confess that airy growth is the giveaway, and sparse foliage the clincher.

Not only are the growth habits of China rosebushes nothing to write home about (unless you're fond of airy growth in general, of course), their blossoms are also disappointing—shapeless, in fact, compared with the families discussed in the previous chapter. Still,

Chinas possess a distinctive naive charm, and the colors of their petals intensify as their blossoms mature. Above all else, however, they bloom throughout summer—a surefire, enviable quality.

Mixed with aggressive dense plants in a border, the sparse growth habits and delicate flowers of China hybrid roses are irresistible. Those you might consider for such plantings are:

COMTESSE DU CAYLA is both dainty and madly colored. Bushes mature to 3 feet by 3 feet and produce drooping, loose, almost single flowers that include red, copper, salmon, and yellow in their complex color schemes. Although foliage is sparse, blooms are abundant and richly scented.

CRAMOISI SUPÉRIEUR forms a low-growing bush with a marked tendency to sprawl. Although its blossoms are small, cupped, and only mildly scented, 'Cramoisi Supérieur' is a free bloomer and gathers its nonfading, clear red flowers in clusters. There is a climbing sport of this variety that is considered to be finer than the bush form and considerably more vigorous.

FABVIER is another ground hugger. Although bushes rarely get taller than 2 feet, they are seldom out of bloom. Mildly scented flowers are bright red,

'MALTON', *technically a Hybrid China, is worthwhile for more than its dazzling blossoms; it proved potent for hybridizing purposes and parented many of the Hybrid Perpetual roses. Although bushes often sprawl, with proper training they behave.*

GOLD OF OPHIR *is a born climber. Best of all, it doesn't mind shade, which it gets plenty of in this thicket of native California willow trees. Although blooms appear sporadically through summer, spring's bounty is glorious — "like a moon on fire," according to M.F.K. Fisher.*

OLD BLUSH *is not merely one of the four original stud roses kidnapped from China in the late eighteenth century, it's also thought to be the prettiest. Dainty blossoms begin life soft pink, then deepen in color as they age, all the while releasing a vanilla-toned fragrance not unlike that of sweet peas, but rosier.*

VIRIDIFLORA, *far better known as 'The Green Rose', doesn't really blossom. Instead, this oddity produces masses of green sepals that resemble blossoms. Arrangers love it. Personally, I can do without it (although I do admire its adamant resistance to disease).*

often streaked with white, and usually drop their petals before fading.

GLOIRE DES ROSOMANES, better known as 'Ragged Robin', was once the most popular understock grown in America. In fact, so many Modern hybrids were grafted onto the rugged root structure of 'Ragged Robin' that the rose soon lost all value as a flower—too bad, in view of its cheery, scarlet, semi-double blossoms growing on a robust bush. In many areas along the coast in southern California, however, miles of gravel roads are still lined with 'Ragged Robin' rosebushes that bloom at least

nine months of the year. That's where I think 'Ragged Robin' looks best—planted in hedges, where mass effect is more important than individual florets.

HERMOSA looks more like a small Bourbon than a typical China—plants are more sturdy than delicate. Lilac-pink blossoms, which appear regularly throughout summer, are cupped and softly fragrant. 'Hermosa' is a favorite in mixed borders. Not only does its size blend well with a host of neighbors so does the shade of its gray-green foliage.

LE VESUVE has persisted in gardens in spite of its reluctant growth habits, no

doubt because of utterly charming blossoms. Nicely scrolled, soft pink buds open into quartered flowers that deepen in color as they age, eventually developing crimson highlights. Plants sometimes reach 5 feet in height, but more usually hover at 3 feet. Flowering is persistent, however, and fragrance is dependable. I've been told that 'Le Vesuve' grows better under glass than outdoors, but I doubt that's true if garden shrubs are granted a sheltered, sunny spot.

MADAME LAURETTE MESSIMY is a favored China hybrid because it mixes so well in borders. Although it can reach 4 feet in a sheltered position, 'Madame Laurette Messimy' more often grows to only 2 feet and about as wide. Regardless of their size, bushes are massed with glossy, gray-green foliage and semidouble flowers that start out copper and end up bright pink, suffused with yellow at the base of each petal.

MUTABILIS is my pick of the Chinas (see entry in chapter 7), mainly because it is rarely out of bloom. 'Mutabilis' is sometimes called the butterfly rose because its whimsical flowers give the appearance of butterflies lighting on the bush—dainty honey-copper buds opening into irregularly shaped pink blossoms that eventually turn crimson. When planted in a sheltered garden position, 'Mutabilis' grows to 8 feet; when in the open, it more usually remains under 3 feet. New foliage is bronze, and although growth is rather twiggy, 'Mutabilis' is thoroughly irresistible.

OLD BLUSH, also known as 'Parsons' Pink China', is not only the prettiest of the stud roses, it's also the one that appears most at home in the garden. Plants of 'Old Blush' are vigorous and produce clusters of dainty, informal pink blossoms that deepen in color as they

'IRENE WATTS' resembles a modern Floribunda because it repeats flowering so often, but it's China to the core. Well-formed buds start out apricot-orange, then take on shades of ivory as blossoms mature, eventually revealing a button-eyes center.

'COMTE DE CHAMBORD' *produces scads of glowing pink, richly fragrant blossoms on a plump shrub. Typical of the Portland family, 'Comte de Chambord' has short stems and foliage tightly packed around its blossoms — what Graham Stuart Thomas calls a "shoulder of leaves."*

'GLENDORA', *an unofficial name, was discovered in an Old Rose garden in Glendora, California. A sufficient number of cuttings were taken to put the rose back into limited commerce. Purists point out that 'Glendora' might actually be a Hybrid Perpetual, but I march with the Portland crowd.*

'PORTLAND ROSE', *named for the Duchess of Portland, is the forerunner of the prestigious Portland family of roses. At first sight, one might easily imagine that the semidouble, cerise red flowers harbor no fragrance. Wrong; perfume is intense.*

age, with a fragrance that many people believe is similar to that of sweet peas. 'Old Blush' is typical of its China family in that it looks best when mixed with other flowers (or climbing in a tree) rather than by itself.

VIRIDIFLORA, undoubtedly a sport of 'Old Blush', would probably not have survived were it not so popular among flower arrangers. Also known as 'The Green Rose', 'Viridiflora' produces "blooms" that aren't really blooms at all but rather masses of sepals, which, together, give the effect of blossoms. The best I can find to say about this

oddity is that it is relatively trouble- and disease free and sure to spark conversation.

PORTLANDS

Although the precise genealogy of Portland roses is still debated, their date of introduction and their origin seem clear. In about 1800 the Duchess of Portland imported a rose from Italy. This *R. paestana*, or 'Scarlet Four Seasons' Rose', was an instant hit because it bloomed repeatedly throughout summer. After marveling over its free-flowering habits, the duchess sent plants

of her remontant discovery to André Dupont, head gardener to Empress Josephine. In gallant honor of their benefactress, the staff at Malmaison named the rose 'Duchess of Portland'. It was only a short time, of course, before French hybridizers had their way with the plants' pollen, and scads of hybrids emerged. Sadly, only a handful remain in commerce.

Portland roses look more like their Damask predecessors than they do anything else. Although Portlands have short stems, the blossoms that form on their tips are shapely. As if to make up for

'GIPSY BOY' *is usually listed among Bourbon roses, but it's actually a Modern Shrub rose and blossoms only once each season. Black-red, nearly scentless blooms feature primrose yellow anthers. The foliage on the tough bushes is leathery, deeply grooved, and abundant.*

'PRINCE CHARLES' *is rarely listed in American rose catalogs, but the Bourbon is insanely popular in Britain. Blossoms formed of loose, crinkled petals are deep reddish purple, veined magenta. Bushes are low on thorns, but flowers are high on fragrance.*

'VARIEGATA DI BOLOGNA' *is perhaps the most famous rose ever hybridized in Italy. Flowers are a showy combination of creamy white petals randomly streaked crimson and purple. Although no two are alike, every flower is soaked with perfume. Blossoms dry well and retain their luminous stripes.*

twiggy branches, foliage is abundant and handsomely embraces the Duchess's fragrant, usually purple (but sometimes pink or white) blooms.

Because of their upright growth, Portlands are favored by landscapers, who appreciate dependable, compact shrubs between 3 and 4 feet tall. Good varieties include:

ARTHUR DE SANSAL grows upright to 3 feet and produces richly fragrant, fully double, crimson-purple flowers with green button-eyed centers. While blooms are unfurling, a pale reverse is obvious; as blossoms mature, petals

quarter and flatten to conceal their lighter undersides. Foliage is light green and ample but is prone to mildew.

BLANC DE VIBERT blossoms over a long period with pure white, lightly cupped, heavily petaled flowers that carry a strong Damask fragrance. Although its foliage is pale green, it's also luxurious and clearly of Gallica heritage.

COMTE DE CHAMBORD grows vigorously and plumply to 4 feet. Flowers are full, quartered, rich pink fading to lilac, and powerfully fragrant. Typical of the Portland family, foliage grows smack

up to the heavy blossoms, forming a handsome rosette.

JACQUES CARTIER is considered by many rosarians to be the finest member of the Portland family. Although it's shorter and not as free a bloomer as 'Comte de Chambord', 'Jacques Cartier' produces blossoms that are lovely and considerably more shapely. Blooms are clear pink, fully petaled, and richly fragrant. (See further discussion in chapter 7.)

PORTLAND ROSE, also known as 'Scarlet Four Seasons' Rose', is the original variety named for the Duchess of

Portland. Although this fine single to semidouble variety rarely grows taller than 3 feet, plants are bushy and well foliated, and they produce masses of cerise red blossoms with prominent golden yellow stamens that harbor a strong Damask fragrance.

ROSE DU ROI is a relatively straggly, not particularly robust member of the Portland clan, but it's a free bloomer and good repeater. Blossoms are double, red with purple mottling, loosely formed, and richly fragrant; foliage is small, pointed, and dark green. It is generally agreed that 'Rose du Roi' is the ancestor from which Modern Roses obtained their clear red color.

BOURBONS

Residents of the Île de Bourbon were fond of encircling their homes with mixed hedges of *R. chinensis* and *R. damascena*. With no assist from mankind, these two roses sufficiently scrambled their pollen to parent a rose that had the best of their respective qualities. Hips from the discovery were sent to the head gardener of King Louis-Philippe, who raised 'Rosier de l'Île de Bourbon'. In turn, hybridizers crossed the seedling with roses of the times, and the Bourbon family emerged.

You may quibble over the growth habits of **'ROSE DU ROI'**, *but never over its ability to repeat flowering. Also, blossoms are richly colored, attractively mottled, and sinfully fragrant. 'Rose du Roi' is credited for introducing clear red to modern hybrids.*

'REINE DES VIOLETTES' *is the favorite rose of certain esteemed rosarians. I'm not swept away myself, but I do admire the blossoms' color transformation from grape purple to Parma violet. Maybe what bothers me is the rude finish—petals dropping all at once. Then again, that fragrance!*

'MADAME PIERRE OGER' *is considered to be one of the most refined of all Bourbon roses. Chalice-shaped blossoms are delicately shaded pinky beige and resemble translucent water lilies. Bushes are also shapely but prone to blackspot.*

Hybridized in 1920, **'ADAM MESSERICH'** *is a newcomer to the Bourbon family. Billowing plants with widely arching canes are almost thornless. Many gardeners believe that the warm pink blossoms of 'Adam Messerich' smell exactly like raspberries.*

Even today, Bourbons unite the best of two rose worlds—the old and the new. Like Old Roses, Bourbons are beautifully colored and fully petaled; like Modern Roses, Bourbon roses blossom until fall. Bourbons also rank among the most strongly perfumed of all roses, and their petals dry well and hold their color (whole blossoms dry nicely, too).

The large shrubs from which Bourbon roses spill their blooms enjoy arching their weighty canes. Because of this natural habit, Bourbons make fine climbers, pillars, and fence huggers.

Bourbons are the first family of roses for whom precise parentage was recorded. When known, ancestry is listed (mothers first), along with the credited hybridizer and year of introduction. Especially worthy Bourbons include:

ADAM MESSERICH is so new on the scene that one of its parents is actually a Hybrid Tea; it nevertheless qualifies as a Bourbon. True to family characteristics, plants grow more happily as climbers or pillars than as shrubs—easily to 5 feet, with vigorous, arching, almost thornless canes. Large, slightly cupped, semidouble blossoms are warm pink and richly fragrant with perfume that some people compare to raspberries. Flowering is profuse in early summer but sporadic and skimpy thereafter. ('Frau Oberhofgartner Singer' x 'Louise Odier' seedling x 'Louis Philippe'), Lambert, 1920.

BOULE DE NEIGE is the most upright and slender of the Bourbons and also the creamiest white (although you wouldn't imagine so from the buds). When flowers first appear, the outside petals are flushed with pink and edged in crimson. As blossoms mature and form themselves in clusters, their petals turn white and reflex into balls of rich

'REINE VICTORIA' *has several wonderful attributes—slender shrubs, pink-shaded-lilac blossoms that are lovingly formed, and an almost unrivaled ability to repeat flowering. Alas, it has a dreadful drawback—an affinity for blackspot.*

'BOURBON QUEEN' *grows as told—either as a tall shrub or a lofty climber. Fragrant blossoms with crinkled petals are shades of rose-pink. Although plants aren't exactly generous with blossoms, they compensate for their stinginess with a generous crop of hips.*

Even gardeners who don't usually care for striped roses fall prey to the charms of **'HONORINE DE BRABANT'** *and its baby pink petals striped randomly with mauve and lilac. Blossoms are deeply fragrant and the robust bushes are relatively thornless.*

perfume. ('Blanche Lafitte' x 'Sappho'), Lacharme, 1867.

BOURBON QUEEN can be grown as a 6-foot shrub or a 12-foot climber; either way, plants are sturdy and tenacious. Sweetly scented, rose-pink flowers with crinkled petals and conspicuous stamens appear in profusion in early summer and selfishly thereafter. As if to compensate for modest blooms in summer, generous hips form each autumn. (Parentage unknown), Mauget, 1834.

COUPE D'HÉBÉ is another Bourbon that grows best as a climber, since plants grow naturally upright and look awkward left unstaked. Fragrant, pale but rich pink, globular flowers are fully double, sometimes quartered. Light green foliage is attractive but prone to mildew. (Precise parentage not recorded), Laffay, 1840.

HONORINE DE BRABANT is the most softly striped member of the Bourbon clan, with large, baby pink blossoms streaked with soft shades of lilac and mauve. Bushes are vigorous but almost thornless, and foliage is plentiful. 'Honorine de Brabant' is a good repeat-bloomer, and blossoms are often most beautiful in fall, when sunlight isn't so harsh that colors bleach. (Origin unknown.)

LOUISE ODIER produces blossoms that are often compared to camellias, since they are more flat than rounded; they are also bright pink and wonderfully perfumed. Because blooms are produced in dense clusters from early summer until late fall, canes arch under their weight, lending grace to an otherwise forthright 5-foot shrub. (Parentage unknown), Margottin, 1851.

MADAME ERNEST CALVAT is a sport of the variety that follows, 'Madame Isaac Pereire', and similar to it in every way except the color of its blossoms, which are light to medium pink. Although I generally prefer softer shades, in this case I prefer the darker version. Fortunately, I don't have to choose, since I have the two Mesdames planted side by side along a 200-foot fence. As if to prove the constancy of their relationship, the two ladies often sport back and forth, providing an even more pleasantly colored spectacle. ('Madame Isaac Pereire' sport), Schwartz, 1888.

MADAME ISAAC PEREIRE is my favorite Bourbon (see entry in chapter 7), probably because, to my nose, it's the most fragrant (many people swear that it's the most strongly perfumed rose ever, but this is a very close call). 'Madame Isaac Pereire' makes a vigorous 7-foot shrub or a rampant 18-foot climber, in either case cloaking itself in thick, deep green foliage. The flowers are huge, hot pink shaded magenta, cupped at first, then quartered, finally reflexed at the petals' edges—dramatic at every stage. (Parentage unknown), Garçon, 1881.

MADAME PIERRE OGER produces some of the most refined blooms of all Bourbon roses—delicate, pinky beige, chalice-shaped flowers that resemble translucent water lilies. This Madame is

'MADAME LAURIOL DE BARNY' *makes people weak in the knees. Lushly fragrant blossoms with silvery pink silky petals nod gracefully on tall shrubs. The Madame is generous with her bounty in early summer, but downright stingy in fall.*

'AMERICAN BEAUTY' *gained enormous popularity purely because of its name. In all honesty, it's a rampant mildewer. Still, when properly grown, the buxom carmine-pink blossoms are a feast for the eyes and nose—fitting for the floral symbol of Washington, D.C.*

'BARONESS ROTHSCHILD' *produces such breathtaking flowers and lush gray-green foliage that you're willing to forgive the fact that perfume is light and bushes are weak. Blossoms considered, the Baroness is worth the extra effort she requires.*

'BARONNE PRÉVOST', *with its old-fashioned button-eyed blossoms, looks older than it is. True to its family of Hybrid Perpetuals, blooms appear intermittently throughout summer. You'll forgive the bushes their thorns in return for their robust growth habits.*

a sport, too—of 'La Reine Victoria', another fine Bourbon. Unlike the Mesdames discussed above, however, 'Madame Pierre Oger' is finer than her parent, probably because of her unique color and form ('La Reine Victoria' is ubiquitous pink). Growth is narrow and upright, to approximately 5 feet, and flowering is nonstop. Alas, blackspot is also unrelenting. ('La Reine Victoria' sport), Verdier, 1878.

MRS. PAUL produces large, soft pink, double flowers that, although somewhat blowsy, are richly fragrant. The bush, too, is rather coarse, though it's certainly vigorous (to heights exceeding 5 feet) and densely packed with plentiful, large-leaved foliage. (Parentage unknown), Paul, 1891.

PRINCE CHARLES, a sport of 'Bourbon Queen', is the most darkly colored member of the Bourbon family, with blossoms that start out purple and then fade to rich lilac. While maturing, individual petals heavily veined with crimson provide a handsome contrast to the flowers' flashy golden yellow centers. Fragrance and recurrence of bloom are light, foliage is large, and thorns are few. (Origin unknown.)

SOUVENIR DE LA MALMAISON, named in honor of the château where Josephine staged her rose revolution, is available both as a bush and as a climber, the latter being the better form, since bushes are too short to do the blooms justice. In either case, blossoms are delicate and blush pink, fading only slightly as they age. Although cupped at first, blossoms mature to more than 5 inches across as they quarter and flatten their sweetly scented petals. When 'Souvenir de la Malmaison' is "on" (usually in warm, dry weather), it's a sight to behold; when weather is damp, it's best to

for this variety is thoroughly ungainly if left on its own. Blossoms, however, are richly red, powerfully perfumed, and produced on long stems; they also recur with pleasing regularity. ('Lord Bacon' x 'Grüss an Teplitz'), Dickson, 1905.

MRS. JOHN LAING was the ultimate hybridizing achievement of Henry Bennett, the man who set the style for roses in Victorian and Edwardian landscapes. The bush is more manageable than most Hybrid Perpetuals, since it grows only to 4 feet in height and not quite as wide. Blossoms are silvery pink, shapely, and richly fragrant and appear repeatedly throughout summer. ('François Michelon' seedling), Bennett, 1887.

PAUL NEYRON is my pet among the Hybrid Perpetuals, producing blossoms that must be seen to be believed—beautifully colored, nicely fragrant, pink and lilac petals that swirl themselves across blooms the size of dinner plates. 'Paul Neyron' matures into a strong, 3-foot, upright bush with large, matte green foliage that is more disease resistant than that of most members of the Hybrid Perpetual family. ('Victor Verdier' x 'Anna de Diesbach'), Levet, 1869.

REINE DES VIOLETTES has a lot going for it besides its lovely, richly perfumed

---

*'**CAPTAIN HAYWARD**' grew first as a bush, then as a climber, as shown here on the walls of England's National Trust garden Mottisfont Abbey. Fully open blossoms become blowsy, but if you pick them, you'll miss the bountiful crop of hips that follow.*

blossoms that start out velvety purple, then fade to soft violet—it grows staunchly upright with almost thornless canes and has soft gray-green foliage. The fault of 'Queen of the Violets' (its English translation) is that blooms shatter and drop their petals almost immediately after they mature. Rosarians hooked on this color, however, don't seem bothered by the premature finish. ('Pius IX' seedling), Millet-Malet, 1860.

ROGER LAMBELIN would probably have been dropped from commerce long ago were it not for the unique color combination of its richly perfumed blossoms—deep maroon with white edging. Otherwise, unless 'Roger Lambelin' is granted a prime garden spot and pampered like no other shrub, it will contract every disease known to roses, most notably mildew and rust. When grown to perfection, however, it has few rivals where showiness is concerned. ('Prince Camille de Rohan' sport), Schwartz, 1890.

VICK'S CAPRICE, a sport of the solid pink rose 'Archiduchesse Élisabeth d'Autriche', is so named because it was discovered by a Mr. Vick of Rochester, New York. The basic color of the intensely fragrant, recurring blossoms is deep pink, but petals are randomly and delicately streaked or flecked with pale pink, lilac, and white. Foliage is large and light green, and the entire bush is relatively thornless. ('Archiduchesse Élisabeth d'Autriche' sport), Vick, 1891.

TEAS

Just like man, the first Tea rose was named 'Adam'. This grandfather to the Hybrid Tea resulted from crossing Bourbon and Noisette roses with two of the notorious China stud roses, 'Hume's Blush China' and 'Parks' Yellow Tea Scented China'. Since everyone agreed that 'Adam' seemed different enough from all other roses to warrant separate botanical nomenclature, and because several people believed that he smelled like fresh tea leaves, 'Adam' was declared the first member of the new family of Tea Scented China roses. In time, the last three names disappeared and the clan became known merely as Teas.

Although I know some dyed-in-the-wool fans of Tea roses who swear that they wouldn't consider being without their old bushes, I think that Teas have hung around mainly from our devotion to their heritage—not a bad reason. A typical Tea rose interspersed in a rose garden makes a terrific visual aid for showing the differences between it and its famous offspring, the Hybrid Tea. The family resemblance, of course, is obvious, but it's also easy to see why the Hybrid Teas are such an improvement—their bushes are not only more vigorous and hardier, they're also far more disease resistant. Still, if you want that clinching prop for a lecture on the historical development of the Modern Rose, you might plant:

ANNA OLIVER is among the more vigorous of the Tea roses, growing on a freely branching bush with attractive mid-green foliage. Fragrant blossoms are two-tone pink—pastel on top, deeper pink on each petal's reverse. (Parentage unknown), Ducher, 1872.

ARCHIDUC JOSEPH is a particularly hardy Tea rose that can be grown either as a bush or as a climber, in either case producing ample, dark green, glossy foliage and few thorns. Blooms that eventually flatten are a mixture of purple and pink petals surrounding blush to yellow centers. ('Mme Lombard' seedling), Nabonnand, 1872.

CATHERINE MERMET is my favorite Tea rose (see entry in chapter 7), probably because it produces superb cut flowers. Alas, it is a bit tender, flourishing only in gardens blessed with temperate climates. Otherwise, it is grown under glass, where it produces lovely, high-centered blooms that are basically blush pink, but with shadings of lilac at the petals' edges. (Parentage unknown), Guillot Fils, 1869.

DUCHESSE DE BRABANT is a particularly fragrant Tea rose, carrying its perfume in large, clear pink to rose-pink cupped blossoms that shower the bush from early spring until fall. Bushes branch freely and are massed in abundant, mid-green, healthy foliage. (Parentage unknown), Bernède, 1857.

LADY HILLINGDON has enjoyed enormous popularity ever since it was introduced in 1910 and has never been

'**WHITE MAMAN COCHET**', *a sport of the famous pink Tea rose, is like its parent in every way except color — creamy white, flushed pink. Either of the Cochets makes a fine companion plant for ornamental grasses — they seem to challenge each other for graceful head nodding.*

'**BRIDESMAID**' *is a sport (spontaneous mutation) of 'Catherine Mermet'. Although both roses are classed as light pink, 'Bridesmaid' is much pinker. Otherwise, she behaves just like her mother.*

'**MONS TILLIER**' *produces miraculous blossoms on two counts. First, color — rosy red shaded salmon and violet. Second, petal arrangement — intricate and irresistible.*

'SAFRANO' *is a lovely Tea rose, even when marred by rain. As its name would suggest, saffron yellow is among the many colors of this sweetly fragrant rose, which also include gold and apricot. Be forewarned, however, that bushes are tender and demand thoughtful winter protection. But fortunately, 'Safrano' performs well in containers, which are easy to protect.*

'LA FRANCE' *caused quite a stir in 1867 when it was declared the forerunner to a whole new race of roses—Hybrid Teas. Although 'La France' proved to be sterile for parenting off-spring, it set the standard for Modern Roses—shapely, urn-shaped, high-centered blossoms.*

'GENERAL GALLIENI' *was enormously popular when he was introduced at the turn of the nineteenth century. Since then, he's fallen out of commerce except among those gardeners hooked on this particular color combination. The General is vigorous and almost thornless.*

out of commerce. Seven years after its debut as a bush, a climbing sport of 'Lady Hillingdon' was discovered, and it has enjoyed even greater success than its parent. While it's true that the rich apricot-yellow color is important to its acceptance, as is its fine perfume, 'Lady Hillingdon' also has beautifully colored foliage and stems. Leaves are not only glossy, they're also a distinctive shade of purplish green, and young shoots are plum-colored—a handsome background for the rather blowsy mature blossoms. Although considered moderately hardy, 'Lady Hillingdon'

is sensitive to cold. ('Papa Gontier' x 'Mme Hoste'), Lowe and Shawyer, 1910.

MAMAN COCHET was once a famous exhibition rose, although it no longer is, having been soundly replaced by its many Modern grandchildren reputed for their stately form. Still, the blooms of 'Maman Cochet' are showy indeed, even though they start out globular. As they mature and rectify their form, the pale pink petals deepen toward their centers and reveal lemon yellow markings. Bushes have leathery, dark green foliage and few thorns. ('Marie van Houtte' x 'Mme Lombard'), Cochet, 1893.

MARIE VAN HOUTTE produces creamy, long, tapered buds tinted carmine-pink and lastingly fragrant. Vigorous bushes cloaked in luxuriant dark green foliage are vigorous but tend to sprawl without support. ('Mme de Tartas' x 'Mme Falcot'), Ducher, 1871.

MONS TILLIER produces tall bushes and abundant blooms for a Tea rose. Individual flowers are not only wondrously colored rose-red, shaded salmon, and violet, they're also intricately petaled. Foliage is particularly lush. (Parentage unknown), Bernaix, 1891.

PAPA GONTIER produces lovely and

lightly scented, semidouble blossoms composed of deep pink petals with a light red reverse. Although foliage is dark green and glossy, it's rather sparse, which is probably why this variety has always been more popular as a greenhouse rose. (Parentage unknown), Nabonnand, 1883.

ROSETTE DELIZY blooms with an irresistible mixture of colors—apricot, buff, and rose-pink. Fragrance is notable, as is the dark bronze foliage. ('Général Gallieni' x 'Comtesse Bardi'), Nabonnand, 1922.

SAFRANO is one of the oldest members of the Tea family and is also a favorite for container planting, which is just as well, since it doesn't perform well in an exposed garden location. Given protection, however, 'Safrano' freely produces sweetly fragrant semidouble blossoms that are saffron yellow tinged apricot. Foliage is mid-green and abundant. (Parentage unknown), Beauregard, 1839.

MY JOURNEY TO 'LA FRANCE'

Soon after I began growing the dowager roses discussed so far, I not only understood why Old Rose enthusiasts love

'LADY HILLINGDON' *is yet another rose more famous as a climber than a bush. Both forms boast glamorous, apricot-yellow fragrant blossoms and handsomely colored foliage and stems. Try to give 'Lady Hillingdon' a sunny spot in the garden; she's sensitive to the cold.*

favorite science teacher had told me about "ROYGBIV," the key word for remembering the colors of the rainbow in order. I realized, however, that I'd never wrap my tongue around a word like "GDACMCPBHPT," the first letters to the 10 families between species and Modern Roses. How to string together Gallica, Damask, Alba, Centifolia, Moss, China, Portland, Bourbon, Hybrid Perpetual, and Tea?

One day while strolling past a border of my favorite Old Roses, I listened to a pirated recording of Maria Callas singing "Norma."

"Why not map this road to 'La France' with a tribute to Madame Callas?" I thought.

"*Genuine Devotees Always Cheer Maria; Childish People Bless High-Pitched Tenors*"—the words tumbled out of my mouth. I realized that it was corny, of course, and never even told anyone about it until recently. I've attempted time and again to improve on my silly phrase, but I keep returning to it.

Make up your own mnemonic saying, but whatever else you do, get to know these beauties that led to the Modern Rose—they pave a handsome road.

---

them so, I fell head over heels for them myself. Also, I finally understood the winding road that led to 'La France', the first Hybrid Tea rose, although it took me longer than it should have to recite the precise route. After growing dozens of members of several families and one from every major clan for more than a decade, I still stumbled over the simplest of questions.

"Tell me, Dr. Reddell," a visitor to my garden would ask, "did this Moss rose here come before or after that Centifolia over there?" My mind would agonizingly grind out the progression of families.

"I've got to make this easier to remember," I swore to myself, "this delayed expertise is embarrassing."

I recalled that when I was a boy my

Soon after I went crazy over Modern Roses, I decided to learn about their ancestors. In the process, I fell head over heels for the entire genus and made up my own mnemonic phrase to keep the dowagers in order.

Modern Roses: 1867 to Now

Roses referred to as Modern—those dating from 1867 until the present—constitute the vast bulk of rosebushes currently in commerce. In fact, of the 150 million rosebushes sold annually throughout the world, at least 80 percent are the types described in this chapter. The immense popularity of Modern Roses is not merely a matter of their being with us for more than a hundred years, it's also because the creators of today's roses are hard at work developing new varieties with extended color ranges, improved disease resistance, and heightened abilities to bloom over prolonged periods.

Personally, I bless the efforts of Modern Rose hybridizers because I relish the security of knowing that I can have roses nonstop from spring until winter. Also, as you'll see in the discussion of the apparent future of roses in chapter 18, breeders are busily creating roses that no one thought possible—varieties that don't require pruning or spraying; in short, no fuss. Still, unless you're blessed with a photographic memory, you, like I, may have trouble remembering the names of

'SWEET VIVIEN' *is sweet indeed, also lightly fragrant and free flowering. Blossoms give the appearance of being single, but they actually contain 17 petals each and reach 3-inch widths before petals reflex. The overall color is pink, but each flower has a white center. Plants are bushy with small, dark, glossy foliage.*

countless new varieties being introduced (the yearly assault of new Miniature roses alone is mind-boggling).

In this chapter, I have tried to strike a balance with what is commercially available and what's worth growing, acknowledging roses still under careful scrutiny as well as those that, although Modern, have already decidedly proven their worth.

HYBRID TEAS

Shortly before 1867, the French hybridizer Guillot wed the Hybrid Perpetual 'Madame Victor Verdier' with the Tea rose 'Madame Bravy' to produce an offspring named 'La France'. Guillot was thrilled with his rosy child because he saw immediately that with its shapely, urn-shaped, high-centered blossoms, 'La France' was indeed different from all roses preceding it. Guillot's French peers agreed that 'La France' qualified as the first member of a chic new race of roses, and agreed temporarily on the name *R. odorata indica*.

Before telling how the name Hybrid Tea officially came to pass, historical accuracy compels me to mention that although 'La France' is generally accepted as the first Hybrid Tea, that honor might actually belong to 'Victor Verdier', a seldom-seen rose hybridized by Lacharme, another

*For reasons I can't fathom, **'INGRID BERGMAN'** hasn't caught on in America, whereas she's a star in England. Blossoms are deep red, beautifully formed, and last well when cut. The dark green ample foliage looks good enough to eat.*

breeder working in Lyons, France. Introduced eight years before 'La France' made its notorious debut, 'Victor Verdier' was the result of a cross between the Hybrid Perpetual 'Jules Margottin' and the Tea rose 'Safrano'.

Horticultural historians revel in the agonies of controversies such as these, but I find it difficult to take a firm position on the argument of which rose should rightfully carry the honor. Although I don't grow 'Victor Verdier' (because I've never been able to get my hands on a healthy bush), I've certainly seen it, and I must admit that it looks every bit as much "Hybrid Tea" as 'La France'. Personally, I believe that Guillot will retain the honor of arriving first from sheer assertiveness, for he was bound and determined that the botanical world acknowledge his find as deserving of a new class among roses. In any case, today all but the most ornery of rosarians agree that 'La France' won the race.

'La France' was not without its problems, however, not the least of which was sterility. What good was the first member of a new race of roses if it could neither sire nor mother offspring? The solution was nearby, just across the English Channel, from the capable hands of Henry Bennett, a Middlesex cattle breeder.

Bennett recognized the potential of those roses hybridized by his French peers, and he drew from his experiences with bovine animals to establish a deliberate breeding platform to improve upon what already existed. Although his early prog-

'ABBEYFIELD' *is a Hybrid Tea whose bushes make fine hedges — they grow staunchly upright to similar heights. Rose-red blossoms are only slightly fragrant, but they're exceptionally large. As you can see in this photograph, 'Abbeyfield' takes well to companion planting.*

eny, which Bennett dubbed "Pedigree Hybrids of the Tea Rose," were nothing special, in 1882 he hit the jackpot when he crossed the creamy Tea rose 'Devoniensis' with 'Victor Verdier' to issue 'Lady Mary Fitzwilliam'—a light pink, intensely fragrant rose that epitomized the stylish qualities that nineteenth-century hybridizers fervently sought. Best of all, unlike 'La France', the Lady was scandalously fertile. While the British rose world was skeptical of earlier pre-

tenders, even the most dubious disbeliever agreed that 'Lady Mary Fitzwilliam' proved beyond doubt that Hybrid Teas had indeed arrived, and the class was promptly accepted.

The French were not to be outdone, and once they got their hands on the sexy 'Lady Mary Fitzwilliam', they bed her with any number of suitors. The premier matchmaker of the day was Joseph Pernet-Ducher, who in 1890 used Bennett's 'Lady Mary Fitzwilliam' as a father (roses are bisexual, and prolific breeders serve double duty as either parent) in developing 'Mme Caroline Testout'—a satiny pink, deeply perfumed beauty that is today more famous in its climbing form than it was then as a bush.

Indebtedness is also owed to Pernet-Ducher for introducing yellow into Hybrid Teas. He did so when he crossed *R. foetida persiana* with the Hybrid Perpetual 'Antoine Ducher', thereby producing 'Soleil d'Or'. Although the French relished the fact that one of their countrymen had singlehandedly brought smartly formed yellow roses into their gardens, it was a dubious honor, for 'Soleil d'Or' and its immediate successors proved addicted to blackspot.

Back in England, Henry Bennett's pollinating expertise strongly influenced other English rose breeders who followed his lead by hybridizing under glass. Foremost was Northern Ireland's Alexander Dickson, who in 1892 won the National Rose Society's first Gold Medal awarded a Hybrid Tea with his pink 'Mrs. W.J. Grant', and Samuel McGredy of Portadown, Ireland, who launched his illustrious hybridizing career in 1910 with the fragrant white 'Mrs. Herbert Stevens'.

Although no American had made an indelible stamp on the hybridization of roses since John Champney in 1811, that was all to change when E. Gurney Hill of Richmond, Indiana, launched a program aimed at the creation of Hybrid Teas. His first success, the rosy red, lightly petaled, intensely fragrant 'General MacArthur'

(today more popular as a climber than as a bush), was introduced in 1905. Once Hill got the picture of what Americans wanted in the way of Hybrid Teas, there was no stopping him, and he introduced more than 20 new varieties within the following decade.

Like their American peers, German breeders weren't to come on strong until after World War I, except for one notable exception—Peter Lambert, who in 1901 introduced 'Frau Karl Druschki'. Although the skyscraping Frau is technically a Hybrid Perpetual (also scentless), today it's customarily lumped with Hybrid Teas in rose catalogs.

While the popularity of roses never slowed, hybridizing them did during both world wars. Especially in Europe, greenhouses were put to more practical use than as sheds for scrambling rose pollen, such as by filling them with tomatoes and other vegetables that grow well under glass. Although the two decades between the wars allowed for a temporary return to floral beauty in the glasshouses, it was not until the end of World War II that the hybridizing of roses became truly big business. Then it went bananas.

By the end of World War II, a hoard of rose hybridizers had joined those already mentioned. In England, the names of Alex Cocker and Edward LeGrice appeared regularly on awards tables; Spain was represented with Pedro Dot; Denmark, with Dines Poulsen; Germany, with Wilhelm Kordes and Mathias Tantau; and France added the Meilland and Delbard

families to their already illustrious line of rose breeders. It was also during this period that American hybridizers forged to the forefront of new rose introductions—a position from which they have never retreated. Fred Howard of Los Angeles led the race, then was shortly joined by the indefatigable Eugene Boerner of Jackson & Perkins and the outrageously successful team of Herbert Swim and Ollie Weeks of Armstrong Roses.

Considerable fuel was added to the fire of American hybridizers in 1930 with the passage of the plant patent law, an amendment to the United States Patent Law, which stated that patentable plants included "any distinct and new variety of plant, including cultivated sports, mutants, hybrids, and newly found seedlings." Plants so patented afford the creator certain rights (including royalties for asexual reproduction) for a term of 17 years. Similar protective acts followed in Europe, including England's Plant Varieties and Seeds Act in 1964.

Hybrid Teas have now been with us for more than a century and a quarter, and introductions number in the tens of thousands. Today's Hybrid Teas are markedly different from those introduced at the turn of the twentieth century—a mixed blessing as far as many rosarians are concerned. Everyone agrees, of course, that increased vigor, disease resistance, and regularity of bloom cycles are all pluses. Furthermore, it is exciting to see an extension of color range—up to a point, that is. The hues of current Hybrid Teas

'ALMONDEEN' *never made a commercial splash after it was introduced in 1984, maybe because it was marketed as a Hybrid Tea rather than as a Floribunda, which it actually is. In any case, slightly fragrant, fully petaled blossoms are a wondrous combination of almond and pink, and foliage is semiglossy, large, and medium green.*

'AVE MARIA' *was a drag on the commercial market, perhaps because the name was wrong for a prissy, high-centered, but only slightly fragrant orange rose. The bush, however, is another matter—upright and swathed in glossy, dark green foliage. 'Ave Maria' has another endearing habit: its flowers almost always occur one-to-a-stem.*

'BLUE NILE', *another in a series of Modern mauve Hybrid Tea roses, is awfully fussy about where it grows. If summers are hot, forget it. Where bushes are suitably cool, however, blooms are ravishing—lovingly formed and drenched in perfume. Foliage is large and olive green. Alas, 'Blue Nile' is prone to mildew.*

are "hot" compared with those of their predecessors; many are considered garish, not blending harmoniously into gardens at large.

Personally, I prefer today's Hybrid Teas to their forerunners, a preference no doubt owing to my addiction to ample bloom and resistance to disease. I agree, however, that many new introductions sport colors so vivid that I, too, am stumped over just what to do with them in the garden.

Another problem in deciding which Hybrid Teas to list is posed by the fickle nature of the buying public and by which colors are in or out of fashion. The issue of

trendiness was perfectly explained 40 years ago in *Roses Illustrated*, a publication sponsored by the Portland Rose Society:

"New and improved varieties become available to the public so swiftly in modern days that few roses, unless outstanding and effective over a wide range of climatic conditions, can anticipate a popularity life span of more than 10 or 15 years in general public interest. Many do not hold the stage even that long."

Nevertheless, I believe that several of the Hybrid Teas discussed here shall remain with us forever (some have already

proven that probability). Others are due to persist until a deserving replacement comes along. The following list of Hybrid Teas is composed of heirlooms, middle-aged beauties, and those fresh off the hybridizing bench:

ADMIRAL RODNEY has been a favorite among rose exhibitors on both sides of the Atlantic for 20 years. The Admiral's huge, exquisitely formed, two-tone pink blossoms are fragrant, and his moderately sized plants are bushy and well foliated but prone to rust. (Parentage unknown), Trew, 1973.

ADOLF HORSTMANN has fragrant, deep

golden yellow blossoms handsomely flushed with salmon. Disease-resistant foliage is mid- to dark green, and bushes are upright growers. Adolf is notably hardy for a Hybrid Tea. ('Colour Wonder' x 'Dr. A.J. Verhage'), Kordes, 1971.

ALEC'S RED is notoriously fragrant, which is no wonder, since its mother is 'Fragrant Cloud', one of the most deliciously fragrant roses ever. Fat, almost black buds open to cherry red flowers that sit atop strong, thorny stems on a mid-sized bush. ('Fragrant Cloud' x 'Dame de Coeur'), Cocker, 1970.

BETTY UPRICHARD qualifies as an heirloom Hybrid Tea. The reason it has managed to stick around is that its shapely salmon-pink flowers have an appealing cloudy reverse on their petals, bushes are extremely free flowering, and foliage is leathery. (Parentage unknown), Dickson, 1922.

BEWITCHED is a hands-down contender for immortality among Hybrid Teas (see entry in chapter 7). Blossoms are huge, fragrant, and clear pink. Bushes cloaked in grayish green foliage are tall and reasonably disease resistant but, alas, rather tender where winters are severe. ('Queen Elizabeth' x 'Tawny Gold'), Lammerts, 1967.

BLUE MOON, as the name would suggest, isn't really blue but rather lilac to lavender. Still, its fully double (40-petaled) blossoms are intensely fragrant, and its bush is upright and blessed with good foliage. ('Sterling Silver' seedling x unnamed seedling), Tantau, 1964.

BOBBY CHARLTON is a fragrant, two-tone pink stunner with exceptionally well formed blossoms. Bushes covered with dark green, leathery foliage grow vigorously upright but are prone to legginess, especially without careful pruning. Hardiness is iffy where winters are severe. ('Royal Highness' x 'Prima Ballerina'), Fryer, 1974.

BRANDY is an exemplary Hybrid Tea in that its blossoms almost always occur one-to-a-stem. Its classic blooms are smartly colored coppery apricot, spiced with fragrance, and complemented by mahogany-tinted foliage. Like the potable after which it's named, 'Brandy' doesn't take well to low temperatures. ('First Prize' x 'Dr. A.J. Verhage'), Christensen and Swim, 1981.

CHARLOTTE ARMSTRONG was queen of the Hybrid Teas for more than a quarter of a century after its introduction, before varieties with stronger necks surpassed it. Long, pointed, blood red buds mature into deep pink, double (35-petaled), fragrant blossoms. Bushes are vigorous, and foliage is dark and leathery. ('Soeur Thérèse' x 'Crimson Glory'), Lammerts, 1940.

CHICAGO PEACE is considered the best of all sports of the famous 'Peace' rose. Like its mother, 'Chicago Peace' is also yellow and pink, but long on pink. Blossoms are ruffled, foliage is glossy and disease resistant, and bushes are extremely hardy. ('Peace' sport), Johnston, 1962.

CHRYSLER IMPERIAL was, for many years, the standard by which red roses were judged. Now it's grown primarily in warm climates where heat is sufficient to open blossoms with 45 petals and mildew isn't a threat. 'Chrysler Imperial' is dark red and richly fragrant, but temperamental. ('Charlotte Armstrong' x 'Mirandy'), Lammerts, 1952.

COLOR MAGIC is my favorite rose (see entry in chapter 7), so you might want to keep that in mind while I rave of its merits. Blossoms that are an everchanging blend of pink, deep rose, and beige reach outlandish sizes and are uniquely fragrant at all stages. Deep love, however, does not blind me to its faults, mainly that it dies back (see chapter 9) like no other rose I've ever known. Still, I wouldn't consider living without it. (Unnamed seedling x 'Spellbinder'), Warriner, 1978.

COMTESSE VANDAL is a favorite among rosarians who admire perfumed Hybrid Teas with classic pointed centers. The Countess's blossoms are salmon-pink with a coppery reverse to their petals. Plants are vigorous, bushy, and well clothed in leathery foliage. (['Ophelia' x 'Mrs. Aaron Ward'] x 'Souvenir de Claudius Pernet'), Leenders, 1932.

CRIMSON GLORY is still widely grown in spite of the fact that more-improved dark velvety red Modern Roses have surpassed it (particularly those blessed with strong necks). True, its scent is virtually irresistible, but its bush is annoyingly asymmetrical. ('Catherine Kordes' seedling x 'W.E. Chaplin'), Kordes, 1935.

DAINTY BESS, as I rationalize in chapter 7, is the finest single-flowered Hybrid Tea

'DIE WELT' *produces blooms that are precisely what Hybrid Tea blooms should look like. Unfortunately, bushes are prone to mildew and are erratic growers. Still, that prissy form is unbeatable; the color combination isn't bad either.*

'HEADLINER', *another Hybrid Tea blend sent to catch up to the fame of 'Double Delight', has a problem with fragrance—it's only slight. Otherwise, blooms are decidedly showy because their 40 petals form exceptionally large flowers. Foliage is large, too; also medium green and glossy. All in all, however, I'll stick with 'Double Delight', thank you.*

'McGREDY'S SUNSET' *was introduced in 1936, making it an old-timer among Modern Hybrid Teas. If you're fortunate enough to get your hands on a plant, you're in for a treat, especially if you like two-tone yellow roses: these petals look as though they've been dipped in scarlet.*

ever hybridized. Although 'Dainty Bess' has only five petals per blossom, they're silvery pink, fragrant, and long lasting, and they surround a center of maroon stamens. Bushes are upright and shapely. ('Ophelia' x 'K. of K.'), Archer, 1925.

DAME EDITH HELEN has hung around the Hybrid Tea family for longer than 65 years in spite of the fact that she doesn't closely resemble many of her kin. As often as not, the Dame's blossoms are quartered, Heritage Rose style. Whatever their globular form, blooms on strong necks are silvery pink and deeply fragrant. (Parentage unknown), Dickson, 1926.

DIAMOND JUBILEE is a free-blooming classic Hybrid Tea, with well-formed, fragrant, pale apricot blooms. Although the flowers are resentful of damp weather, bushes are strong growers and handsomely foliated. ('Maréchal Niel' x 'Feu Pernet-Ducher'), Boerner, 1947.

DIE WELT sticks around for an instant refresher course on what a classic Hybrid Tea should look like. Yellow blossoms brushed with orange are downright prissy, but you've got to hand it to them—they've certainly got form. Alas, this stately bush is mildew-prone and an erratic grower. (Seedling x 'Peer Gynt'), Kordes, 1976.

DOUBLE DELIGHT caused a splash when it was introduced as an All-America Rose in 1977. Small wonder, it's quite a splashy rose (see entry in chapter 7): no two richly fragrant blossoms are alike but rather are randomly blushed red over cream. ('Granada' x 'Garden Party'), Swim and Ellis, 1977.

DUET is the quintessential workhorse among roses, with armloads of two-tone pink blossoms regularly occurring on ong stems with glossy foliage—another immortal beauty discussed in chapter 7. ('Fandango' x 'Roundelay'), Swim, 1960.

ELECTRON has lost ground in popularity recently, not because rosarians aren't still fond of its large hot pink blooms but rather because they're fed up with its viciously thorny, runty bush and its constant need for disbudding. Still, 'Electron' is a free bloomer. ('Paddy McGredy' x 'Prima Ballerina'), McGredy, 1973.

ERNEST H. MORSE holds a soft spot in my heart because I once won a rose trophy with two of its powerfully fragrant, turkey red blossoms. Bushes are upright growers, foliage is dark, and stems are maroon-brown. (Parentage unknown), Kordes, 1964.

ÉTOILE DE HOLLAND was once the dark red fragrant rose to beat. Nowadays it's rarely seen as a bush, although the climber still enjoys popularity. Blossoms today are just as richly colored and powerfully perfumed as they were decades ago; unfortunately, the plant is yet highly susceptible to infestations of mildew. ('General MacArthur' x 'Hadley'), Verschuren, 1919.

FIRST LOVE is one of the first roses I fell in love with. Clear pink, perfectly formed buds shaded with mahogany open to rather blowsy blossoms with only 25 petals. Foliage is good, as is the upright growth habit, and blooms appear regularly. Reliable budwood seems to be on the wane. ('Charlotte Armstrong' x 'Show Girl'), Swim, 1951.

FIRST PRIZE, a veteran exhibition rose, is a triumph of Gene Boerner's hybridizing career. Where contented, bushes of 'First Prize' grow upright; otherwise,

plants spread low and blooms have short stems. Blossoms are knockouts, beginning mid-pink flushed deep rose and eventually revealing an ivory heart. Fragrance is light, but foliage is dark and leathery. ('Enchantment' seedling x 'Golden Masterpiece' seedling), Boerner, 1970.

FOLKLORE is labeled *Rosa vulgaris* in my garden. Bushes are skyscrapers, sometimes requiring a ladder for harvesting. On the other hand, plants form impenetrable hedges and the long-stemmed yellow and shrimp pink blooms are pleasantly fragrant. ('Fragrant Cloud' x unidentified seedling), Kordes, 1977.

FRAGRANT CLOUD wins my vote for the most fragrant Modern Rose ever, placing it firmly in the immortal category (see entry in chapter 7). Although the color of its lipstick red blossoms isn't to everyone's taste and its oversized dark green foliage is highly mildew-prone, 'Fragrant Cloud' possesses a heady perfume that makes such complaints seem almost petty in comparison. (Unnamed seedling x 'Prima Ballerina'), Tantau, 1968.

GARDEN PARTY was an All-America Rose Selection in 1960 and is still a favorite among many rosarians in spite of the fact that roses of the same color combination have surpassed it. Large, slightly fragrant blossoms are white, tinged pink at the petals' edges. Although bushes are vigorous, they're especially prone to mildew. ('Charlotte Armstrong' x 'Peace'), Swim, 1959.

GRANADA was an All-America Rose Selection in 1964 and is still going strong. Its

most impressive colors include vermilion, scarlet, and lemon yellow, the combination of which is fluorescent. Blossoms are smallish for a Hybrid Tea, but they're intensely fragrant and faithfully among the first to bloom each season. ('Tiffany' x 'Cavalcade'), Lindquist, 1963.

GRANDPA DICKSON, better known in the United States as 'Irish Gold', is a classic among yellow Hybrid Teas. Blossoms are large but exceedingly well shaped and sweetly fragrant; bushes are thorny and sparsely covered with mid-green foliage. (['Kordes' Perfecta' x 'Governador Braga da Cruz'] x 'Picadilly'), Dickson, 1966.

HARRY WHEATCROFT is named after a flamboyant character who fancied himself to be a fine talent scout in the world of roses, as indeed he was. This rose is actually a sport of 'Picadilly', although here the blossoms are yellow on the petals' outsides and red-and-yellow-striped on the insides—as madly showy as the man himself. ('Picadilly' sport), Wheatcroft, 1972.

HELEN TRAUBEL, except for her notoriously weak necks, is one of the loveliest apricot-pink roses ever hybridized. Bushes are tall and vigorous, foliage is ample and matte green, and the large blossoms are as fragrant as a honey pot. Alas, those necks (although many gardeners couldn't care less). ('Charlotte Armstrong' x 'Glowing Sunset'), Swim, 1951.

HELMUT SCHMIDT is unique among yellow Hybrid Teas for its exquisitely shaped blossoms. Although bushes tend to sprawl rather than grow upright, their foliage is

'MAID OF HONOR' *is officially classified as yellow, but mine are beige; they also frequently blossom in sprays rather than one-to-a-stem. No matter, this is a fine rose and a lofty grower with mid- to dark green, disease-resistant foliage. The Maid also has a bad habit of sporting back to her father, 'Folklore'—a far less desirable Hybrid Tea.*

'MON CHÉRI', *a child of 'Double Delight', isn't nearly so famous as its father, but it, too, is a spiffy combination of colors. Petals range in color from dark red through pink to glowing yellow. Although blossoms are only lightly fragrant, they're nicely framed in foliage that remains mahogany red long before it turns emerald green.*

'PARADISE' *is so unusually colored that photographs rarely look real. Besides dramatically combining mauve and ruby red in a blend previously unheard of, 'Paradise' is sweetly fragrant. Its blooms are also almost always perfectly formed, with petals surrounding a bull's-eye center.*

disease resistant and handsome. Where I garden, Helmut is stingy with bloom, but I plant him anyway, strictly out of admiration for those warm yellow, perfectly formed blossoms. ('New Day' x unnamed seedling), Kordes, 1979.

HONOR was a member of the trio of roses with which Bill Warriner swept the All-America Rose awards in 1980 (the other two were 'Love' and 'Cherish'). 'Honor' is a mighty classy rose. Its bushes are skyscrapers (mine reach 7 feet at summer's end), its foliage is dark green (watch out for mildew), and its blossoms are pure white and become enormous before they

finish opening. (See entry in chapter 7.) (Unnamed seedling x unnamed seedling), Warriner, 1980.

INGRID BERGMAN, for some reason, is far more popular in Europe than she is in the United States. Fragrant double blossoms are deep red and occur regularly on a dense bush heavily clothed in dark green, semiglossy foliage. (Unnamed seedling x unnamed seedling), Poulsen, 1983.

IRISH ELEGANCE is one of the world's favorite single-petaled Hybrid Tea roses. Bushes are growers and freely produce large, five-petaled flowers that combine deep pink, scarlet, bronze, and gold.

(Parentage unknown), Dickson, 1905.

JOHN WATERER is a large (44-petaled), classically formed, crimson Hybrid Tea that's also fragrant. Bushes are strong upright growers with ample dark green foliage. ('King of Hearts' x 'Hanne'), McGredy, 1970.

JOSEPHINE BRUCE persists in popularity in spite of two serious flaws: an awkward, angular bush and disease-prone foliage. On her plus side, Josephine is richly fragrant and one of the most purely colored of all crimson roses. ('Crimson Glory' x 'Madge Whipp'), Bees, 1949.

JULIA'S ROSE, the brown rose, is an

oddity among Hybrid Teas. Its color isn't actually brown, more like parchment tan. Blooms are well formed and have a spicy fragrance. Alas, the bush is puny. ('Blue Moon' x 'Dr. A.J. Verhage'), Tysterman, 1976.

JUST JOEY is one of the few Modern Roses that's equally treasured by rosarians addicted to Heritage Roses. Its blossoms are beautifully colored shades of apricot and deliciously fragrant. Although 'Just Joey's' bushes are rather runty, they rank among the most floriferous of Hybrid Teas, and their blooms are appealingly oversized. (See entry in chapter 7.) ('Fragrant Cloud' x 'Dr. A.J. Verhage'), Cant, 1972.

KING'S RANSOM was an All-America Rose Selection in 1962 and the most popular yellow Hybrid Tea for almost 20 years thereafter. Blossoms are fragrant, shapely, and golden yellow and sit atop strong necks. 'King's Ransom' bushes are vigorous and foliage is dark green and glossy. ('Golden Masterpiece' x 'Lydia'), Morey, 1961.

LADY ALICE STANLEY is a dowager among Hybrid Teas. Her fragrant blossoms are packed with 70 petals that are soft pink with a deeper pink reverse. Bushes are angular but graceful in growth, and foliage is rich. (Parentage unknown), McGredy, 1909.

LADY ROSE is treasured among exhibitors because of its long, pointed buds and high-centered blossoms, which are also salmon-colored and fragrant. Bushes are vigorous growers and amply clothed

in mid-green foliage. (Seedling x 'Traümerei'), Kordes, 1979.

LADY X is another exhibition rose praised less for its natural beauty than for its perfect form. Lightly fragrant blossoms are an arrangement of mauve petals that formally quill themselves around a high center. Bushes grow staunchly upright and foliage is leathery but mildew-prone. (Seedling x 'Simone'), Meilland, 1966.

LA FRANCE, generally agreed to be the first Hybrid Tea, has lost considerable vigor since its introduction (although that's not why its necks are weak; they always were). 'La France' is still widely grown, however, not simply out of sentiment but also because of its powerfully fragrant, silvery-to-rose-pink, heavily petaled blossoms. ('Madame Victor Verdier' x 'Madame Bravy'), Guillot, 1867.

LAKELAND is only slightly fragrant in spite of having 'Fragrant Cloud' as a mother. Its blossoms are large, shell pink, and nicely formed. Bushes are upright and foliage is plentiful. ('Fragrant Cloud' x 'Queen Elizabeth'), Fryer, 1976.

LOS ANGELES has ensured its popularity not only because of its large, fragrant, coral-and-gold blossoms but also because it's such a good stud rose. Bushes tend to spread, but foliage is leathery and dark green. ('Mme Segond Weber' x 'Lyon Rose'), Howard, 1916.

MADAME BUTTERFLY, a sport of 'Ophelia', is more famous than the rose from which it mutated. Like 'Ophelia', 'Mme Butterfly' is fragrant and beautifully shaped. It's also more strikingly

colored—a deeper pink than its mother and suffused with yellow at the base of each petal. Bushes are thin, but they're reliable bloomers. ('Ophelia' sport), Hill, 1918.

MALA RUBINSTEIN isn't as great as either of its parents, but it's a fine rose. Rich pink blossoms appear with steady regularity on a nice bush with abundant, matte-green foliage. Many people rave about Mala's strong scent. I'm not bowled over, but I like it. ('Sea Pearl' x 'Fragrant Cloud'), Dickson, 1971.

MCGREDY'S YELLOW sports unfading, buttercup yellow, cupped, fragrant blossoms on a bush that has semi-glossy foliage tinted bronze. Bushes are low growers but abundant bloomers. ('Mrs. Charles Lamplough' x ['The Queen Alexandra Rose' x 'J.B. Clark']), McGredy, 1934.

MEDALLION has fragrant, exceptionally large blossoms in an appealing color— pale pink to apricot. They come on a nice bush too—tall, upright, and shapely. If you cut roses to enjoy indoors, remember that you have to wait awhile to cut 'Medallion'—until the bud shows signs of unfurling. Then, it's "Katie-bar-the-door." Another immortal rose, discussed in chapter 7. ('South Seas' x 'King's Ransom'), Warriner, 1973.

MICHÈLE MEILLAND was the first rose fathered by 'Peace' the most famous rose in the world. Ms. Meilland's blossoms are basically buff but are heavily shaded salmon-pink. Bushes are short but vigorous. ('Joanna Hill' x 'Peace'), Meilland, 1945.

'ROYAL HIGHNESS' *was an All-America Rose Selection almost 30 years ago, but it's still one of the most elegant blooms in all of rosedom, particularly in bud. Although it's classified as light pink, 'Royal Highness' looks white next to most pink roses. In classic Hybrid Tea form, blooms form one-to-a-stem.*

'SHEER BLISS' *is still rather new to rosedom (it was an All-America Selection in 1987), but I think it's destined to stick around for a good while. White roses with carmine edges are hardly unusual, but ones that smell this nice are rare.*

'TOUCH OF CLASS' *is scentless, no way around it. In compensation, buds and half-open frilly blooms are a cheerful shade of orange. Then a color transformation begins that ends up with pink, fully open blossoms. Stems are long, and the bush is generous with its bounty.*

MISS ALL-AMERICAN BEAUTY was first known as 'Maria Callas' in Europe. I think Maria must have been relieved when her namesake was introduced as 'Miss All-American Beauty' in the United States, for I can't imagine that she approved of the color—hot neon pink. The bush, however, has a lot going for it, including dark green, glossy leaves. The fragrant, heavily petaled blossoms are often on stems too short to do the blooms justice. ('Chrysler Imperial' x 'Karl Herbst'), Meilland, 1965.

MISTER LINCOLN is the world's favorite dark red rose. Black-red buds open to cherry red blossoms, fragrant at all stages. Bushes are upright and almost naturally urn-shaped; foliage is large but susceptible to mildew. Still, 'Mister Lincoln' is ensured immortality, as discussed in chapter 7. ('Chrysler Imperial' x 'Charles Mallerin'), Swim and Weeks, 1965.

MRS. OAKLEY FISHER is one of the most beautiful of all single-flowered Hybrid Tea roses. Fragrant, bright apricot-yellow blossoms with amber stamens appear in clusters on thorny mahogany stems clothed in bronze-green, glossy foliage. (Parentage unknown), Cant, 1921.

NATIONAL TRUST will keep your disbudding fingers busy if you intend to grow its flowers one-to-a-stem. Blossoms that appear artificial because of their flawless showy form are cherry red and scentless. Bushes are thick, densely foliated, and heavily thorned. ('Evelyn Fison' x 'King of Hearts'), McGredy, 1970.

NEW DAY still goes around as 'Mabella' in Europe, where it was hybridized. Large, fragrant, mimosa-yellow blossoms appear regularly on a bush disappointing in vigor. Stem length is highly variable. ('Arlene Francis' x 'Roselandia'), Kordes, 1977.

OLYMPIAD was named in honor of the 1984 summer Olympic Games in Los Angeles and was an All-America Rose Selection that same year. Except for its thorough lack of fragrance, 'Olympiad' is a fine rose—scarlet, flawlessly formed, and long stemmed. ('Red Planet' x 'Pharaoh'), McGredy, 1984.

OREGOLD was an All-America Rose Selection in 1975 and has been losing ground ever since. Although it's true that its softly fragrant blossoms are as sensationally colored as rich butter, they often appear misshapen and bloom far too infrequently. When 'Oregold' is "on," however, it's hard to ignore. ('Picadilly' x 'Colour Wonder'), Tantau, 1975.

PARADISE, an All-America Rose Selection in 1979, bowled over the rose world when it was introduced. Even though mauve roses were no longer rare, one with petals edged ruby red was. Besides the dramatic color combination (admittedly not to everyone's taste), 'Paradise' has exemplary form and is sharply fragrant. Alas, its foliage is distressingly problematical. ('Swarthmore' x unnamed seedling), Weeks, 1978.

PASCALI, from Belgium, is considered by many Modern Rose enthusiasts to be the finest white Hybrid Tea ever hybridized. I happen to believe that honor belongs elsewhere, but I'll never be without my bushes of 'Pascali'. Not technically pure white, 'Pascali' is so close that it's not worth quibbling about. Blossoms form atop thin but strong, long stems on upright bushes with handsome foliage. A winning rose. ('Queen Elizabeth' x 'White Butterfly'), Lens, 1963.

PEACE is the most famous rose in the world, not only because of its intrinsic values but also due to considerable hoopla surrounding its introduction (see entry in chapter 7). No two blossoms are alike, but all are golden to pale yellow flushed with rose-pink. Foliage is dark and glossy. (['George Dickson' x 'Souvenir de Claudius Pernet'] x ['Joanna Hill' x 'Charles P. Kilham'] x 'Margaret McGredy'), Meilland, 1945.

PEAUDOUCE is marketed as 'Elina' in the United States, but I prefer its European name. Although it's classified as yellow, 'Peaudouce' is much closer to white, so ivory are its yellow markings. Bushes are vigorous and freely produce large blossoms on good straight cutting stems. A knockout of a rose, especially if the thought of mildew doesn't scare you. ('Nana Mouskouri' x 'Lolita'), Dickson, 1985.

PERFUME DELIGHT lives up to its name with sumptuous fragrance. Blooms are large and hot pink, but bushes are slow to repeat. Leathery foliage verges on oversized. ('Peace' x ['Happiness' x 'Chrysler Imperial'] x 'El Capitan'), Weeks, 1973.

PETER FRANKENFELD, like 'Perfume Delight', is hot pink. Although the blossoms are only slightly fragrant, they occur faithfully all season on tough thorny bushes with disease-resistant foliage. (Parentage unrecorded), Kordes, 1966.

PICADILLY has never performed as well for me as it does elsewhere. Then again, I'm not mad for this particular bold color combination of scarlet and yellow or for faintly scented roses in general. Where it grows well, the thorny shrub of 'Picadilly' is vigorous and its foliage dark and shiny. ('McGredy's Yellow' x 'Karl Herbst'), McGredy, 1960.

PICTURE is a beloved buttonhole rose in England. Its pure pink blossoms are nicely formed but only lightly fragrant; bushes are short and thorny but nicely foliated and floriferous. (Parentage unknown), McGredy, 1932.

PINK PEACE is not a sport of 'Peace', but the famous rose does figure incestuously in its parentage. If you happen to like enormous, neon pink, sinfully fragrant roses, by all means have a look and sniff at 'Pink Peace'. Although bushes are upright growers, they're not exactly vigorous and their pale matte green foliage is susceptible to mildew. As if in shame of those flaws, blossoms have an appealing habit of closing their petals at night. (['Peace' x 'Monique'] x ['Peace' x 'Mrs. John Laing']), Meilland, 1959.

POLAR STAR, known equally well as 'Polarstern', took a while to reach American shores but finally did so at the beckoning hands of exhibitors who recognized a winner when they saw one. Blossoms are creamy white and elegantly formed. Unfortunately, fragrance is virtually nonexistent and bushes are nondescript. (Parentage unknown), Tantau, 1982.

PORTLAND TRAILBLAZER probably won't be popular much longer because fragrant dark red roses with nicer growth habits are sure to take over. In the mean-

'HAWAIIAN SUNSET' *is a fine choice for gardeners who like informal Hybrid Teas. Perhaps because the blossoms have up to 50 petals each, mature flowers have a whimsical form. Their color is not to be sneezed at, however, nor is their fruity fragrance.*

'CORDON BLEU' *combines a classy range of colors from apricot to begonia pink. The form of individual blossoms is loose, but because flowers usually occur in sprays of three, the mass effect is thoroughly pleasant.*

'FUNKHUR' *has no fragrance, but it certainly isn't short on color (some say it is garish). The bushes on which the eye-blinking, yellow-edged-red blossoms appear are upright and massed with medium-green, glossy foliage.*

time, 'Big Chief' (as 'Portland Trailblazer' is known in Europe) is a leggy grower but a winner. ('Ernest H. Morse' x 'Red Planet'), Dickson, 1975.

PRESIDENT HERBERT HOOVER is an eternally popular bicolor—rose-gold petals with a buff reverse. Stems are long, necks are strong, and foliage is tough. Because bushes lean toward lanky growth, forethought should be given to complementary companion planting. ('Sensation' x 'Souvenir de Claudius Pernet'), Coddington, 1930.

PRIMA BALLERINA is deep pink and large of flower. By the time they're fully open, blossoms become appealingly blowsy and never lose their deep fragrance. Bushes are sturdy, thorny, low growers. (Seedling x 'Peace'), Tantau, 1957.

PRISTINE is my hands-down vote for the rose of the 1970s. Read its full description in chapter 7, but for now, rest assured that its graceful, white-edged-crimson blossoms flower on staunch, if thorny, voracious bushes. An all-time winner. ('White Masterpiece' x 'First Prize'), Warriner, 1978.

RED DEVIL is aptly named, for this rose will woo you into growing it in spite of the fact that it's a stingy bloomer. Still, the slightly fragrant blossoms that manage to appear are large and high centered. ('Silver Lining' x 'Prima Ballerina'), Dickson, 1970.

ROSE GAUJARD is a fine rose that's not likely to enjoy wide appeal because of its unusually colored blossoms—red and silver petals with a paler reverse. Bushes are vigorous, foliage is dark and glossy, but fragrance is faint. ('Peace' x 'Opera' seedling), Gaujard, 1957.

ROYAL DANE is my favorite rose from Denmark's Poulsen family. Decidedly fragrant, rosy bronze and rich orange blossoms are produced in abundance on a bush covered in dark green, glossy foliage. ('Super Star' x ['Baccara' x 'Princess Astrid'] x 'Hanne'), Poulsen, 1971.

ROYAL HIGHNESS has two fatal strikes against it: affinities for mildew and botrytis. What a pity, for when 'Royal Highness' performs well, she's irresistible. Perfect pink-but-almost-white buds form atop long cutting stems heavily clothed in dark green foliage that looks (but isn't) impervious to disease. Blooms are shapely until the three-quarters-open stage, at which time they become formless. If you garden where both days and evenings are dry and warm, by all means try Miss Highness. If weather becomes damp, keep a sprayer ready. ('Virgo' x 'Peace'), Swim, 1962.

SHEER BLISS grows so well where I garden that it seems as though it were hybridized just for my region. So, I'm biased. Bushes are hard workers, producing one long stem after another with a perfectly formed blossom perfectly parked on top. White-edged deep-pink roses aren't unique, but one that smells this nice is. An All-America Rose Selection in 1987 and a fine choice. ('White Masterpiece' x 'Grand Masterpiece'), Warriner, 1987.

SILVER JUBILEE is the crowning achievement in hybridizer Alec Cocker's career. Named in honor of the silver anniversary of Queen Elizabeth's reign, the rose is a showstopper if properly grown. Blossoms, which tend to be small unless disbudded one-to-a-stem, are shaded salmon- and copper-pink. Fragrance is only moderate,

but foliage is large and abundant. (['Highlight' x 'Colour Wonder'] x ['Parkdirektor Riggers' x 'Picadilly'] x 'Mischief'), Cocker, 1978.

SIR HARRY PILKINGTON has only 30 petals, but they're perfectly placed. Blossoms are large, bright red, and long on form. Fragrance isn't strong and bushes could use a bit more vigor. ('Inge Horstmann' x 'Sophia Loren'), Tantau, 1974.

SUMMER SUNSHINE is a cheerful rose indeed. Its luscious yellow color is constant, and fragrance is strong enough to pronounce it pleasantly scented. Buds are long and well formed; blossoms are another matter—blooms may be shapely, but just as often they're cuppy. Growth is upright, and foliage is dark. ('Buccaneer' x 'Lemon Chiffon'), Swim, 1962.

SUNNY SOUTH, perhaps the most famous rose hybridized in Australia, blooms in a rich combination of pink flushed carmine and yellow. Fragrance is strong, and bushes are vigorous. ('Gustav Grünerwald' x 'Betty Berkeley'), Clark, 1918.

TALISMAN is still widely grown, especially by people who had already planted it before 'Sutter's Gold' came along. In fragrance and color, however, these two roses are quite similar, although foliage of 'Talisman' is light green and not entirely plentiful. ('Ophelia' x 'Souvenir de Claudius Pernet'), Montgomery, 1929.

THE DOCTOR is an extremely popular vintage Hybrid Tea. It has only 25 petals, but 'The Doctor' has arranged them perfectly—fragrant silvery pink scrolls with a satiny sheen. Although they remain

close to the ground, bushes are vigorous (except for an affinity for blackspot). ('Mrs. J.D. Eisele' x 'Los Angeles'), Howard, 1936.

TIFFANY is a treasure among rosarians who like elegant buds that mature into deeply fragrant, buxom blossoms. In spite of the fact that it's classified as a pink blend, you might as well think of it as pink with hints of yellow at the base of each petal. Bushes are vigorously upright, and stems are long. ('Charlotte Armstrong' x 'Girona'), Lindquist, 1954.

TOUCH OF CLASS makes me feel ambivalent. I like so much about this rose—its perfectly formed flowers that start out orange and end up pink; its long stems; its glossy, dark green foliage and upright growth. Still, I despise it as a harbinger of mildew and for its scentless blossoms. If perfume doesn't matter to you, however, and you don't mind spraying, 'Touch of Class' is a stunner. ('Micaëla' x ['Queen Elizabeth' x 'Romantica']), Kriloff, 1984.

TROPICANA, I believe, has singlehandedly given Modern Roses a bad name. The problem lies mainly in its shocking neon orange color, although there are other faults, including dingy foliage and affinity for mildew. I know gardeners who swear 'Tropicana' is fragrant. To me, it smells no better than cardboard. ([Seedling x 'Peace']) x ([Seedling x 'Alpine Glow']), Tantau, 1960.

VIRGO is a favorite among Hybrid Tea aficionados. Pointed white (often blushed pink) buds are long, and blossoms are large and high centered, but only mildly perfumed. Bushes are random in their growth habits; some are vigorous, but an equal number are weak. In all cases, foliage is matte and prone to mildew. ('Blanche Mallerin' x 'Neige Parfum'), Mallerin, 1947.

WENDY CUSSONS is immensely more popular in Europe than in the United States, probably because Americans don't lack for roses somewhere between red and bright pink. Still, Wendy is worth a second look because of her beautifully formed, deeply fragrant blossoms and her strong bushy growth. ('Independence' x 'Eden Rose'), Gregory, 1963.

WHISKY MAC is treasured for the golden amber color of its blossoms but even more so for its lusty perfume. Blooms are shapely, and the bushes on which they appear have dark green, lustrous foliage. Unfortunately, plants are low on vigor and niggardly in flowering. (Parentage unknown), Tantau, 1967.

WHITE WINGS is an offspring of 'Dainty Bess', the most famous five-petaled Hybrid Tea in the world. 'White Wings' has attained considerable notoriety, too, chiefly due to creamy white petals surrounding garnet red stamens. Bushes are strong growers, flowers are pleasantly scented, and stems are long. ('Dainty Bess' x unknown seedling), Krebs, 1947.

*'**MOONSPRITE**' is an underappreciated Floribunda, probably because the only gardeners who can grow it well are those in warm climates. Blossoms can have up to 80 petals each! Although basically creamy white, each petal has a golden touch at its base.*

FLORIBUNDAS

Whereas there is legitimate controversy over whether French or English hybridizers first established Hybrid Teas as a freestanding class of roses, there is no such debate when it comes to Floribundas. The creator of this family of cluster-flowered roses was, without doubt, Dines Poulsen of Kvistgaard, Denmark.

Early in the twentieth century, the Poulsen family of rose breeders, like other Scandinavians, had grown weary of large-flowered rose varieties that couldn't stand up to cruel winters. Determined to create a new race of roses capable not only of withstanding plummeting temperatures but also of blooming over an extended season, in 1911 Dines Poulsen crossed the red Polyantha 'Mme Norbert Levavasseur' with the Rambler 'Dorothy Perkins' to produce 'Ellen Poulsen', a short rosebush with pink flowers that, although not remarkably different in appearance from its Polyantha mother, proved extremely hardy. Then Poulsen tried another father, the Hybrid Tea 'Richmond', which, when crossed with the original Polyantha seed parent, resulted in a variety he named 'Rödhätte' ('Red Riding Hood')—a free-blooming, semidouble, cherry red rose that not only blossomed in large clusters and proved to be extremely hardy but also displayed growth habits significantly different from those of Polyantha roses.

While Dines laid the foundation for the rose family about to emerge, his brother Svend brought the Poulsens a step closer to their goal when he entered the hybridizing act. In 1924, from a single cross of the Dwarf Polyantha 'Orléans Rose' and the Hybrid Tea 'Red Star', Svend produced two worthwhile seedlings—the semidouble pink 'Else Poulsen' and the single red 'Kirsten Poulsen'. The flowers on both sisters were large compared with those of their Polyantha predecessors and were arranged in attractive clusters that appeared regularly throughout summer.

The Poulsen clan continued their efforts with notable results such as the scarlet 'Karen Poulsen', introduced in 1932, and 'Poulsen's Yellow', which debuted in 1939 as the world's first yellow, dwarf, clustered-flowered rosebush. In recognition of a mighty contribution to rosedom and because most varieties were named for their family members anyway, collectively these new introductions became known as the "Poulsen roses." Soon, however, hybridizers from around the globe contracted Floribunda fever and called their offspring Hybrid Polyanthas—a classification that lasted until the early 1950s, when, because of remarkable advances in color, growth habits, and flower size, the name Floribunda was officially accepted.

Precisely as when pollen from Hybrid Teas first became accessible, when that from Floribundas hit the open market the rose world went berserk. Breeders from every hybridizing family mentioned thus far took up the cause, but no one more successfully than Eugene Boerner of America's formidable firm of Jackson & Perkins. So prodigious were his efforts, Boerner was given the name "Papa Floribunda."

Today, just as when they emerged, Floribundas are valued for the massed effect they contribute to the well-landscaped garden. As a group, they are hardier and more disease resistant than Hybrid Teas and somewhat more generous in their flowering. Although not as numerous as Hybrid Teas, scads of Floribundas have been introduced in the twentieth century. Especially meritorious varieties include:

ALLGOLD produces bright buttercup yellow blossoms both singly and in clusters on a vigorous compact bush with small, light green foliage. Fragrance is light, but blooms are abundant. ('Goldilocks' x 'Ellinor LeGrice'), LeGrice, 1956.

AMBER QUEEN is famous for the universally popular, amber-yellow color of its blossoms. Foliage is large and has a copper sheen. Fragrance is moderate. Because of the nicely colored blooms and since bushes grow low to the ground, 'Amber Queen' is a popular landscape rose. ('Southampton' x 'Typhoon'), Harkness, 1984.

ANGEL FACE wins my vote as the best mauve rose ever (see entry in chapter 7). Powerfully fragrant blossoms are frilly, and petals surround a boss of golden yellow stamens. Bushes are low growers, and foliage is dark and plentiful. (['Circus' x 'Lavender Pinocchio'] x 'Sterling Silver'), Swim and Weeks, 1968.

APRICOT NECTAR is an award-winning (All-America Rose Selection, 1941) Flo-

'AMBER QUEEN' *is a hit among land-scapers because its bushes are low growing and well behaved. Plump buds develop into cupped blossoms that are nothing to sneer at either—handsomely colored amber and yellow and accompanied by flattering foliage with a copper sheen.*

'BETTY PRIOR' *has all but dropped from commerce, but it was the single-petaled Floribunda to beat in 1935. When in full bloom, bushes are literally showered in clusters of fragrant, carmine-pink blossoms whose petals are ruffled and centers golden. Plants of 'Betty Prior' grow moderately and blossom in nice regularity.*

'CHERISH' *is anything but just another pink Floribunda; it's a classic. The bush hugs the ground and looks puny until you go to cut its blooms. Although they usually mass themselves together in sprays, every bloom seems perfectly formed. All this and fragrance too!*

ribunda from America's tireless hybridizer, Gene Boerner. Intensely fragrant blossoms are a blend of apricot, pink, and gold. Plants are bushy, and foliage is dark and glossy. (Unnamed seedling x 'Spartan'), Boerner, 1965.

CATHEDRAL made a big splash when it was introduced, even winning an All-America award. In only a decade it seemed to slip into obscurity and was no longer generally commercially available. That's a pity, for 'Cathedral' is a fine rose, especially if you like apricot-orange. Although blossoms carry only a light scent, they arrive both singly and in sprays on a

moderately sized bush with disease-resistant, shiny, olive green foliage ('Little Darling' x ['Goldilocks' x 'Irish Mist']), McGredy, 1975.

CHERISH is a classy Floribunda, with blooms that rival Hybrid Teas for grace and form. Lightly fragrant blossoms are coral-pink, sometimes freckled near the petals' edges. Bushes are low, spreading growers, and foliage is large and exceptionally dark. ('Bridal Pink' x 'Matador'), Warriner, 1980.

CHINATOWN is one of the taller-growing Floribundas, usually to at least 4 feet. Strongly fragrant blossoms are primarily

yellow but are often edged in pink. Bushes are vigorous growers and free-bloomers. ('Columbine' x 'Cläre Grammerstorf'), Poulsen, 1963.

CITY OF BELFAST is an attention getter. Scarlet blossoms are double, cupped, and formed in trusses that often camouflage entire bushes. Foliage is glossy, but fragrance is virtually nonexistent. ('Evelyn Fison' x ['Circus' x 'Korona']), McGredy, 1968.

DAINTY MAID is likely to live in fame because it was one of the parents of the forerunner to David Austin's English Roses (discussed later in this chapter). Single

'CHINATOWN' *is a hybridizing triumph for Denmark's Niels Dines Poulsen. Not only are blossoms an appealing shade of yellow, they're often edged in complementary pink; they're also always lusciously fragrant. Bushes of 'Chinatown' grow considerably taller than do most Floribundas.*

'ESCAPADE' *is a free-bloomer of large clusters of rose and violet semidouble blossoms with white centers around vivid yellow stamens. Alas, fragrance is only moderate. Bushes nicely clothed in glossy, light green foliage are frisky growers.*

'GRÜSS AN AACHEN' *has been with us since 1909, and newly propagated plants still grow in number each year. Small wonder; only the cruelest of hearts could resist the large, fragrant, pink-to-white blossoms that occur regularly all summer. Foliage is nice and leathery.*

flowers carried in large clusters are silvery pink with a darker reverse. Although there is no distinguished fragrance to the blossoms, bushes are vigorous and compact. ('D.T. Poulsen' × unknown), LeGrice, 1940.

ESCAPADE produces large clusters of fragrant blossoms whose petals are a blend of rose and violet. Bushes branch freely and cover themselves in light green foliage. ('Pink Parfait' × 'Baby Faurax'), Harkness, 1967.

EUROPEANA is considered by many rosarians to be the finest Floribunda ever hybridized (see entry in chapter 7). Al-

though only lightly fragrant, blossoms are ruby red, perfectly formed, and arranged in large, heavy trusses. Foliage remains mahogany red until just before blooms mature, then it turns dark green. ('Ruth Leuwerik' × 'Rosemary Rose'), de Ruiter, 1963.

EVENING STAR produces sprays of white and pale yellow blossoms that are faintly scented. Bushes are vigorous and upright. I've never been able to grow this rose as well as friends in warmer climates do. Still, I wouldn't care to be without it. ('White Masterpiece' × 'Saratoga'), Warriner, 1974.

EYE PAINT is an eye-catcher. Tall bushes with plentiful small foliage shower themselves with sprays of lightly fragrant, bright red flowers that have a white eye and a center of golden yellow stamens. (Unnamed seedling × 'Picasso'), McGredy, 1975.

FRENCH LACE was originally intended to be a greenhouse rose, but it proved to grow so well outdoors that it won an All-America Rose Selection in 1982. Slightly fragrant, ivory to pastel apricot blossoms have flawless form and occur in sprays of from three to a dozen blooms each. Thorny stems are thin but strong; foliage is small

'MARGARET MERRIL' *is one of the most fragrant Floribundas ever. Not only do the blush white blossoms smell like lemons, they are also beautifully formed and long lasting on or off the bush. Blossoms spend so much time maturing that by the time they fully roll back their petals, stamens have turned dark brown. Foliage is dark green and distinguished.*

'OLD MASTER' *is one in a series of Sam McGredy's "hand-painted roses," in this case a blend of carmine and white that never seems to duplicate itself from one fragrant bloom to another. Bushes are vigorous growers and mighty producers.*

'PICASSO', *introduced in 1971, was the first of hybridizer Sam McGredy's "hand-painted" roses. Although it's technically a pink blend, most blooms are downright red, except for white eyes and silvery white undersides. Foliage is sparse near blooms but dense below, and plants are upright. Be careful if you landscape with 'Picasso'; he doesn't look good near most other roses.*

and dark. ('Dr. J.A. Verhage' x 'Bridal Pink'), Warriner, 1981.

GENE BOERNER is a fitting tribute to its hybridizer, and an All-America Rose Selection in 1969. Flowers are high centered, double, and deep pink but have no particular fragrance. Bushes are upright and vigorous, with glossy foliage. ('Ginger' x ['Ma Perkins' x 'Garnette Supreme']), Boerner, 1968.

GERANIUM RED is another classic Floribunda hybridized by Gene Boerner. As advertised, blossoms are geranium red, also heavily petaled and intensely fragrant. Bushes sport dark, glossy foliage.

('Crimson Glory' x unnamed seedling), Boerner, 1947.

GRÜSS AN AACHEN has never fit comfortably into any category—it was hybridized before the Floribunda class came into being, and because it's virtually sterile, no one has been able to observe familial characteristics among offspring. Any rose family would be proud to claim 'Grüss an Aachen', however, because it's a fine rose. Large, richly fragrant, cunningly formed, flesh pink to white flowers are produced all season on a low-growing, rounded plant that rarely rises above 3 feet. ('Frau Karl Druschki'

x 'Franz Deegen'), Geduldig, 1909.

ICEBERG is considered by many to be the best rose in the world. Were it more fragrant, I'd probably agree. As is, 'Iceberg' is surely one of the very best (see entry in chapter 7). Blossoms formed in large trusses are icy white; foliage is light and glossy green. ('Robin Hood' x 'Virgo'), Kordes, 1958.

INTRIGUE, because of its downright unnatural color, is decidedly not one of my favorite roses, but many people think me wrong. Blossom color has been described as reddish purple to ripe plum. Petals are ruffled, fragrance is intense, and foliage is

'PLAYGIRL' *is the daughter of 'Playboy' (no comment). Although not quite as flashy as her father, 'Playgirl' is an eye-blinker because of the dazzling combination of hot pink petals around stamens the color of bubbling butter. Flowers occur mostly in sprays, and foliage is abundant on an upright bushy plant.*

'SARATOGA', *a Floribunda, is supposed to be loveliest when all of the blooms in a spray open at the same time, in this case meaning that the center blossom should have been removed before the side buds developed so far. Then again, it looks good this way, too, doesn't it?*

'SEXY REXY', *as its name would imply, has proved to be a virile stud in current hybridizing trends. It's also an arbitrator among rose enthusiasts, since, like Modern hybrids, it blossoms all season long; like Old garden roses, its intricately formed blossoms have whimsical form.*

dark and semiglossy. ('White Masterpiece' x 'Heirloom'), Warriner, 1984.

IVORY FASHION is a Modern Rose that appeals even to rosarians devoted to Heritage Roses. Its blossoms are richly fragrant, large, shapely, and semidouble (17 petals). Foliage is leathery, and bushes are vigorous. ('Sonata' x 'Fashion'), Boerner, 1958.

LAVENDER PINOCCHIO has become more famous as a parent than as a variety all its own because of its fragrant, unusually colored blossoms—light chocolate to pinkish lavender. Foliage is leathery, and plants are bushy yet compact. ('Pi-

nocchio' x 'Grey Pearl'), Boerner, 1948.

LITTLE DARLING may be adorable, but it certainly isn't little—bushes are vigorous and spreading, often climbing. Spice-scented blossoms, however, are a lovely combination of pink, gold, and apricot. Foliage is leathery and dark. ('Captain Thomas' x ['Baby Château' x 'Fashion']), Duehrsen, 1956.

MARGARET MERRIL hit the big time in Europe long before it took North America by storm. Now both continents revel in Margaret's lemon-scented, deeply fragrant, blush white blossoms and matte, dark green foliage. (['Rudolph Timm' x

'Dedication'] x 'Pascali'), Harkness, 1977.

MATANGI and the rose following, 'Old Master', are two of hybridizer Sam McGredy's breathtaking "hand-painted" roses—blossoms that appear painted by hand because colors are randomly accentuated. In the case of 'Matangi', lightly fragrant, mottled orange-red blossoms have a white eye, and their petals have a silvery reverse. Foliage is small but plentiful, and plants are bushy and upright. (Unnamed seedling x 'Picasso'), McGredy, 1974.

OLD MASTER has white petals that look as though shades of red have been carefully applied to them, fading to brush strokes at the petals' edges. The sweetly scented blossoms are large and semidouble (15 petals), and the bushes on which they freely appear are vigorous and bushy. (['Maxi' x 'Evelyn Fison'] x ['Orange Sweetheart' x 'Frühlingsmorgen']), McGredy, 1974.

PLAYBOY is a dazzling rose, with single-flowered clusters of blossoms that are glowing yellow splashed with red, and emerald green, disease-resistant foliage that looks as if it's been hand-polished. (See a further description in chapter 7.) ('City of Leeds' x ['Chanelle' x 'Picadilly']), Cocker, 1976.

SARATOGA wins my vote as the crowning achievement in Gene Boerner's illustrious hybridizing career. Fragrant, double, creamy white, gardenia-shaped blossoms appear in irregularly sized clusters on a vigorous upright bush. ('White Bouquet' x 'Princess White'), Boerner, 1963.

SEA PEARL is, I believe, a Floribunda that's here to stay (see entry in chapter 7). Sweetly fragrant, shapely, double (24-petaled) blossoms are composed of pink petals whose reverse is a handsome blend of apricot and yellow. 'Sea Pearl' is exceptionally tall among Floribundas. ('Kordes' Perfecta' x 'Montezuma'), Dickson, 1964.

SEXY REXY would probably have withstood the Floribunda race for its blossoms alone, but, as its name would suggest, it's proven to be a potent stud for breeding, thereby ensuring longevity. Softly fragrant blooms have more than 40 salmony

pink petals each, which flatten as they mature into an Old Rose formation. Light green foliage is glossy, and the plants are bushy. ('Seaspray' x 'Dreaming'), McGredy, 1984.

SIMPLICITY, when introduced in 1979, was marketed as a "living fence" because it grew densely upright on its own roots and produced an outrageous number of blooms. Since then it has also proved to be a fine Floribunda for cut flowers. Lightly fragrant blossoms are mid-pink and formed in sprays. Although blooms are technically semidouble (18 petals), they open flat. ('Iceberg' x unnamed seedling), Warriner, 1979.

SUMMER FASHION hasn't received nearly the recognition it deserves. Sharply fragrant blossoms are an enchanting combination of white, soft yellow, and pink. Foliage is large and medium green; bushes are thorny and low to the ground, yet produce good cutting stems. ('Precilla' x 'Bridal Pink'), Warriner, 1985.

GRANDIFLORAS

While the United States had consistently followed England's lead as far as Modern Rose nomenclature was concerned, in 1954 the two countries parted ways. In that year, California's Dr. E. Lammerts achieved the hybridizing triumph of his career—'Queen Elizabeth', a skyscraping rosebush with panicles of soft pink blossoms occurring in one cluster after another from late spring through fall.

"Oh, our Lammerts has established a new breed of roses," American rosarians

must have said at the time. "Surely this rose deserves a new class."

The English took a more conservative view. In spite of the fact that they recognized that the 'Queen Elizabeth' bush was taller than that of any clustered-flowered rose they had seen to date, the British were leery about creating a new class, preferring instead to number the Queen along with other Floribundas.

Although anyone who's met me knows that I'm as American as the Union Label and I'm sensitive to what must have been the thinking at the time, I split the blanket with my fellow American rosebuddies when it comes to this dispute. I believe that in the 1950s American rosarians charged with separating roses into this and that class truly believed (prayed, perhaps) that other roses would soon be hybridized that equaled 'Queen Elizabeth' in stature. Unfortunately, none ever quite has. Nevertheless, in the spirit of an enthusiastic reception for 'Queen Elizabeth' in America, a new class was created just for her—Grandiflora. Liz was/is grand all right, but deserving of a whole new class? I think not.

Perhaps in an effort to ward off criticism for their hasty decision, the American rosarians charged with defending the new rose subdivision laid down qualifications that future roses deserving the Grandiflora name would have to meet—namely with their blossoms. Whereas sprays from Floribunda rosebushes were supposed to display clusters of blossoms at all stages (from buds to fully open blooms), those meeting the new Grandiflora class should have clustered blooms that were not only comparable in form to those of Hybrid Teas but should furthermore flower at the same stage of development. In the United States, these "rules" are still obeyed when Floribundas and Grandifloras are entered for competition in rose shows, while in the United Kingdom, roses being exhibited are either "large-flowered" or "clustered-flowered" blooms—period.

The Grandiflora class is vexing in the garden, too. It's quite difficult, for instance, to explain to a novice rose grower why the lofty 'Queen Elizabeth' and the comparatively runty 'White Lightnin'' are both classified as Grandifloras, especially when that aspiring rosarian has just admired the towering 'Sea Pearl', only to be told that it is a Floribunda. As you've already read for yourself, there are ample rose categories to commit to memory without creating needless additions. Perhaps Americans will someday follow the wisdom of their British rose peers by referring to all clustered-flowered Modern Rose bushes as Floribundas. Until then, in the United States (and in Canada), there are some fine roses currently marketed as Grandifloras. They include:

AQUARIUS was an All-America Rose Selection in 1971 and clearly deserved the honor. 'Aquarius' is prolific, almost naturally urn shaped as a bush, and covered in thick, disease-resistant foliage. My solitary complaint with this fine Grandiflora is that its blooms are smaller than aver-

age. On the other hand, they occur in such large sprays that it doesn't seem to matter. Buds are dark pink, blossoms are light pink, and the gradual lightening is a marvel to watch. Fragrance is mild. (['Charlotte Armstrong' x 'Contrast'] x ['Fandango' x ('World's Fair' x 'Floradora')]), Armstrong, 1970.

ARIZONA aptly fits its name. Blossoms are an eye-grabbing blend of the blazing colors of an Arizona sunset—golden yellow, bronze, and brownish red. Fragrance is strong; bushes are tall, upright growers; and foliage is dark, glossy, and leathery. Sprays are enormous and occur on long cutting stems. Often you can't find centers with a road map, but the color combination may well win you over anyway. ([[('Fred Howard' x 'Golden Scepter') x 'Golden Rapture'] x [('Fred Howard' x 'Golden Scepter') x 'Golden Rapture']]), Weeks, 1975.

CAMELOT has fallen out of favor with the rose-buying public since its selection as an All-America Rose in 1965, except, of course, with people who like large sprays of oversized blossoms. Color is shrimp pink, fragrance is spicy, and bushes are tough and tall. ('Circus' x 'Queen Elizabeth'), Swim and Weeks, 1964.

CRYSTALLINE is a newcomer to the Grandiflora class, but it's already a firebreather among people fond of exhibiting roses. Although it performs best where summers are hot, 'Crystalline' is a free bloomer of sprays of fragrant, pure white blossoms on a moderately sized, well-behaved bush of moderate disease-resis-

tance. ('Bridal Pink' x 'Blue Nile' seedling), Carruth and Christensen, 1982.

GOLD MEDAL gets my vote for the rose of the 1980s and one of the best yellows ever. 'Gold Medal' is a workhorse, producing scads of rich yellow, fragrant blossoms on a well-behaved bush with good foliage. (See entry in chapter 7.) ('Yellow Pages' x 'Shirley Laugharn'), Christensen, 1983.

PINK PARFAIT is a Grandiflora that makes you worry about classification. Should it have been classed as a Floribunda since it's forever in bloom? Faintly fragrant, small, shell pink blossoms with a hint of yellow are freely produced on a moderately sized, bushy plant. ('First Love' x 'Pinocchio'), Swim, 1960.

PRIMA DONNA won an All-America award in 1983 but may well be out of commercial availability before it reaches its twentieth birthday. Fuchsia-pink roses aren't rare, so a rose of this color has to be fragrant to stick around, and 'Prima Donna' isn't. Bushes, however, are tall, vigorous, and free blooming. ([Unnamed seedling x 'Happiness'] x 'Prominent'), Shirakawa and Nakashima, 1983.

QUEEN ELIZABETH, as I've already confessed, is my idea of the best Grandiflora ever. Not for the meek, the Queen is a lofty grower and a mighty producer. (See entry in chapter 7.) ('Charlotte Armstrong' x 'Floradora'), Lammerts, 1954.

SCARLET KNIGHT is more popular in Europe than in America, partly because it was hybridized in France, where rose varieties often linger past their prime.

'TOURNAMENT OF ROSES' *breaks the rule of Grandifloras looking best in sprays. As you can see for yourself, blossoms that come one-to-a-stem are nice, too (but don't count on them as often as clusters).*

'QUEEN ELIZABETH' *was the first Grandiflora rose and it's still the best. The Queen is a regal grower and blossoms with panicles of dawn-to-mid-pink blooms. Never try to stifle her lofty habits; 'Queen Elizabeth' pouts if pruned too low. Properly grown, stem length is outrageous.*

'GOLD MEDAL' *is one of the finest Grandiflora roses ever hybridized and still one of the best all-around yellow roses of the entire genus. Not only are its fragrant blossoms smartly colored yellow through gold, 'Gold Medal' bushes are among the last of all roses to give up flowering each year.*

Crimson ovoid buds open to cupped scarlet blooms, tinged black. Fragrance is light, but foliage is leathery. (['Happiness' x 'Independence'] x 'Sutter's Gold'), Meilland, 1966.

SHREVEPORT was named after the city that headquarters the American Rose Society. Although I'm not generally fond of roses color-classed orange, I like this one with its muted coloring. Blossoms are clustered, usually in threes, sometimes more; foliage is large and toothed; and plants are vigorous growers. ('Zorina' x 'Uwe Seeler'), Kordes, 1981.

SONIA is one of the few garden roses that grows better under glass than in the garden (although it's considerably more fragrant when grown outdoors). Blossoms are pink suffused with coral and salmon. Bushes are short and particularly free blooming, often with one blossom per stem. ('Zambra' x ['Baccara' x 'Message']), Meilland, 1974.

TOURNAMENT OF ROSES's long suit is the color of its blossoms—shades of pinky beige. Blooms are also fragrant and freely produced in sprays. Alas, most stems are short and weak. ('Impatient' x unnamed seedling), Warriner, 1989.

WHITE LIGHTNIN' was the first white Grandiflora ever to win an All-America Rose Selection award. Although I believe that it should have been classed as a Floribunda, that doesn't detract from its merit. Above all else, blossoms have a distinct citrus fragrance, and bushes are clothed in handsome foliage. 'White Lightnin'' doesn't perform well where summers are cool, but with enough heat those frilly white blooms become dazzling. ('Angel Face' x 'Misty'), Swim and Christensen, 1980.

MINIATURES

Mysterious clouds hover over the original Miniature rose much the way they do over the land where it undoubtedly first blossomed—China. *R. chinensis*, as hybridizers will attest, is a highly unstable species, often producing widely divergent growth patterns within a single variety. It is not unreasonable, therefore, to imagine that many years ago (centuries perhaps), a genetic event occurred that resulted in a dwarf clone. According to Peter Beales, that fine British rosarian and hybridizer, "Even though it does not exist today, *Rosa chinensis minima* would have been the obvious name and, therefore, we can accept that it came via Mauritius, having been found there by one Robert Sweet in about 1810, as was reported by the well-known and highly respected botanist Lindsey in 1920."

Documentation is sketchy over the arrival of the Miniature rose in England; spotty, too, about its debut in France, although historians report that Miniature roses enjoyed moderate popularity in both countries as a pot plant. Then in 1918 an officer of the Swiss army medical corps named Roulet spotted Miniature roses growing in a small Swiss village. Roulet so believed that the diminutive roses had commercial value that he propagated them under the name *R. rouletii*. It was only a short matter of time before plants found themselves in the hands of hybridizers eager to improve the strain.

Credit for the first Miniature rose ever hybridized goes to the Dutch breeder de Vink, who in 1936 crossed 'Rouletti' with the Dwarf Polyantha 'Gloria Mundi' to produce 'Peon', which had attention-grabbing red flowers with a white eye. 'Peon' was popular with the Dutch, but it took a journey to North America for true fame. When the pioneering rosarian Robert Pyle of Pennsylvania saw 'Peon', he not only recognized its potential but also that a name change would ensure commercial success. 'Peon', therefore, was renamed 'Tom Thumb', and the Miniature rose was off and running. To the delight of hybridizers eager to try their hand at enhancing the fashionable tiny-rose rage, young Tom proved to be a prodigious stud, and broods of Miniature roses emerged.

Although the pioneering contributions of Roulet, de Vink, Spain's Pedro Dot, and a handful of other European hybridizers are still recognized, today the overwhelming success of Miniature roses is credited to Ralph Moore of Visalia, California. Moore was fascinated by the potential of the Miniature rose and perceived its infinite potential—mossing, rambling, and striping, as well as varieties that, if properly parented, could blossom with bantam versions of Hybrid Tea flowers or whimsical forms of Antique grandparents. Most contemporary catalogs offering Miniature roses are

generously peppered with credits to Ralph Moore.

Once "Minis" caught on, they spread like gossip, to the point that one can hardly keep up on current introductions. Minis are not without their adversaries, especially those rosarians who point out that Miniature roses are "supposed" to be *truly* miniature—not just their blos-

At Garden Valley Ranch, we grow Miniature roses at the foot of taller plants — here, in front of lavender, rosemary, Bourbon roses, and Lombardy poplars. Make certain you check on the growth habits of the Miniatures you select; some are actually small shrubs.

soms and foliage but their bushes as well (originally capable of fitting under a tea-cup)—not plants that rival the stature of many Floribundas. On the contrary, landscapers are quick to defend current Miniature rose introductions, pointing out that they are invaluable for low-grow-ing, nonstop-blooming additions to the garden at large.

In any case, Miniature roses seem to have carved out a permanent spot in today's world of roses. Although there are jillions to choose among, varieties worthy of consideration include:

BABY BETSY MCCALL is a vigorous but short, compact bush that produces small, light pink, cupped flowers with 20 petals. ('Cécile Brünner' x 'Rosy Jewel'), Morey, 1960.

BEAUTY SECRET is no secret among Miniature fanciers who like cardinal red, double blossoms up to 1½ inches wide. Foliage is glossy and leathery. ('Little Darling' x 'Magic Wand'), Moore, 1965.

BLACK JADE has buds that are about as black as dark red roses ever become. Blossoms are deep red and double, foliage is dark and semiglossy, and bushes rarely top 2 feet. ('Sheri Anne' x 'Laguna'), Bernardella, 1985.

'MINNIE PEARL' *is classified as a pink blend, but it's often downright coral. Bushes are exceptionally vigorous and tall for a Mini, and they are agreeably disease resistant as well. Foliage is appropriately small, medium green, and semi-glossy.*

'MAGIC CARROUSEL' *is one of America's favorite Minis, not just because it's so easy to grow but also because of its florid combination of colors. A florist who sells Miniature roses for boutonnieres told me that she uses 'Magic Carrousel' more than any other Miniature rose.*

'JEAN KENNEALLY' *is a spiffy Miniature rose; so are its bushes, which often tower over other Minis. Not only are blossoms well-colored shades of apricot, they occur freely in clusters on fine cutting stems.*

CUPCAKE produces clusters of soft pink, heavily petaled blossoms that last well as cut flowers. Bushes are low growers (usually under 1 foot) and relatively thornless. ('Gene Boerner' x ['Gay Princess' x 'Yellow Jewel']), Spies, 1981.

DRESDEN DOLL, thanks to hybridizer Ralph Moore, was the world's first Miniature Moss rose. Blossoms are shell pink and highlight bright yellow stamens. ('Fairy Moss' x unnamed Moss seedling), Moore, 1975.

DWARFKING produces carmine, double, cupped flowers on a bush that remains low growing and compact. Foliage is glossy. ('World's Fair' x 'Tom Thumb'), Kordes, 1957.

EASTER MORNING is an ivory white classic. Blossoms with as many as 60 petals occur regularly on a bush that's low growing, vigorous, and clothed in glossy foliage. ('Golden Glow' x 'Zee'), Moore, 1960.

GOURMET POPCORN is so markedly different from 'Popcorn', the rose from which it sported, that it warrants separate description. Bushes grow vigorously to more than 2 feet and cascade themselves with clusters of semidouble blossoms with golden yellow centers. The bonus of disease resistance makes 'Gourmet Popcorn' an ideal landscape rose. ('Popcorn' sport), Desamero, 1988.

GREEN ICE produces buds and fresh flowers that are soft greenish white. Tiny white glossy leaves cover a plant that's dwarf but bushy. ([*R. wichuraiana* x 'Floradora'] x 'Jet Trail'), Moore, 1971.

HEARTBREAKER is a floriferous and trouble-free newcomer to the mini scene. Blossoms are cream with a deep pink edge, and bushes are naturally rounded to just under 2 feet. ('Crystalline' x 'Magic Carrousel'), Carruth, 1990.

HOLY TOLEDO is generally considered to be the finest commercially available

'LILIAN AUSTIN' *has some good things going—she's reliable in producing fragrant salmon-pink-shaded-yellow blossoms on a hardy, disease-resistant bush. Disappointing even to the hybridizer, however, this variety lacks "Old Rose" charm. Still, Lilian manages to compete well among fine free-blooming Modern Shrub roses.*

'GERTRUDE JEKYLL', *named in honor of the trendsetting British gardener, is one of the most strongly perfumed of all English roses. Although the rich-pink blossoms start out small, by the time they mature, they're buxom and shapely.*

'GRAHAM THOMAS' *isn't famous simply because it's named after Britain's most esteemed rosarian, its vibrant color helps, too. Some gardeners say it screams yellow; others are crazy about the strong color. Mature plants take on considerable heft.*

David Austin's *A Handbook of Roses*, the catalog from his nursery, now lists more than 80 varieties of English Roses in colors ranging from blood red to pristine white, grouped by (supposed) height. I haven't grown them all, but here are a dozen I happily recommend:

CLAIRE ROSE, as already mentioned, was the first English Rose I fell for. That was in part, no doubt, because of the size and color of its flowers—large, shallow-cupped blossoms intricately formed from massive numbers of blush pink petals.

Austin claims not only that Claire is fragrant but also that her only fault is that "petals tend to spottle with age if there has been rain." This freckling tendency couldn't concern me less; it seems only fair for blossoms *this* large that last *so* long. I quarrel with the claim for fragrance, however, since to my nose Claire has no distinguishing perfume whatsoever.

CRESSIDA, I believe, will be recorded in history as one of Austin's triumphs, primarily because it serves double duty as a climber or a sprawling shrub. It was the blooms, however, that won me over—informal arrangements of myrrh-scented, pinky beige petals with an apricot reverse. (See chapter 7.)

DAPPLE DAWN is my personal favorite among the single English Roses. A sport of 'Red Coat', 'Dapple Dawn' is, I think, superior to its parent. Bushes of 'Red Coat' blossom freely with flowers that begin life clear scarlet but end up with dull brown overtones. 'Dapple Dawn', on the other hand, is fresh from start to finish—delicate pink petals, veined throughout with deep pink, entirely encircling a boss of long, golden yellow stamens. Like its parent, 'Dapple Dawn' is ideal for hedges and mass

'HERITAGE' *is the most famous of all English roses because of its alluring shell-pink blossoms, which have an appealing cupped shape and notorious fragrance. Best yet, bushes are free flowering.*

'MARY ROSE' *has only one obvious draw-back—her large rose-pink blossoms are only slightly fragrant. Otherwise, the thorny bushes are a snap to prune, and she's the first of the English roses to bloom each year (often the last, too).*

'PROSPERO' *doesn't prosper unless well cultivated; even then, it grows only to about 2 feet. When contented, however, its blossoms are knockouts—crimson through purple to mauve petals uniting in classic Old Rose formation. Fragrance is classic, too. Still, not a rose for the average gardener.*

plantings. According to Austin, whether plants of 'Dapple Dawn' and 'Red Coat' are grown as bushes or as shrubs makes an enormous difference in quantity of bloom. When they're pruned as 4-foot bushes, there are reportedly "two very big flushes of bloom, whereas when grown as shrubs, the flowering is spread out over the season." Fragrance in both varieties is only slight, if detectable at all.

ENGLISH GARDEN is one of the most beautiful yellow roses I know, old or new. Although the bush is on the short side for an English Rose, it produces intricate blossoms of staggering symmetry. The color is basically buff-yellow, paling to cream at the petals' edges. Foliage is light green, and fragrance is comparable to that of Tea roses.

GERTRUDE JEKYLL displays more Old Rose qualities than do most other English Roses, undoubtedly because one of its parents is the famous Portland rose 'Comte de Chambord'. Because of this heritage, 'Gertrude Jekyll' is among the most strongly perfumed of Austin's roses. Although buds start out small and scrolled, they quickly mature into buxom, rich pink, rosette-shaped blossoms. For me, bushes grow to 4-foot heights and almost as wide.

GRAHAM THOMAS is one of the most popular English Roses for two reasons. First, it is named for the most beloved rosarian in Britain, but more important, it blossoms in a deep yellow color that is unmatched among Old Roses and rare among Modern hybrids. Blossoms are medium-sized and deeply cupped and have a strong Tea rose fragrance. Leaves are smooth (perhaps because 'Iceberg' numbers among its ancestors), and bushes are almost as wide as they are tall.

HERITAGE made the biggest splash in

'WIFE OF BATH' *flowers with warm pink blossoms so delicate that it's easy to image that the bush is fragile, too. Wrong. This fine David Austin creation matures into a no-nonsense little shrub that flowers regularly. Best of all, blooms are strongly scented of myrrh.*

'WISE PORTIA' *is smart enough to grow on a better bush than 'Prospero' does, but still not with the vigor one would hope for. When pleased with her placement in the garden, however, Portia gives freely of deep rose, purple, and mauve blossoms that are heavy in perfume and last well when properly harvested.*

'YELLOW CHARLES AUSTIN', *a sport of 'Charles Austin', is considered to be an improvement over its parent because of its appealing pale yellow color. Otherwise, growth and bloom habits are virtually identical— exceptionally tall (verging on ungainly) and niggardly with flowers (although the show in fall is almost as impressive as spring's).*

America of all English Roses when they were introduced, which is hardly a surprise, since Austin himself considers it "perhaps the most beautiful English Rose." Although bushes of 'Heritage' are admirably bushy and free branching, I think that the enormous success of this hybrid is due to its irresistible shell pink color and also because the blossoms are perfectly cupped and richly fragrant. As a final bonus, the robust bushes are remarkably free flowering. (See chapter 7.)

LEANDER is touted as the healthiest and most disease-resistant variety of all the English Roses, reaching heights of 8 feet and taller. Alas, 'Leander' is not a free repeat-bloomer, although its bushes are literally showered with flowers in spring. For those hooked on deep apricot flowers with fruity fragrance, however, quantity of blossom is secondary to quality. Individual blossoms are smallish, but they're produced in handsome sprays.

LILIAN AUSTIN is the most Modern-looking of the English Roses, since its semidouble flowers with wavy petals resemble Modern hybrids rather than Old garden roses. Its strong point is its growth habit—low, moundlike, and arching. Although the color of the fragrant blossoms

(salmon-pink, tinted orange and apricot) looks out of place in most mixed borders, a few bushes planted together make a fine statement. The disease-resistant shrubs are quick to repeat their flowers.

MARY ROSE produces flowers that are only slightly fragrant, but its bush is a pruner's dream—it will perform as told. Large rose-pink flowers that are informally cupped and loosely filled with petals are likely to be the first of the English Roses to appear and the last to give up bloom. Plants are free branching and robust, but they're exceptionally thorny.

PERDITA is considered to be one of the

best all-around English Roses. Although bushes rarely grow taller than 3 feet, in one season they produce an amazing number of medium-sized, fully double, light apricot blossoms that are richly fragrant. Foliage is ample, dark green, and disease resistant, and stems are a handsome shade of reddish brown.

THE COUNTRYMAN, like 'Gertrude Jekyll', owes much of its appearance to its Portland rose ('Comte de Chambord') ancestry. Like 'Lilian Austin', 'The Countryman' is valued for its contribution to the landscape, since its bushes arch and prettily nod their blossoms. Although the Countryman's bush is rather short, its leaves are long and its blooms are large, deep pink, heavily petaled, and richly fragrant.

I asked David Austin if he had favorites among his roses or some that he thought would outlast others.

"Those are two different questions," he pointed out thoughtfully. "I suppose 'Heritage' numbers among my favorites, but so do some of the simpler varieties," he admitted. Going on to explain how he resists reacting commercially to his hybrids, Austin spoke as though he were quoting from his own book:

"In the breeding of the English Roses it has always been my aim first of all to hybridize, and then to select for the overall beauty of the plant. That is to say, for the charm, character, and fragrance of the flower, for the elegance and grace of growth and leaf. Only then do I consider the more practical aspects of reliability, toughness, disease resistance, and freedom and regularity of flowering, vital though these undoubtedly are. The tendency has too often been to see the rose as a machine for the production of flowers. The rose, it has been assumed, would automatically be beautiful. This unfortunately is not so. I really cannot see that the practical has much value without the aesthetic."

Neither can I.

After having grown David Austin's roses for more than 10 years, I fear that a good number of varieties suffer from transatlantic blues—a malady I've observed in many roses. Before learning to diagnose the condition, I couldn't figure out why so many fine Modern American roses never catch on in England or why some varieties I see in gardens all over Britain aren't marketed in the United States. Now, of course, I realize that it's all a matter of certain roses traveling well and others preferring to stay near home.

Many roses, particularly Modern varieties, don't perform identically from garden to garden. In America, for instance, roses that shine in Portland, Oregon, may pout in Portland, Maine, and vice versa—which is why roses selected All-America are grown all over the country before being voted on, so that regional differences average out. Truly great roses, of course, transcend locales, even those as wide as the Atlantic Ocean—immortals such as the majestic pale pink Grandiflora 'Queen Elizabeth' hybridized by California's Lammerts; 'Peace', the dazzling no-two-alike yellow Hybrid Tea created by France's Meilland; or 'Sea Pearl', the salmon-apricot Floribunda beauty introduced by Harkness of England. There are many more stars, but an even greater number of international also-rans that perform satisfactorily only on one continent or the other.

When you consider the vast differences between the climates of the United States and the United Kingdom, it makes sense that the Atlantic Ocean shouldn't be a runway for roses. When most English gardeners are deciding whether to carry galoshes as well as umbrellas, their Yankee counterparts are deliberating over which strength sunscreen to apply and whether or not to also wear a sun visor. Why, then, *should* our roses grow the same? I've never, for instance, been able to cultivate the splendid 'Silver Jubilee' (a fabulous two-tone pink Hybrid Tea hybridized by Cocker) as well as I've seen it grown all over England. Instead, I settle for 'Color Magic', another pink bicolor Hybrid Tea (but hybridized in America by William Warriner)—hardly a compromise.

In defense of hybridizers, I understand why their breeding platforms are heavily biased in favor of roses that perform well close to home. Why shouldn't stellar varieties loom in one's mind while imagining prospective parents? In the case of Austin's roses, however, I'm afraid that means that certain varieties pay a luxury tax for performing best near Albrighton, England. By perform, I mean bloom. Some varieties such as 'Graham Thomas', 'Claire Rose', and 'Yellow Charles Austin' actually grow far larger in California than they do anywhere in England. Blossoming, however, is another matter.

In my garden, for example, the roses just mentioned blossom in early summer as though they had been hybridized with Petaluma, California, in mind. The outrageous show lasts a good six weeks. Then plants seem to say, "Okay, that's it for blooming for a while, let's vegetate." Bushes then spend a good portion of each summer growing as though they had never imagined so much warm sun and haven't figured out how to respond to it modestly. For these aggressive varieties, repeat blooming is skimpy and fall's show is a relative dud. In contrast, in England these varieties seem perfectly at home repeating their blooms as advertised.

So why the overwhelming success of David Austin's roses in America? In retrospect, I think it seems predictable. Another rose revolution like the one Empress Josephine staged early in the nineteenth century was long overdue. Also, ever since the first Hybrid Tea was introduced, old-fashioned varieties have wandered in and out of vogue every few decades, and here were roses that not only looked like Antiques but rebloomed as well!

In time, I believe that many American gardeners will do one of two things: (1) Stop pretending that Austin roses are truly everblooming in our gardens and gratefully accept recurrent flowers as lagniappe,

or (2) plant only those mid-sized and small English Roses that grow modestly and repeat-bloom with acceptable faith.

Although I'm not certain what I'll ultimately decide, many Austin roses are growing in my garden for good.

David Austin considers **'L.D. BRAITH-WAITE'** *to be one of his very finest deep crimson varieties because of its free-blooming characteristics. Moderately sized bushes grow about as wide as they do tall and blooms are loosely formed but fragrant.*

Famous Cousins

he five families discussed in this chapter—Rugosas, Noisettes, Polyan-thas, Hybrid Musks, and Shrub roses—are perhaps deserving of a more presti-gious lumping than "Famous Cousins." In some cases, members of these families have become considerably more notorious than their predeces-sors. I know several fine rosarians whose entire rose gardens are composed exclusively of varieties mentioned in this chapter. Although most of the roses discussed here are repeat-flowering varieties, those that aren't handily compensate by blossoming copiously over a period of several weeks early each summer.

RUGOSAS

All Rugosa hybrid roses evolved from *R. rugosa*, a tough old dowager native to northern China, Korea, and Japan. Drawings of this original Rugosa rose date from A.D. 1000, yet it surely flourished long before. *R. rugosa* has a lot going for it, not the least of which is hardy vigor—a constitution of iron and rambunctious growth to 8-foot heights with equal spread. Thorns are tough and plentiful, and the decidedly disease-resistant foliage is roughly textured. Large, lightly fragrant, violet-rose flowers blossom throughout summer and are

'NATHALIE NYPELS' *makes no effort to conceal the dominance of her China rose ancestry with blossoms that are large for a Polyantha; they're also exceptionally well scented and occur on a low-growing plant that can be trained to serve double duty as a ground cover.*

whose bush is noticeably smaller than those of the other Grootendorsts. (*R. rugosa rubra* x 'Mme Nobert Levavasseur'), de Goey, 1918.

FRAU DAGMAR HARTOPP is a favored Rugosa among landscape gardeners because its bushes mass so well and are foolproof to prune. It is also blessed by people fond of cut flowers because it blooms repeatedly over a long season. Richly fragrant blossoms are satiny pink, and petals surround creamy white stamens. (Parentage unknown), Hastrup, 1914.

HANSA is a poor man's 'Roseraie de l'Hay'. Although it's similarly colored deep crimson-purple, 'Hansa' grows to only half the height of 'Roseraie de l'Hay' and isn't as fragrant. On the other hand, its bushes don't grow taller than 4 feet, making 'Hansa' more manageable in the landscape. It's also freeflowering. (Parentage unknown), Schaum and Van Tol, 1905.

LADY CURZON isn't a lady at all, if given her way—contented bushes easily grow 8 feet tall and just as wide. Although flowers don't recur, they almost make up for it by showering whole shrubs in early summer. Flowers are large, fragrant, and iridescent pink; stamens are golden. (*R.*

macrantha x *R. rugosa rubra*), Turner, 1901.

ROBUSTA is robust indeed, producing scads of single, scarlet, lightly fragrant flowers on a thorny vigorous bush well clothed in dark green foliage. 'Robusta' makes a fine prowler-proof hedge, and its bushes remain in blossom all season. (*R. rugosa* x unnamed seedling), Kordes, 1979.

Before buying a rose called Grootendorst, find out what its first name is. **'F.J. GROOTENDORST'** *has scentless dull crimson flowers, but three of its sports are not only more modestly colored, they're fragrant, too.*

'ROSERAIE DE L'HAY' *is named for the famous garden in Paris—and a fitting tribute it is. Blossoms are reddish purple and richly fragrant. Although bushes set few hips, they're adamantly resistant to disease.*

'RUSKIN' *is not without problems or virtues—it has bad growth habits and blossoms only once each year, but its fragrance is ravishing and the makeup of each crimson-purple bloom is perfection. If you decide to grow 'Ruskin', plan to prune it by half each year or to train it to climb; otherwise, plants get clumsy.*

'SARAH VAN FLEET' *is a robust young lady (bushes scramble quickly to 7-foot heights). Foliage is roughly textured and thorns are abundant, but the clear pink blossoms are delicate, fragrant, and formed in comely clusters.*

R. RUGOSA ALBA is not only a sport of the already discussed *R. rugosa*, it's also a decided improvement. Whereas the species rose is beloved in spite of the color of its flowers, the white sport is treasured because of it. *R. rugosa alba* produces large, fragrant, five-petaled blossoms on an ironclad shrub that will take up more than its allotted space if you're not careful. It grows exceptionally well on its own roots, to the point of invasiveness. Then again, it does bloom all summer long. (Origin unknown), classified in 1870.

ROSERAIE DE L'HAY, named for the sensational garden near Paris, is appreciated best by people who like reddish purple roses. Assuming one does, 'Roseraie de l'Hay' is a winner—a bushy, disease-resistant shrub that yields armloads of large, fragrant blossoms with creamy stamens. Hips are few. (Unknown sport from *R. rugosa*), introduced by Cochet-Cochet in 1901.

SARAH VAN FLEET is another robust Rugosa, growing to 7 feet, with ample, roughly textured leaves and nasty thorns. In contrast, blossoms are delicate, fragrant, clear pink, and formed in clusters. Said to be a cross of *R. rugosa* x 'My Maryland', but this parentage is supposedly in doubt. Van Fleet, 1926.

SCABROSA may be a seedling from *R. rugosa* or even a misplaced hybrid. In either case, its parentage is lost. Shrubs grow vigorously to 5 feet and produce masses of fragrant, large (up to 6 inches across), single, cerise pink blossoms with paler stamens. Introduced by Harkness in 1926.

SCHNEEZWERG is distinguished among Rugosas for its foliage alone, which is dark and shiny rather than mid-green and coarse. Otherwise, 'Snow Dwarf', as 'Schneezwerg' is also known, is not par-

ticularly interesting, except that its small, white, scentless blossoms are pure white and are followed by crops of rich red hips. (*R. rugosa* ×unknown Polyantha), Lambert, 1912.

NOISETTES

I have included the Noisette family here rather than with Climbers for two reasons. First, Noisettes were developed long before most Climbing roses were hybridized; and second, with proper training, some varieties make fine, lax shrubs.

John Champney, an early-nineteenth-century rice farmer in South Carolina, produced a rose he named *R. moschata hybrida*, later renamed 'Champney's Pink Cluster'. Whether or not Champney himself mixed the pollen (many claim it was accidental), it seems certain that *R. moschata hybrida* came to be when 'Parsons' Pink China' (one of the original China stud roses) was mated with a Musk rose. The affair resulted in a climbing rose that flowered throughout summer.

Next, Philippe Noisette, a nurseryman also working in Charleston, bettered Champney's mark when he sowed seeds of the pink-clustered rose and gave birth to 'Blush Noisette', which, although not as tall as either of the supposed parents, blossomed recurrently with clustered flowers that smelled strongly of cloves.

Philippe then sent seeds to his Parisian brother, Louis, who apparently not only understood on sight the potential of these new roses but also how to improve them and, finally, how best to market them as a new garden rage. Louis's scheme

'ALISTER STELLA GRAY' *is a particularly graceful climbing Noisette rose. Buds are butter-yellow, but by the time they finish unfurling into mature blossoms formed in large clusters, the petals are creamy-white.*

worked, for the American seedlings fancied their French lovers and notorious children were born. With an assist from Tea roses, the Noisettes broadened their color range and their blossoms became more beautifully shaped. Thanks to 'Parks' Yellow China', yellow emerged. The French adored "their" new Noisettes.

Before the end of the nineteenth century, however, Noisettes had gone out of fashion. Their decline in popularity was not only due to younger roses taking their place but also because hybridizers were faced with the same diploid/tetraploid problem as mentioned for Rugosas: Although new hybrids developed, they were sterile because of their parents' chromosome incompatibility.

Noisette roses are famous as perfumed free-bloomers, whose flowers' petals are silky and softly colored. Their hardiness is not always what one would choose, and several fine varieties demand the luxury of a southern walled exposure. Still, they are deserving of special care, and worthwhile cultivars still readily available in commerce include:

AIMÉE VIBERT, a supposed cross between a Noisette and *R. sempervirens*, was introduced in France in 1828 by Vibert. Aimée is an unusual rose because she closely resembles Rambling roses but

'CHAMPNEY'S PINK CLUSTER,' *discovered by a rice farmer in South Carolina, is the original Noisette rose, but it still enjoys enormous popularity because its bushes are hardy, vigorous, and incredibly floriferous.*

blooms throughout summer. Blossoms are small but double, are pure white, and carry a faint trace of musk scent. Plants easily climb to more than 15 feet or form a graceful arching shrub. Tender.

ALISTER STELLA GRAY, grown either as a climber or as a shrub, is a particularly graceful Noisette. Tight yellow buds mature into quartered, tea-scented, creamy white blossoms formed in clusters. (Parentage unknown), Gray, 1894.

I planted this rose at the base of a 15-foot tree stump. In one year, it had engulfed half of its support; in another, it finished the job. Flowering is continual throughout the blooming season and splendid in autumn.

BLUSH NOISETTE, believed to be a sport of the first Noisette rose, was introduced by France's Noisette in 1817. Unless trained on a wall, 'Blush Noisette' forms a short, bushy shrub. However they're grown, plants produce copious numbers of spice-scented flowers that start out as rosy buds and develop into buff-pink blossoms.

CÉLINE FORESTIER is a slow-growing variety that never reaches the size of other family members but is a treasure anyway. Richly fragrant blossoms are formed from pale yellow petals with notable substance. At maturity, blooms quarter petals around a button eye. Céline grows best on a warm, sunny wall.

CHAMPNEY'S PINK CLUSTER, the first Noisette rose, is widely grown today and not from sentiment alone. Plants are vigorous, hardy, and floriferous over a long season. Rose-pink buds open into clusters of lighter pink flowers, fragrant at all stages.

GLOIRE DE DIJON is thought to be the result of a cross between an unidentified Tea rose and 'Souvenir de la Malmaison', the famous Bourbon rose. Whatever the parenting, the issue is superb—yellow-tinted-apricot blossoms are large and richly fragrant. Blooming is steady, and foliage is tough and leathery. Jacotot, 1853.

LAMARQUE, although winter-tender, is praised for the distinct color of its large but delicate blossoms (pale lemon yellow) and for its sharp but clean fragrance. 'Lamarque' grows well under glass. ('Blush Noisette' x 'Parks' Yellow China'), Maréchal, 1830.

MADAME ALFRED CARRIÈRE is my pet among Noisettes, as discussed further in chapter 7. Although her blossoms often lack traditional shape, they're consistently large, white-blushed-pink, and fragrant. In addition, Madame is a robust grower and a free-bloomer. Schwartz, 1879.

MARÉCHAL NIEL was, for more than 25 years, *the* climbing yellow rose to grow because its pure yellow, deeply perfumed, classically formed blossoms were unique among late-nineteenth-century roses. 'Maréchal Niel' had annoying growth habits, however, which were soon to spell its demise. It is so tender that it can be grown successfully only in staunchly temperate climates or, better yet, under glass. This finicky Noisette is thought to be a seedling of 'Cloth of Gold' and was introduced by Pradel in 1864.

RÊVE D'OR is another tender Noisette, but it's a rampant grower where contented. Although blossoms are only lightly fragrant, they're yellow flushed salmon and informally but nicely shaped. Flowering is acceptably recurrent, and foliage is abundant and glossy. ('Madame Schultz' seedling), Ducher, 1869.

POLYANTHAS

In or about 1860, Guillot (the same French hybridizer who graced the world with its first officially recognized Hybrid Tea) planted seeds from the climbing *R. multiflora*, a parent of many a Rambling rose. Instead of producing single white flowers like those of their parent, seedlings (some of which had semidouble and double forms) blossomed in varying shades of pink. Unfortunately, the majority of these surprising offspring proved sterile. One, however, formed a hip, and Guillot was quick to harvest its seeds and replant them. To his great delight, the plants that followed weren't ramblers at all but instead short, compact bushes that enjoyed a prolonged season of bloom.

It is now generally agreed that Guillot's great find was actually the result of Mother Nature's hand at mixing pollen from *R. multiflora* with that gadabout China stud rose, 'Old Blush'. Two of the seedlings showed such promise that Guillot decided to introduce them under the names 'Paquerette' and 'Mignonette', both of which produced large sprays of

'CHINA DOLL' *was a latecomer to the Polyantha clan, but she gained immediate acceptance because of her free-blooming attitude. Although the small blooms are only mildly scented, they're formed in pretty trusses of blossoms with 24 petals each. Low-growing, naturally mounded bushes are well clothed in leathery foliage.*

'LITTLE WHITE PET' *is a dwarf sport of the Rambling 'Félicité et Perpétue', but there's nothing small about its performance — scads of fragrant, heavily petaled pompon flowers on a rounded disease-resistant plant. Many rose suppliers list 'Little White Pet' among Modern Shrub roses rather than Polyanthas. It's a winner in either group.*

'MARGO KOSTER' *is a member of a highly variable family of roses that keep changing colors. Margo's original shade was salmon-pink, but orange has since crept in. Some of the Kosters like to climb.*

rosy pink, pompon flowers that faded to white as they aged. Because neither variety grew taller than a foot (which is why English rosarians refer to this family as Dwarf Polyanthas), it was clear that a new class of roses had been born—one that was to play an important role in the development of subsequent roses valued for their contributions to landscape gardening.

In spite of the fragile blossoms that they so freely produce in cluster after cluster, Polyanthas are tough and demand little in the way of cultivation, including from the soil in which they're

planted. Pruning is incidental, too, consisting mainly of thinning and the removal of dead growth. The single negative among this hardy little group of roses is an only slight fragrance from their blossoms.

Finally, although they're technically not pure Polyantha, I include three roses here that could just as well be listed with China roses: 'Cécile Brünner', 'Perle d'Or', and 'Jenny Wren', all of which (at least in America) have become irrevocably associated with the Polyantha clan. In each case, one parent actually *is* a Polyantha; besides, these winsome roses display all of the desirable family char-

acteristics associated with the family. Choice Polyantha varieties include:

BABY FAURAX rarely grows taller than 1 foot and produces multiple tiny, cupped flowers that many people call blue but that are actually reddish violet. Lille, 1924.

CÉCILE BRÜNNER found its way into my chapter on immortal roses (see entry in chapter 7), but not entirely from personal favoritism. This rose is so overwhelmingly ubiquitous, both in Europe and in America, that it's often the only rose people know the name of. Still, it's a classic and a mighty producer of tiny,

'AUTUMN DELIGHT' *is one of the lowest-growing Hybrid Musks; it's also a sight to behold each fall, when bushes are showered with sprays of sweetly fragrant flowers that change in color from creamy yellow to glistening white.*

'BELINDA' *isn't as famous a Hybrid Musk as it should be, especially for those in search of an everblooming hedge. Plants are vigorous, smothered in dark green, handsome foliage, and free with large trusses of mid- to deep pink, fragrant blossoms. Although spring blossoms are nothing to sneer at, autumn's are even nicer.*

'ERFURT' *produces blossoms that are only mildly fragrant, but they just don't stop coming. They're also magnificently colored— bright pink with white centers and clusters of golden yellow stamens that darken as they age.*

lightly scented, perfectly formed blossoms of pale to mid-pink. 'Cécile Brünner' is available as a bush, as a climber, and in white (thanks to an albino sport). Pernet-Ducher, 1881.

CHINA DOLL grows low to the ground, but its mounded bushes are showered with leathery foliage and large trusses of small, cupped, rose-pink blossoms with petals colored mimosa yellow at their bases. Fragrance is no stronger than mild, but blossoming is profuse. ('Mrs. Dudley Fulton' x 'Tom Thumb'), Lammerts, 1946.

JENNY WREN produces large blossoms for a Polyantha, but they're still small and

formed in open sprays. Blooms are prettily colored light apricot to salmon-pink and are strongly perfumed. Foliage is dark and abundant. ('Cécile Brünner' x 'Fashion'), Ratcliffe, 1957.

KATHARINA ZEIMET produces blossoms that are more delicate than those of most other Polyantha roses. They're also double, pure white, and formed in large clusters (to 50 blooms each). ('Étoile de Mai' x 'Marie Pavié'), Lambert, 1901.

MADAME JULES THIBAUD is a peach-pink sport of 'Cécile Brünner' and similar in every way, except that there is no climbing sport.

MARGO KOSTER is a late member of a riotous family. The Kosters are famous among rose surnames for their ability to sport new varieties. The lineage began with 'Tausendschon', a Climber, which sported a short bush. Four sports later Margo appeared, and she is generally agreed to be the family favorite. She has also sported herself, but her original color is salmon-pink. Koster, 1931.

MARIE PAVIÉ makes a twiggy but relatively thornless bush that produces delicate creamy white blossoms. Foliage is large and rich green. (Parentage unknown), Alégatière, 1888.

MIGNONETTE is one of the original Poly-anthas. Its blossoms are usually rose-pink but sometimes creamy white spotted wine red. Blossoms are individually small, but they occur in panicles of up to 50 blooms each. Guillot Fils, 1880.

PAUL CRAMPEL, introduced in 1930, was one of the first roses ever to be colored vermilion. Bushes liberally produce clusters of small flowers with white eyes and grow erectly to 2 feet; foliage is light green. (Parentage unrecorded), Kersbergen, 1930.

PERLE D'OR is often called 'Yellow Cécile Brünner' even though it has parentage all its own. All in all, 'Perle d'Or' is a stronger rose than 'Cécile Brünner', sweeter in aroma, and more deeply colored—pinkish apricot fading to cream. Although there is no documentation, 'Perle d'Or' is thought to be the result of a cross between an unidentified Polyantha and 'Madame Falcot', a Tea. Rambaud, 1883.

HYBRID MUSKS

At the dawn of the twentieth century, a German nurseryman named Peter Lambert planted a seed from (he claimed) a self-fertilized cross of 'Aglaia'—a Rambler originally derived from a cross between *R. multiflora* and 'Rêve d'Or', a Noisette. This seedling, which Lambert christened 'Trier', demonstrated marked advantages over its parent, most notably its growth habit, which was shrubby rather than rambling. As a further bonus, unlike its mother, 'Trier' repeated its bloom cycle.

Lambert fancied his 'Trier' and crossed it extensively, eventually producing a line of roses he marketed as 'Lambertiana'. Alas, the breed never caught on with the buying public, who viewed them simply as oversized Polyanthas.

Then the Reverend Joseph Pemberton, a clergyman turned avid gardener in England's County Essex, tried his hand at improving 'Trier' by crossing it with various Polyanthas, Noisettes, Hybrid Teas, and Tea roses. It is at this point in the development of the Hybrid Musk roses that history becomes clouded, for Pemberton seems to have had an aversion to keeping a stud book for recording precise parentage. Instead, he preferred (and even instructed his pupils) to "develop an eye" for the desired qualities that new roses were to assume.

To complicate the heritage of the Hybrid Musk roses even further, Pemberton turned over the responsibility for introducing his hybrids to a nurseryman named J.A. Bentall, who not only joined in the hybridizing process himself but also convinced his wife, Anne, to champion the breeding program while he was off fighting in World War I. Although Anne's record keeping was no more diligent than Pemberton's, she obviously had talent, for it was she who bred 'Ballerina' and 'Buff Beauty', two of the world's favorite Hybrid Musk roses.

The name of this family of roses seems destined to stick even though it's a classic horticultural misnomer. Hybrid Musk roses have little to do with the true Musk rose except for their vague lineage via Noisette roses and a fragrance that embraces a musky quality in an otherwise sophisticated bouquet. Although they didn't make much of a splash when their family first appeared, Hybrid Musk roses were "rediscovered" in the 1960s and have enjoyed popularity ever since.

The majority of Hybrid Musk roses in commerce today grow into graceful 5- to 6-foot shrubs that bloom profusely in early summer and modestly in autumn. Properly cultivated, Hybrid Musks should be thought of as Modern shrub roses and should be planted, fertilized, and pruned with the same careful attention given to recent hybrids. Varieties worthy of attention include:

AUTUMN DELIGHT, as advertised, is a joy late in the rose season when it freely showers its bushes with sprays of sweetly fragrant flowers that change in color from yellow buds to creamy white blossoms with red stamens. One of the lowest-growing Hybrid Musks, it rarely tops 3 feet. (Parentage unrecorded), Bentall, 1933.

BALLERINA may not be typically Hybrid Musk, but it certainly is a stunner. Individual soft pink, white-eyed flowers are tiny (to 1 inch), but they mass themselves in giant trusses (to 100 blossoms each) and form at the ends of long, graceful stems. Although they carry only a light fragrance, blooms last exceptionally long on or off the bush. (Parentage unknown), Bentall, 1937.

'FELICIA' *makes a superb hedge rose because she's not shy when it comes to heft. Blossoms are a plus, too; packed with perfume, they undergo a nice color transformation, beginning with apricot-salmon buds.*

'KATHLEEN' *is among the tallest of the Hybrid Musk roses. Although the two-tone pink flowers formed in clusters are only moderately fragrant, they're followed by a flashy display of orange hips.*

'LAVENDER LASSIE', *another sleeper in the Hybrid Musk family, is an ideal selection for training on a fence, especially if a bench is placed nearby for enjoyment of the fine fragrance. Lavender-pink blossoms open flat and occur regularly on healthy bushes.*

BISHOP DARLINGTON has large, semidouble, cream to flesh pink blossoms with a yellow glow and a distinct perfume of musk. Bushes are vigorous, and foliage is dark green. ('Aviateur Blériot' x 'Moonlight'), Thomas, 1926.

BUFF BEAUTY achieved immortality among Hybrid Musk roses, as I speculate in chapter 7, primarily because of its color. Although blossoms range in hues from mid-apricot to buff-yellow, they always appear edible and smell terrific. Shrubs have a tendency to sprawl but are easily shaped. (Parentage unknown), Pemberton, 1939.

CORNELIA blossoms with large sprays of small flowers that are quite formal with distinct rows of petals around stamen-clustered centers. They're also strongly fragrant and flushed coral and pink, blending nicely with the bronze foliage. 'Cornelia' is a portly maiden, rarely growing taller than 5 feet but considerably wider. (Parentage unknown), Pemberton, 1925.

ERFURT has blooms that look single but actually have enough petals to make the bloom technically semidouble. It's also wondrously colored—bright pink blossoms with white centers and clusters of golden yellow stamens. Fragrance is only

slight, but blossoming is nonstop. ('Eva' x 'Réveil Dijonnais'), Kordes, 1939.

FELICIA, like her sister 'Cornelia', is a hefty lass. Flowering is reliable, however, and strongly fragrant blossoms are nicely shaded apricot-salmon, fading as they mature. Because her bushes respond well to shapely pruning, 'Felicia' forms a fine hedge. ('Trier' x 'Ophelia'), Pemberton, 1928.

FRANCESCA is praised for the pleasant apricot-yellow coloring of her large, semidouble blossoms and for their pungent Tea rose perfume. 'Francesca' makes a fine bush, too, growing to heights of more

'ALCHEMIST' *flowers only once each year, and its blooms take an eternity to mature, but all such matters are gratefully accepted when you get a load of the divinely scented, intricately segmented yolk-yellow to apricot-gold blossoms.*

'ARTHUR HILLIER' *has a charming way of spilling blossoms along the entire length of its arching canes. Although blooms have only five petals each, and are only slightly fragrant, they're reliable and exquisitely colored rose-crimson.*

'COCKTAIL' *is a surefire attention-getter; blooms are an eye-blinking combination of geranium red and primrose yellow. Bushes of 'Cocktail' often grow as wide as they do tall and work superbly as the focal point in a strategic garden spot.*

than 6 feet and giving freely of broadly arching canes. Stems are dark; foliage is large, glossy, and dark green. ('Danaë' x 'Sunburst'), Pemberton, 1928.

KATHLEEN is a particularly tall Hybrid Musk—to more than 8 feet. Moderately fragrant blossoms are deep pink, opening to blush pink, almost-single flowers packed in large clusters. Flowering is followed by the production of showy orange hips. ('Daphne' x 'Perle des Jeannès'), Pemberton, 1922.

MOONLIGHT might be so named because of its reputed fondness for growing 20 feet up trees. Small white flowers are semi-double and are formed in sprays that get larger as the season grows. 'Moonlight' carries a fragrance that is as purely musk as any flower. ('Trier' x 'Sulphurea'), Pemberton, 1913.

PAX is the most popular Hybrid Musk rose in the United States, chiefly because of its agreeable, tall but graceful growth habits and for its sprays of fragrant, semidouble, creamy white blossoms. Stems are brown; foliage is dark green. ('Trier' x 'Sunburst'), Pemberton, 1918.

PENELOPE is one of the most reliable performers among the Hybrid Musk roses. Shrubs that grow as wide as they do tall form clusters of salmon buds. Then pale pink blossoms develop that eventually fade to white, retaining a strong musky fragrance all the while. Coral pink hips form in fall. ('Ophelia' x 'Trier'), Pemberton, 1924.

PROSPERITY is distinguished among Hybrid Musk roses because of its upright growth habits. So, instead of bending from its tendency to sprawl, branches arch because of the weight of their richly fragrant, ivory white blossoms held in large trusses. Foliage is dark green and lustrous. ('Marie-Jeanne' x 'Perle des Jardins'), Pemberton, 1919.

'CONSTANCE SPRY' *is the matriarch of David Austin's English roses, but she's a monstrous shrub to gardeners. Although she blossoms only once each year, Constance makes up for infrequency with bountiful fragrant blossoms that resemble peonies.*

'FRANK NAYLOR' *is a free-bloomer, producing scads of musk-scented single red blossoms with a yellow eye. In order to grow Mr. Naylor well, forewarned gardeners stay on the prowl for mildew.*

'FIMBRIATA' *is sometimes listed as a Hybrid Rugosa but just as often as a Shrub rose. However it's classified, 'Fimbriata' is famous for distinctively fringed petals similar to those of dianthus (pink). As one would hope, the gossamer pale pink blossoms are sweetly scented, and shrubs are well behaved.*

TRIER, as already discussed, was the original Hybrid Musk rose. Although 'Trier' is now considered to be relatively unimportant compared with his offspring, he's still grown because bushes are strongly upright and free flowering with small blossoms that are fragrant, semidouble, and creamy white. Tiny red hips shower shrubs each fall. 'Trier' is thought to be a natural seedling of 'Aglaia'. Lambert, 1904.

WILHELM is the German cousin of the predominantly English Hybrid Musk roses. 'Wilhelm' is a free-bloomer of lightly fragrant, dark claret, semidouble flowers carried in large clusters. Foliage is deep green and particularly disease resistant. ('Robin Hood' x 'J.C. Thornton'), Kordes, 1944.

SHRUB ROSES

Among roses, shrubs differ from bushes in gracefulness. Whereas Modern Rose bushes are bred for remontancy even at the risk of stiff growth habits, Shrub roses were hybridized with the complete gardener in mind—that person who cannot focus only on how regularly blossoms appear but who must also consider how entire plants blend into the garden at large.

Unlike the roses in preceding chapters, shrub roses have widely divergent family trees. Although the vast majority of these roses have a Hybrid Tea as one parent, the other parent may be anything from an ancient species rose to a sassy Floribunda.

Shrub roses do possess a couple of common traits, namely robustness and ease in cultivation, making them right up the alley of gardeners who like colorful, showy roses on naturally graceful plants that are short on demands. And although most cultivars are recurrent in their flowering, some aren't. From a

The bushes of **'FRÜHLINGSMORGEN'** *are the smallest of the three sibling Shrub roses hybridized by Kordes in Germany, but her blossoms are perfectly formed. Depending on how bright the sun is, blooms vary in shades of pink.*

'GOLDEN WINGS' *looks like a species rose and is every bit as hardy. The large fragrant blossoms are handsomely colored sulphur yellow and bushes are resistant to disease and practically thornless.*

'HEBE'S LIP' *is often listed as a Damask, sometimes as an Eglanteria, but it's marketed as a Shrub because of its exceptionally obedient habits. Although it flowers only once each season, blooms are stunning—creamy white, edged with pink.*

'VEILCHENBLAU', *actually a rambler, is often grown as a loose-headed shrub because gardeners are so eager to include its color in the landscape. Purple-violet flowers with white centers intensify in color as they age. Fragrance is fresh from start to finish.*

R. DUPONTII *clearly isn't a species rose because it often flowers repeatedly. Pleasantly scented blossoms are formed from white petals around pronounced golden brown stamens. R. dupontii is a late bloomer, blossoming later than most similar roses.*

'HANSEAT' *blossoms with delicate clusters of faintly scented, five-petaled, two-tone pink flowers, but the bushes on which they bloom are anything but delicate—quickly to 6 feet and taller if not aggressively pruned.*

vast array of choices, I've chosen the following Modern Shrub roses for particular consideration:

ALCHEMIST has only one bloom cycle each year, but it's long and magnificent, with blossoms taking so long to open that you get to know them intimately before they mature. Sharply fragrant petals start out yolk yellow, but before they finish scrolling across blossoms the size of large saucers, they take on shades of apricot and gold. Best of all, you have a choice: 'Alchemist' will grow either as a tall shrub or as a moderate climber. ('Golden Glow' x *R. eglanteria*), Kordes, 1956.

ALOHA can't seem to decide whether it's a shrub or a climber, and consequently it doesn't grow truly satisfactorily as either (shrubs are floppy and climbers are short). One might wonder, then, why I chose to include it here. Well, its fragrant blossoms are another matter—deep rose-pink on the outsides and lighter within. Plants of 'Aloha' look best when planted at the tops of walls so that their drooping blossoms can be viewed head-on from below. ('Mercedes Gallart' x 'New Dawn'), Boerner, 1949.

BLOOMFIELD ABUNDANCE produces clusters of small roses with pale pink petals so perfectly arranged that they look like miniature Hybrid Tea blossoms; they're also dead ringers for 'Cécile Brünner', except that the shrubs they grow on are twice as tall and their sepals are longer. (Nurserymen tell me that plants of the true 'Bloomfield Abundance' no longer exist and that the rose marketed under this name is actually a sport of 'Cécile Brünner'.) ('Sylvia' x 'Dorothy Page-Roberts'), Thomas, 1920.

BONICA, in 1987, was the first Shrub rose ever awarded the coveted All-America Rose title. As I confess in chapter 7, I think that 'Bonica' is the first wave of tomorrow's roses—free blooming, disease resistant, and not fussy over whether or not it's regularly pruned. Pale pink blossoms with only a faint hint of perfume adorn shrubs regularly. (([*R. sempervirens* x 'Mlle Marthe Carron'] x 'Picasso'), Meilland, 1981.

CERISE BOUQUET is not for the faint of heart. Bushes grow to 12-foot heights and just as wide. In spite of such bulk, 'Cerise Bouquet' is a graceful rose—its branches arch, and its clustered cherry-crimson blossoms are carried on willowy, individual stems. Fragrance is fruity; foliage is small, abundant, and grayish green. (*R. multibracteata* x 'Crimson Glory'), Tantau, 1958.

CLAIR MATIN at first glance appears to be no more than another Modern Shrub rose that grows vigorously and blossoms with lightly fragrant, pale pink flowers. If you keep an eye on these shrubs, however, you'll notice that 'Clair Matin' blooms more regularly than do most of its siblings. It also grows happily as a climber. ('Fashion' x ['Independence' x 'Orange Triumph'] x 'Phyllis Bide'), Meilland, 1960.

COCKTAIL is another vigorous shrub that grows almost as wide as it does tall. The color of the five-petaled, clustered blossoms is dazzling—geranium red with a primrose yellow base. Fragrance is slight but crisp, and foliage is dark and leathery. (['Independence' x 'Orange Triumph'] x 'Phyllis Bide'), Meilland, 1957.

CONSTANCE SPRY, the mother of David Austin's English Roses is a showstopper only once each year, but the bounty of blossoming handily makes up for infrequency. From a distance, blooms resemble peonies because of the incredible size they assume by maturity. Heavily petaled flowers with outer petals that reflex gracefully are rich pink and, to some noses, smell strongly of myrrh. Because bushes reach gargantuan sizes, they are often grown as climbers or against large walls. ('Belle Isis' x 'Dainty Maid'), Austin, 1961.

FOUNTAIN produces blossoms that rival Hybrid Tea roses in form. Although blooms have only 35 petals each, they're large, intensely fragrant, and pure crimson. Bushes grow almost as wide as they do tall and have an abundance of dark green foliage that's tough as nails. (Parentage unknown), Tantau, 1970.

FRANK NAYLOR has the most complicated precise lineage of any rose I know. Its prolific flowers, on the other hand, couldn't be simpler—five-petaled single red blossoms with a yellow eye and a scent of musk. Alas, Mr. Naylor is highly susceptible to mildew. (['Orange Sensation' x 'Allgold'] x ['Little Lady' x 'Lilac Charm'] x ['Blue Moon' x 'Magenta'] x ['Cläre Grammerstorf' x 'Frühlingsmorgen'] x ['Little Lady' x 'Lilac Charm'] x ['Blue Moon' x 'Magenta'] x ['Cläre Grammerstorf' x 'Frühlingsmorgen']), Harkness, 1978.

FRED LOADS is considered by many rosarians to be a giant Floribunda. Clusters of fragrant semidouble blossoms are blended salmon and vermilion. Foliage is abundant, dark green, and disease resistant. ('Dorothy Wheatcroft' x 'Orange Sensation'), Holmes, 1968.

FRITZ NOBIS has a single major flaw that keeps it from earning a top spot among Modern Shrub roses: it blooms only once each year. As if in compensation, blossoming is abundant. Perfectly pointed buds open their clove-scented, semidouble petals into beautifully formed blossoms of salmon-pink. After blooming, shrubs sport dark red hips that persist well into winter. ('Joanna Hill' x 'Magnifica'), Kordes, 1940.

FRÜHLINGSANFANG is one of three Modern Shrub roses introduced by Germany's Kordes clan with a prefix that translates as "spring" in English. 'Frühlingsanfang' is the most aggressive of the trio, with shrubs that reach 10 feet by 10 feet. Lightly scented blossoms are large, single, and ivory-white and occur intermittently throughout summer. ('Joanna Hill' x *R. spinosissima altaica*), Kordes, 1950.

FRÜHLINGSGOLD compensates for blooming only once each year with unrivaled hardiness and ease of cultivation. Although buds are tinged crimson, they mature into primrose yellow blossoms with conspicuous butter yellow stamens. Fragrance is strong, and bushes are tough. ('Joanna Hill' x *R. pimpinellifolia hispida*), Kordes, 1937.

FRÜHLINGSMORGEN is not as robust as her two sisters, nor are her blossoms as strongly perfumed. But the single blossoms are perfectly formed around long maroon stamens. Depending on how

R. MICRUGOSA *sounds as though it should be a species rose and it looks like one, too. Prickly shrubs grow to moderate sizes and give freely of light pink flowers with fat yellow centers. Splendid crops of orange-red hips follow flowering.*

'SUNNY JUNE' *is sunny indeed, with golden yellow, five-petaled blossoms and reddish apricot stamens. 'Sunny June' also has a pleasant disposition and dark green, healthy foliage. Because she's so adaptable to where she grows and because she easily reaches 8-foot heights, 'Sunny June' is sometimes grown as a climber (better yet as a pillar).*

'FRITZ NOBIS' *is another shrub that blossoms only once each year. In defense of Mr. Nobis, the show is spectacular, with showers of blush-pink to soft-salmon double blossoms. The orange hips that form in fall are small but festive.*

bright the sunlight is when flowering occurs, petals range in color from rose-pink to light pink. (['E.G. Hill' x 'Cathrine Kordes'] x *R. spinosissima altaica*), Kordes, 1942.

GOLDBUSCH usually grows wider than it does tall, but it gives freely of semidouble, bright yellow blossoms that carry a distinct Tea rose scent. Flowering is intermittent during summer, with a decent crop each fall. (Parentage unknown), Kordes, 1954.

GOLDEN WINGS has the whimsical appeal of a species rose (indeed, its parentage is closely tied to two *R. pimpinellifolia*

species roses). Large flowers are single (usually with five petals, although there can be more), sulphur yellow (with golden brown stamens), and pleasantly fragrant. Bushes are relatively thornless and hardy. ('Soeur Thérèse' x [*R. spinosissima altaica* x 'Ormiston Roy']), Shepherd, 1956.

JAMES MASON typifies why the gardening public is so confused over roses. Named for the fine British actor, 'James Mason' is often listed as a Gallica rose because his mother is part Gallica and his father entirely Gallica. But the rose was hybridized in 1982 by the famed British

rosarian Peter Beales, technically making it a Modern Shrub. Very confusing.

However it's classed, 'James Mason' is a stunning rose. Pure crimson petals arranged in two rows surround a boss of brilliant yellow stamens. Fragrance is strong and bushes are densely foliated, but blossoming is restricted to early summer. ('Scharlachglut' x 'Tuscany Superb'), Beales, 1982.

KASSEL, unlike her German siblings, is not reliably winter-hardy, nor are her blossoms subtly colored. Clusters of slightly fragrant, orange-red flowers appear regularly throughout summer on a sprawling bush that can be trained to climb. ('Hamburg' x 'Scarlet Else'), Kordes, 1957.

LAVENDER LASSIE, sometimes listed along with Hybrid Musk roses, grows and blossoms more like a large Floribunda. Rosette-shaped, pale lavender or lilac-pink flowers form in large trusses and weigh down arching branches. Regularly recurring blossoms are pleasantly fragrant; bushes are neat and are disease resistant. ('Hamburg' x 'Mme Norbert Levavasseur'), Kordes, 1960.

LITTLE WHITE PET is a terrific rose for people whose gardens can't afford the space required by most Modern Shrub roses. Although bushes often grow slightly wider than tall, they rarely exceed 2 feet in either direction. Pompon-shaped, sweetly fragrant flowers formed in clusters are packed with tiny pure white petals. Shrubs of 'Little White Pet' are rarely out of bloom and are seemingly impervious to disease. ('Félicité et Perpétue' sport), Henderson, 1879.

MARJORIE FAIR is the rose for people who wish 'Ballerina' were red. 'Ballerina' is Marjorie's mother, and she passed on three good habits—forming trusses of fragrant tiny flowers, blooming all summer long, and resisting disease. The single blossoms are ruby red and white-eyed. ('Ballerina' x 'Baby Faurax'), Harkness, 1978.

NEVADA takes the cake among Modern Shrub roses, as I admit in chapter 7. Blossoms (which appear mostly in early summer but sometimes again in fall) are wide, semidouble, and rich creamy white and cling to branches right to their tips. Bushes are adamantly resistive to disease, except, I'm told, blackspot. (Parentage not precise), Dot, 1927.

NYMPHENBERG is a hefty maiden but a graceful rose that trains well on a pillar. Semidouble blossoms formed in clusters are salmon-pink at the edges and deep yellow in the center. Fragrance is strong, foliage is dark green, and bushes are vigorous and faithful rebloomers. ('Sangerhausen' x 'Sunmist'), Kordes, 1954.

PEARL DRIFT was supposed to be a climber, or so its hybridizer imagined when he mated Climbing parents. Instead, 'Pearl Drift' remains compact (although it stubbornly sprawls). Flowering, however, takes place over a long period and features large, semidouble, white-flushed-peach-pink blossoms that are mildly scented. Foliage is shiny and pale green. ('Mermaid' x 'New Dawn'), LeGrice, 1980.

PLEINE DE GRÂCE is the perfect rose for distant garden spots—it will eat them up. Bushes ramble into monstrous sizes, but they shower themselves once each year in masses of creamy white, five-petaled, fragrant blossoms, followed by huge numbers of orange-red hips. ('Ballerina' x *R. filipes*), Lens, 1983.

SALLY HOLMES has, for reasons I cannot fathom, remained relatively unknown in the United States, whereas it's been a rage in England ever since its introduction. From a distance, shrubs of 'Sally Holmes' look like rhododendrons, so clustered are the flowers at the tips of graceful branches. Blossoms are not only fragrant, they're also exceptionally long lasting as cut flowers. (See further discussion in chapter 7.) ('Ivory Fashion' x 'Ballerina'), Holmes, 1976.

SPARRIESHOOP is my favorite Shrub rose (see Chapter 7). Well planted and maintained, 'Sparrieshoop' grows to the size of a small car, or, trained properly, to enormous climbers or pillars. Blossoms are composed of bright, clear pink, wavy petals that surround large centers of brilliant yellow stamens. The fragrant blooms on long cutting stems last well on or off the decidedly disease-resistant plants. ('Baby Chateau' x 'Else Poulsen' x 'Magnifica'), Kordes, 1953.

THE FAIRY is often included with Polyanthas because its flowers are similar. Its growth, however, is decidedly shrubby and wider than tall. Nearly scentless blossoms are small, soft pink, and arranged in flat sprays. Flowering is continuous and foliage is small and glossy. ('Paul Crampel' x 'Lady Gay'), Bentall, 1932.

SIX

Rambling Roses

American gardens used to be fairly dull as far as Climbing roses were concerned. The only Climbing rose native to the United States is *R. setigera*, commonly known as the prairie rose, which doesn't grow tall and blossoms

poorly with scentless, dark-pink-fading-to-white, single flowers.

Matters weren't much rosier in Europe, where the only Climbers native to Britain were *R. arvensis* (another loser that would rather sprawl than climb) and the evergreen *R. sempervirens* (which originated along Mediterranean shores and wasn't hardy much farther north).

As English trade with China grew during the eighteenth century, so did interest in the Climbing roses tradesmen reported seeing during their journeys. It was only a matter of time before plantsmen had to see for themselves.

In 1792, Lord Macartney led a British mission to Peking. Among Macartney's staff was George Staunton, a knowledgeable horticulturist who managed to gain entry to two nearby provinces, where he discovered *R. bracteata*, later dubbed the Macartney rose.

Eleven years later, the prestigious Royal Horticultural Society sent William Kerr to China, specifically to search for

'ROYAL SUNSET' *is one of the most underappreciated Climbing roses in America. A winner on all counts, 'Royal Sunset' has beautifully colored blossoms that are rich in fragrance and foliage that's disease-resistant, leathery, and abundant.*

plants. Kerr struck paydirt in Canton, where he found a double white rampant Climber that he named *R. banksiae banksiae* in honor of Lady Banks, the wife of the director of the Royal Horticultural Society at the time. A second mission was dispatched a few years later that resulted in *R. banksiae lutea*, a double yellow goldmine. The single versions of Banksian roses were soon to follow.

Mid-nineteenth-century rose breeders wanted more Climbing roses, but travel in China was still strictly monitored. Robert Fortune, an avid English plant collector, found a way around these restrictions—he shaved his head, grew a pigtail, and dressed in Chinese clothing, thereby gaining entry to a wealthy mandarin's garden and leaving with an immortal Climber now known as 'Fortune's Double Yellow' as well as 'Gold of Ophir'.

By the dawn of the twentieth century, the drive for more Climbing roses was raging and travel constraints were easing. Sir Henry Collet found *R. gigantea* in Burma; Ernest H. Wilson, the most prolific plant finder China had ever known, laid claim to *R. sinowilsonii* in 1904, *R. rubus* in 1907, *R. filipes* in 1908, and *R. multibracteata* in 1910.

American rose hybridizers weren't sitting still either. Soon after the arrival of

'BOBBIE JAMES' *is a Rambling rose for brave gardeners. Plants are so robust that they demand support almost from the moment they're planted. When in full bloom, bushes shower themselves in weighty clusters of fragrant creamy-white cupped blossoms.*

R. wichuraiana late in the nineteenth century, billowing roses emerged, including 'Dorothy Perkins', 'American Pillar', and 'Dr. W. Van Fleet' (which went on to sport the famous repeat-flowering 'New Dawn').

Before discussing the fine cascading roses that emerged during the nineteenth and twentieth centuries from the hands of American and European hybridizers, however, it's crucial to understand the significant role that Mother Nature has played by creating sports.

Sports, as you recall, are spontaneous mutations that result in either a different-colored rose or one with a different growth habit. Rose sports occurred in nature long before man recorded them. Who knows how long ago, for instance, *R. foetida* decided that it was no longer content only with bright yellow flowers and, all on its own, produced the eye-blinking *R. foetida bicolor*, better known as 'Austrian Copper'.

Sometimes roses enjoy a spontaneous mutation that doesn't alter the color of the sport, merely its growth habits. When that change involves an urge to climb, sprawlers are born.

Finally, in this chapter I have made the arbitrary definition of Ramblers to include species roses and their near hy-

'RAMBLING RECTOR' *is a house eater among Rambling roses, devouring anything in sight. On the other hand, when grown into a majestic tree with a comfortable bench nearby, as it is here in St. Albans, England, the Rector is a religious experience.*

'DEBUTANTE' *is considered to be one of the best all-around pink Rambling roses ever. Blossoms are not only distinctly fragrant, they're also held in dainty clusters and change colors from start to finish — rose-pink fading to cameo pink. In agreeable contrast to her delicate blossoms, plants of 'Debutante' are notably robust.*

'ETAIN' *is classified as an orange blend, but its trusses of lightly fragrant flowers are actually salmon-pink. Plants are vigorous Ramblers, and their glossy, dark green foliage is practically evergreen.*

'GOLDFINCH' *is less vigorous than most Rambling roses, but if space is a problem, this rose might be the ticket. Yellow petals with random shades of primrose surround golden brown anthers. Foliage is glossy and stems are almost thornless.*

brids that bloom only once each season, Climbers for those roses that repeat their blooms over summer, and Ground Covers for roses that grow more horizontally than vertically (see further discussion in chapter 17). In some cases, roses listed in one of these three categories first grew as bushes but have achieved greater fame as climbers; hence their inclusion here rather than with their original form.

RAMBLERS

Before you skip this section because you insist on roses that have more than one period of blossom each year, consider that some of the varieties discussed here number among the most beloved roses in the world. In time, the fact that they blossom only once each year is rendered incidental.

Ramblers are unrivaled in their ability to shower plants with blossoms from bottom to top. With some varieties, blossoming lasts two months; others bloom only half that long. Still, it doesn't seem to matter. As mentioned by Christopher Warner (Britain's wizard of Climbing roses) while discussing the coppery pink 'Albertine', "It is perhaps surprising that a rose that has only three weeks of bloom should have remained so long a favorite." Obviously, it says something about the quality of the bloom.

Gardeners' favoritism for Ramblers has doubtlessly developed because no other roses can so thoroughly devour an unsightly shed, camouflage an entire rickety roof, or engulf a dead stump. Some Ramblers grow well in live trees (particularly deciduous ones so that coexistence can be arbitrated at pruning time). Grown into trees, they show to their best advantage because they can be viewed from below—always their best angle.

If you've never witnessed the glories

'FRANCIS E.' LESTER' *blossoms with single-petaled flowers formed in huge trusses. The blooms that start out clear pink but fade to white resemble apple blossoms but smell like a fruit compote. Foliage is distinctfully tapered and glossy.*

R. BANKSIAE LUTEA, *like all members of the Banksian family of roses, knows no bounds when it comes to spread. Although it's hardier than most other Banksias, it's not as fragrant. Still, it's a blooming fool.*

'THALIA' *doesn't grow large, but it happily rambles and flowers profusely. Although individual flowers are small, they mass nicely in clusters and emit a hearty rose fragrance. 'Thalia' is a terrific choice among Ramblers for gobbling up a split rail fence.*

of a cycle of blossoms from a Rambling rose, you owe yourself the favor. However long the show lasts, when it comes to staging, no roses top Ramblers such as:

ALBÉRIC BARBIER, the first of a trio of *R. wichuraiana* hybrids, is a vigorous but somewhat tender Rambler that likes to grow horizontally, making it a natural for low fences. Fat yellow buds open into large, creamy, double flowers with quartered petals and a scent of green apples. Although there's a chance of a modest repeat bloom in fall, I wouldn't count on it. (*R. wichuraiana* x 'Shirley Hibberd'), Barbier, 1900.

ALBERTINE, as mentioned, takes less than a month to stage its show each year, but what a show it is! Reddish buds develop into coppery pink, richly fragrant, ragged but charming blossoms. Plants are thorny and slightly prone to mildew. (*R. wichuraiana* x 'Mrs. Arthur Robert Waddell'), Barbier, 1921.

ALEXANDER GIRAULT achieved immortality in one planting—at the famous Roseraie de l'Hay in Paris, where it smothers a backdrop at one edge of the garden. 'Alexander Girault' blooms in a profusion of clustered, reddish salmon flowers that are packed with fragrant quilled petals

around a green button eye. Foliage is profuse, shiny, and resistant to disease. (*R. wichuraiana* x 'Papa Gontier'), Barbier, 1909.

AMERICAN PILLAR, perhaps due to its name alone, was the most popular Rambler in the United States for several decades after its introduction. Now it's been replaced by more gracefully blooming, mildew-resistant Ramblers. Scentless, single, bright pink blossoms with white centers are produced in large clusters during midsummer. ([*R. wichuraiana* x*R. setigera*] x unnamed red Hybrid Perpetual), Van Fleet, 1902.

BELLE OF PORTUGAL was bred at the botanical gardens in Lisbon, so it's no surprise that it's not entirely winter-hardy. Where winters are temperate, however, the Belle is a favorite landscape rose, especially on the eaves of houses with Victorian gingerbread. Long and pointed buds open into flesh pink blossoms with silky quilled petals that loosen as they age but always retain a strong, fruity fragrance. (*R. gigantea* x 'Reine Marie-Henriette'), Cayeux, 1903.

BOBBIE JAMES is a house eater among Ramblers, but also one of the most beautiful when in full, majestic bloom. Large heads of deeply fragrant, creamy white, semidouble, cupped blossoms with bright yellow stamens shower whole plants, which reach easily to 25 feet. Give this rose strong support. (Thought to be a hybrid from *R. multiflora*), Sunningdale Nurseries, 1960.

CHEVY CHASE isn't fragrant or exceptionally well colored, but he has other things going for him, including a constitution of iron when it comes to resisting disease. Hardy, aggressive plants produce multitudes of small, double, crimson blossoms packed with petals and formed in dense clusters. (*R. soulieana* x 'Éblouissant'), Hansen, 1939.

'FÉLICITÉ ET PERPÉTUE' is one of rose-dom's favorite ramblers and for good reasons — it's exceptionally hardy, almost evergreen, requires little attention at pruning time, and will tolerate shade. Besides all that, nicely scented blossoms are milky white, profuse, and complement nearby flowering companions.

DEBUTANTE closely resembles 'Dorothy Perkins', but has two marked advantages—finer rose-pink color and resistance to mildew. Blossoms start out cupped, then quill their petals as they open and fade in, but not lose, color. Many compare the fragrance of 'Debutante' to that of primroses. (*R. wichuraiana* x 'Baroness Rothschild'), Walsh, 1902.

DOROTHY PERKINS was introduced in America in 1901 and ruled the fragrant rose-pink Rambler class for some time afterward. Growth is supple and vigorous but prone to mildew. (*R. wichuraiana* x 'Mme Gabriel Luizet'), Jackson & Perkins, 1901.

EXCELSA, sometimes called 'Red Dorothy Perkins', has masses of small, globular, crimson flowers with white centers. Taller than but not as fragrant as her predecessor, 'Excelsa' is also susceptible to mildew. Otherwise, it makes a fine weeping standard. (Parentage unknown), Walsh, 1909.

FÉLICITÉ ET PERPÉTUE, named for two Christian martyrs and also for the daughters of its breeder (gardener to the Duc d'Orléans), is a Rambling classic. Not only is it exceptionally hardy, its ever-green foliage persists into winter and its bushes don't need pruning. Besides all that, it will tolerate shade. Milky white pompon blossoms are profuse and nicely scented (some say of primroses) and have button eyes. (Parentage unknown), Jacques, 1827.

FRANCIS E. LESTER is named for its breeder, who also founded California's

---

*If you want to see Rambling roses grown to perfection, visit the Roseraie de l'Hay just outside Paris. Here, '***EXCELSA***' is strutting its stuff. As long as you can control powdery mildew, 'Excelsa' is a beauty.*

famous nursery Roses of Yesterday and Today. The single flowers that form in large trusses start out clear pink but fade to white, resembling apple blossoms but smelling like a fruit compote. Foliage is tapered, long, and glossy green. ('Kathleen' seedling), Lester, 1946.

GOLDFINCH has fruit-scented, yolk yellow buds that take on hints of apricot before they fade to white buttonlike flowers. Foliage is shiny, and bushes are practically thornless. 'Goldfinch' happily grows into a lax arching shrub. ('Hélène' x unknown rose), Paul, 1907.

KIFTSGATE, thought to be a sport of *R. filipes* and often sold under that name, wins the prize for voracity among Ramblers. 'Kiftsgate' knows no bounds, and owners of mature plants like to talk in terms of how many hundreds of square feet their specimens cover. Blossoms shower plants with massive corymbs of small, single, creamy white flowers with yellow stamens and good perfume. Introduced from western China in 1908.

LADY GAY is treasured by gardeners who like 'Dorothy Perkins', but don't care to put up with her mildew. Although she doesn't grow quite as tall as her lookalike, and blooms later, 'Lady Gay' produces clusters of blossoms that are colored a more agreeable rose-pink. (*R. wichuraiana* x 'Bardou Job'), Walsh, 1905.

PAUL'S LEMON PILLAR graces a wall near the entrance of Mottisfont Abbey, an Heirloom rosarian's dream garden, and few people pass that rose in full bloom without walking over for a closer look.

Fat, greenish yellow buds open into large, creamy yellow blossoms with artfully scrolled petals and a delicious fragrance. ('Frau Karl Druschki' x 'Maréchal Niel'), Paul, 1915.

PURITY, as its name would suggest, has uncompromisingly white blossoms; it's also hardy, vigorous, and adaptable—growing equally well as a climber, pillar, or freestanding shrub. (Unnamed seedling x 'Mme Caroline Testout'), Hoopes, 1917.

RAMBLING RECTOR lives up to its name by religiously scrambling over anything it's planted near—fences, stumps, shrubs, trees, roofs, any unclaimed territory. Blossoming consists of heads of small, semidouble, creamy white flowers with yellow stamens and a pungent perfume. Small hips form in autumn. (Origin unknown), introduced in 1912.

R. BANKSIAE BANKSIAE is one member of a closely knit family of roses, all of whom share a reputation for fragrance, an affinity for rapid growth to heights in excess of 25 feet, and a tenderness to winter. Although it's not the oldest Banksian rose, *R. banksiae banksiae* is the most fragrant—scented, many claim, of violets. Flowers are less than 1 inch, fully petaled, pure white, and shaped like rosettes. As with all members of the family, wood is almost thornless, and foliage is long, light green, and shiny. (Origin unknown), introduced by William Kerr in 1807.

R. BANKSIAE LUTEA is a carbon copy of *R. banksiae banksiae* except that it's deep

to pale yellow, somewhat hardier, and not as fragrant. (Origin unknown), introduced by J.D. Park in 1824.

R. BANKSIAE LUTESCENS is brighter yellow than *R. banksiae lutea*, but more important, its blossoms are single rather than double. Introduced in England in 1870.

R. BANKSIAE NORMALIS, probably the oldest Banksian rose, was the last to be introduced. Native to western China, *R. banksiae normalis* is single, snow white, and superbly scented. Introduced in England in 1877.

SEAGULL is the rose of choice for people who like the looks of 'Kiftsgate' and 'Rambling Rector' but can't afford that much room (it's also a companionable rose for growing in live trees). Although blossoms are small, they're abundant, semidouble, centered with yellow stamens, and sweetly fragrant. Foliage is large and semiglossy. (Parentage unknown), Pritchard, 1907.

THALIA is a typical Rambler from *R. multiflora*—vigorous in its clustered production of small, double, white flowers with a fine fragrance. Plants are hearty but not voracious. (*R. multiflora* x 'Paquerette'), Schmitt, 1895.

THE GARLAND is the product of a cross between two species roses. Although the offspring has characteristics of both species, it blooms like neither. Blossoms are semidouble and open from pink buds into creamy white blossoms with quilled petals and a scent of sweet oranges. 'The Garland' will obediently form a pillar,

'SANDER'S WHITE' *is usually grown as a rambler, but it serves double duty as a groundcover. However it's grown, blossoms form in large clusters and emit a powerful fragrance. Beloved in England, the variety is rarely (and unfortunately) cultivated in America.*

'JOSEPH'S COAT' *has always seemed a bit garish to me, but loads of people think I'm all wet where this dazzling bicolor is concerned. 'Joseph's Coat' grows as well as a lax shrub as a climber, but colors are just as assaultive.*

'LAWRENCE JOHNSTON', *named in honor of the founder of Hidcote (one of Britain's prized National Trust gardens), is about as clear yellow as roses get. Blossoms are fragrant, and they're accompanied by abundant, shiny foliage.*

climb trees, or mass its growth into a sprawling shrub. (*R. moschata* x*R. multiflora*), Wells, 1835.

CLIMBERS

Climbers, as already agreed, differ from Ramblers in that they blossom repeatedly throughout the season. The Climbing roses mentioned here also have larger flowers and bloom in a wider range of colors than do Ramblers. As for whose blossoms are more beautiful or refined, that, of course, is in the eye of the beholder.

Keep in mind that climbers not listed here appear elsewhere throughout this text. The bulk of the Noisette roses discussed in the previous chapter, for instance, are better grown as climbers than as lax shrubs. Then, from Chinas through Miniatures, repeat-blooming roses that once grew only as shrubs have sported Climbing clones of themselves. Some roses, such as the Hybrid Tea 'Sutter's Gold', sported a climber the same year the rose was introduced into commerce. Others, such as the fabulous Bourbon rose 'Souvenir de la Malmaison', have taken their own sweet time (50 years) in getting around to climbing.

If you've fallen in love with a rosebush but dream that it will someday sport a climber, check to see if it already has—fistfuls have. Otherwise, you might consider these:

ALTISSIMO, as I admit in chapter 7 while discussing its probable immortality, is a fine climber (pillar, too). Seven-petaled blossoms are blood red and surround a mass of golden stamens; they're also fragrant and last well on or off the bush. ('Tenor' x unidentified rose), Delbard-Chabert, 1966.

AMERICA was an All-America Rose award winner in 1976 in honor of the U.S. bicentennial, and a fitting selection it

'MRS. SAM MCGREDY' *was never much as a bush, but the Climbing sport is a doozy. Fragrant blossoms are a vivid combination of scarlet, copper, and red. Alas, the glossy reddish bronze foliage is no stranger to blackspot.*

'PHYLLIS BIDE' *resembles a Rambling rose more than a Climbing, but it's a climber all right, and it blossoms repeatedly to prove it. Although blooms are irregularly shaped, they're nicely colored and sweetly fragrant.*

'CLAIR MATIN' *is a blooming fool, with fragrant, pale pink, semidouble flowers occurring with remarkable regularity over a long season. Plants mature into large (but graceful) shrubs only slightly taller than wide. With proper training, shrubs can be forced to climb. In any case, foliage is dark green and leathery.*

was. 'America' has more than 40 fragrant coral petals per bloom, arranged in perfect symmetry at all stages of maturity. If you train 'America' on a wall, in order to avoid mildew be certain to give it some breathing room (see chapter 17). ('Fragrant Cloud' x 'Tradition'), Warriner, 1976.

DEVONIENSIS, the Climbing form, is a sport of the Tea rose bush hybridized in 1838. Although tender to winter however it's grown, 'Devoniensis' grows well climbing a south wall even in cruel climates. Powerfully fragrant blossoms are creamy white but are also suffused with pink and apricot. (Parentage unknown), introduced by Pavitt in 1858.

DON JUAN is highly rated by the American Rose Society, probably for its willingness to produce large, velvety, dark red blossoms packed with perfume. Foliage is dark, leathery, and glossy, and plants are moderate growers. ('New Dawn' seedling x 'New Yorker'), Malandrone, 1958.

DORTMUND is one of a race of exceptionally hardy roses hybridized by Kordes of Germany. Its flashy single blossoms are bright red and have golden yellow stamens smack-dab in the middle of eye-blinking white centers. Dark green, glossy foliage resembles that of holly (and is similarly tough). If you want a second crop of blossoms, it's important to harvest the first crop of seed-bearing hips. (Seedling x *R. kordesii*), Kordes, 1955.

GOLD OF OPHIR, also known as 'Fortune's Double Yellow', as mentioned earlier, was discovered in China by Robert Fortune when he gained entry to a wealthy mandarin's garden. Sweetly scented blossoms are a dazzling copper, golden orange, yellow, and buff-white. Foliage is mid-green, and wood is almost thornless. (Parentage unknown), Fortune, 1945.

'ROSARIUM UETERESEN', *the name, doesn't trip lightly off the tongue, but the rose is easy in every way. Plants perform exactly as told and have handsome toothy foliage and richly fragrant, densely petaled blossoms.*

'RAUBRITTER' *is the most quintessential Ground-cover rose, and no specimen is photographed more often than this one at Mottisfont Abbey, home to the rose collection of Britain's esteemed Graham Stuart Thomas. Shrubs rarely mound taller than 3 feet, but easily stretch to 8 feet, with clusters of cupped, soft pink flowers.*

'NOZOMI' *is an amazingly versatile rose — it will climb, cover the ground, or grow into a specimen weeping standard (tree rose). Blossoms are so small they qualify for Miniature rose status; foliage is small, too, but glossy and plentiful.*

Because 'Gold of Ophir' was the favorite childhood rose of my late friend M.F.K. Fisher and also because I heard that it would tolerate shade, I placed three bushes near a thicket of deciduous native willow trees. Probably because of the dense summer shade, the plants took a seeming eternity to climb those willows. Now, however, they're more than 15 feet long, and early each summer, they shower themselves in flowers that, as Mary Frances rightfully declared, "look like moons on fire."

GOLDEN SHOWERS is to Climbing roses what 'King Alfred' is to daffodils—vivid yellow, early, and profuse. Although blossoms open fairly quickly (they have fewer than 30 petals each), they're large and fragrant and feature attractive red anthers. Because 'Golden Showers' naturally grows upright, it makes a fine pillar rose and is rarely without blossoms. Foliage isn't worth mentioning, except that it has a tendency to mildew. ('Charlotte Armstrong' x 'Captain Thomas'), Lammerts, 1956.

HANDEL, in spite of its near scentlessness, is an enormously popular Climber both in Europe and in the United States because of the unusual coloring of its flowers' petals—cream, edged pink. Fall's blossoming is almost as spectacular as summer's, and although foliage is glossy olive green, it's prone to blackspot. ('Columbine' x 'Heidelberg'), McGredy, 1965.

JOSEPH'S COAT has always been problematical for me. The first time I saw a climber of 'Joseph's Coat' in full bloom, I thought it garish, and I haven't changed my mind. Admittedly, I'm in the vast minority, for several gardeners I know wouldn't dream of living without the cavalcade of colors offered by 'Joseph's Coat'. Bright yellow buds flushed with orange mature into vaguely fragrant red

blossoms flushed pink. Because it's not particularly robust, 'Joseph's Coat' grows well as a loose shrub. ('Buccaneer' x 'Circus'), Armstrong and Swim, 1964.

LAWRENCE JOHNSTON is a vigorous climber and profuse early bloomer. Loose, cupped, sharply fragrant flowers are clear yellow and appear especially bright against the abundant shiny green foliage. Although I've not seen it for myself, I'm told that 'Lawrence Johnston' is susceptible to blackspot. ('Mme Eugène Verdier' x *R. foetida persiana*), Pernet-Ducher, 1923.

MME CAROLINE TESTOUT has been a treasured Climbing rose for almost a century because its first burst of bloom occurs midseason, when most Climbing roses are well past their first flush. Flowers are lightly scented, large, globular, and, depending on weather, some shade of silvery rose. Wood is thorny, and foliage is dull mid-green. Mme Testout is a sport from the bush rose raised by Pernet-Ducher from a cross between 'Mme de Tartas' and 'Lady Mary Fitzwilliam'. The climbing form was introduced by Chauvry in 1901.

MAIGOLD is sometimes listed as a Shrub rose rather than as a Climber; in truth, it's somewhere in between but consistently vigorous. Although 'Maigold' is viciously

*'**DORTMUND**', like other roses from Kordes of Germany, is exceptionally hardy. It also produces dazzling red blossoms with white centers and vivid yellow stamens. Foliage resembles that of holly and is just as shiny.*

thorny, its lush, shiny foliage is hardy and exceptionally resistant to disease; it's also an early bloomer. Buds streaked red open into golden yellow blossoms with a powerful scent of honey. ('Poulsen's Pink' x 'Frühlingstag'), Kordes, 1953.

MARÉCHAL NIEL, in spite of its extreme sensitivity to cold, was so popular when it was introduced in 1864 that Victorians built lean-to greenhouses simply to house it. Blossoms are large, apricot-yellow, and strongly scented of tea. Foliage is sparse, light green, and glossy. Plants are unhappy in humid conditions. 'Maréchal Niel' is believed to be a seedling of 'Cloth of Gold'. Introduced by Pradel in 1864.

MEG has 10 petals per flower, placing it midway between a single and a semidouble blossom. Its flowering effect, however, is nearly unsurpassed. Peachy apricot, pungently fragrant blossoms with russet stamens and wavy petals are large and formed in clusters. Because it has rigid stems, 'Meg' is more easily grown against a wall rather than as a vining climber. Believed to be the result of a cross between 'Paul's Lemon Pillar' and 'Madame Butterfly'. Gosset, 1954.

MERMAID is an immortal rose even though it's not one I selected for discussion in

---

'DR. W. VAN FLEET' *has been eclipsed in popularity by its own progeny—'New Dawn', which blossoms repeatedly. Although the Doctor enjoys only one flush of bloom, his plants grow considerably taller than those of his daughter.*

'MADAME DRIOUT', *a climbing Tea rose, requires coddling to perform well. Rewards for such efforts are considerable, however, including shapely buds that open flat. Quartered fragrant blossoms are reddish pink, often flecked with white.*

'CHAPLIN'S PINK COMPANION', *a R. wichuraiana hybrid, is more tastefully colored than its immediate predecessors. Though still bright, blossoms are silvery pink. Plants are vigorous and foliage is glossy.*

'ICEBERG' *has been available as a Climber for years in England, but has only recently become commercially available in America. This particular plant had been in the ground only 15 months when this photograph was taken. Astounding!*

chapter 7. Although it has many endearing qualities, the most appealing is its willingness to accept shade. Perfumed blossoms are single but large (more than 5 inches each), are lemon yellow, and have golden brown stamens that persist even after petals fall. It may be slow to start, but once 'Mermaid' takes hold, it's a voracious grower. Wood is slightly brittle, making early training mandatory; foliage is narrow, glossy, and abundant. 'Mermaid' is considered tender. (*R. bracteata* x unidentified yellow Tea rose), Paul, 1917.

MRS. SAM MCGREDY, as a bush, was cursed with gangly growth habits. Then a climbing sport emerged and Mrs. McGredy could amble all she pleased. Fragrant blossoms are blindingly showy—scarlet-copper, heavily flushed with red. Foliage is glossy, reddish bronze, and susceptible to blackspot. ('Donald Macdonald' x 'Golden Emblem' x [seedling x 'The Queen Alexandra Rose']), McGredy, 1929. The climbing sport was introduced by Buisman in 1937.

NEW DAWN was the first rose ever to be patented, which is ironic, in that it's a sport. Unlike the once-flowering rose from which it sported, 'New Dawn' repeats well throughout summer. Medium-sized blossoms are apple-blossom pink and fruitily fragrant. Foliage is light green, glossy, and adamantly resistive to disease, and plants are decidedly hardy. 'New Dawn', a climbing sport of 'Dr. W. Van Fleet', was discovered by Somerset Rose Nursery in 1930.

PHYLLIS BIDE closely resembles Rambling roses because its small flowers are formed in clusters. But unlike Ramblers, 'Phyllis Bide' regularly repeats its flowering. Irregularly shaped blossoms are pale gold, shaded pink, and sweetly fragrant. Like the flowers, foliage is small but plentiful; wood is almost thornless. ('Perle d'Or' x 'Gloire de Dijon'), Bide, 1923.

ROSARIUM UETERESEN is an unusually adaptable climber because it scrambles up pillars, permits rigid training on a wall or fence, or serves equally well as a large weeping standard. Foliage is large, profuse, medium green, and distinctly toothed. Although the salmon-pink blossoms are crammed with petals, they eventually open flat and emit a fragrance that many people compare to that of green apples. ('Karlsruhe' x unidentified seedling), Kordes, 1977.

ROYAL SUNSET is one of the most beautiful Climbing roses I've ever seen (I'm told that's because it grows best near where I garden, but I sincerely doubt that report). Blossoms are a rich shade of apricot and strongly fragrant. Foliage is not only abundant, it's also leathery, dark green, and disease resistant. ('Sungold' x 'Sutter's Gold'), Morey, 1960.

SHOT SILK never amounted to much as a bush, but what a climber it sported! The undeniable attribute of this variety is embodied in the deeply fragrant blossoms of silky salmon petals shot with yellow. Foliage is glossy and mid-green. (See further discussion in chapter 7.) ('Hugh Dickson' seedling x 'Sunstar'), Dickson, 1924. The climbing sport was introduced by Knight in 1931.

SOMBREUIL is another immortal Climbing rose (see entry in chapter 7). Creamy white blossoms brushed lightly with pink are heavily petaled but mature into flat, rosette-shaped flowers of exquisite form

and a deliciously clean tea scent. It's also entirely hardy. Although precise parentage is not documented, 'Sombreuil' is thought to be a seedling of a Hybrid Perpetual rose named 'Gigantesque'. Robert, 1850.

SUTTER'S GOLD still gets my vote as the best all-around yellow Hybrid Tea, although I prefer to grow it as a climber rather than as a bush. Deep yellow buds flushed reddish gold open quickly to clear yellow blossoms with whimsical form. Fragrance is sensational at all stages. Stems are long and accompany dark green, leathery foliage. ('Charlotte Armstrong' x 'Signora'), Swim, 1950.

GROUND COVERS

Roses described in this section aren't ground covers in the usual sense because they aren't meant for walking on. For landscaping, however, procumbent roses are invaluable because they grow wider than tall. Although Ground-cover roses are unsurpassed for concealing stumps or broad unsightly garden areas, they're also useful in mixed garden borders. Desirable varieties include:

FAIRYLAND grows no taller than 2 feet but twice as broad. Rosy pink blossoms formed in sprays are small, semidouble, strongly fragrant, and recurrent throughout summer. Foliage is glossy, and plants are winter-hardy. ('The Fairy' x 'Yesterday'), Harkness, 1980.

FERDY is tall for a ground cover (to 3 feet), but it spreads to 6 feet. Salmonpink blossoms that appear in clusters in

early summer and again in fall are scentless but profuse. Foliage is abundant, light green, and disease resistant. (Unnamed Climbing seedling x 'Petite Folie' seedling), Keitoli, 1984.

MAX GRAF is best known as the Rugosa hybrid that eats up banks of unclaimed land. 'Max Graf' is a quintessential Ground-cover rose because it rarely grows taller than 2 feet but sends out long shoots that root themselves to travel farther. Although it only flowers once each year, the prolific blossoms are single, pale pink, and fruit scented. (*R. rugosa* x *R. wichuraiana*), Bowditch, 1919.

NOZOMI, often listed as a climbing Miniature rose, also makes a fine ground cover, particularly in rock gardens. Trusses of flat, slightly fragrant, pearlpink blossoms appear in midsummer against small, glossy foliage. Growth rarely exceeds 1-foot heights but spreads more than 5 feet. 'Nozomi' also makes a fine weeping standard. ('Fairy Princess' x 'Sweet Fairy'), Onodera, 1968.

RALPH'S CREEPER, named in honor of the indefatigable American Miniature rose hybridizer Ralph Moore, is a fine choice for those who want to cover their ground with small, bright red blossoms that have bright white eyes. Plants are particularly vigorous for a Miniature and disease resistant as well. ('Papoose' x 'Playboy'), Moore, 1988.

RAUBRITTER, which matures into a low spreading mound, is a favorite Groundcover rose in Europe but has only recently caught on in America. Because of their deeply cupped formation, the mildly fragrant, nonrecurring blossoms of 'Raubritter' resemble those of Old Roses and are formed all along the length of thorny branches with dark green, wrinkled, leathery foliage. Stay on the watch for mildew. ('Daisy Hill' x 'Solarium'), Kordes, 1936.

RED BLANKET reliably grows twice as wide as tall. Small, semidouble, rose-red, faintly fragrant flowers are repeatedly produced in clusters on prickly plants blessed with dark, glossy foliage. ('Yesterday' x unnamed seedling), Ilsink, 1979.

SEA FOAM is conventionally listed as a shrub, but because of its decided preference for hugging the ground, I think of 'Sea Foam' as either a ground cover or, better yet, a wall hanger. When well-cultivated, bushes are showered with exceptionally well formed, white to cream, slightly fragrant double blossoms. Foliage is small, glossy, and tough. The parentage is bewilderingly incestuous: ([[('White Dawn' x 'Pinocchio') x ('White Dawn' x Pinocchio)] x ['White Dawn' x 'Pinocchio']), Schwartz, 1964.

SMARTY, hybridized by the same breeder as 'Red Blanket' and having similar parentage, bears remontant sprays of seven-petaled pink blossoms with a fruity fragrance. Plants have bright green, matte, disease-resistant foliage. ('Yesterday' x unnamed seedling), Ilsink, 1979.

'FERDY' *is a big girl, growing twice as wide as tall. Although blossoms are small and nearly scentless, they're plentiful, double, and nicely colored salmon-pink. The light green foliage is also small, but abundant.*

SEVEN

Fifty Immortal Roses

I've always maintained that there are too many varieties of roses in commerce and that it's becoming worse each year, with more hopefuls than we can ever keep track of or names we can commit to memory. *Modern Roses 10*, the

most current Rose Grower's definitive listing of varieties, lists more than 16,000 cultivars!

During those years I fretted over choosing among so many different roses, I suffered a recurring dream that always turned into a nightmare. It started well, with my arrival at heaven's gates, but matters took a sharp turn when a surly archangel appeared to inform me that my allotted celestial land would hold only 12 rosebushes and that I must declare which they were to be, within an hour.

The first night these nagging images appeared to me, I

awoke from deep slumber and couldn't go back to sleep until I had completed the first draft of my list. The next day, obvious substitutions occurred to me, so, of course, I had the dream again and bettered my selections.

Although I altered my choices countless times during those years of delicious agony, they always came from roses discussed

'COLOR MAGIC', a pink blend deliciously fragrant Hybrid Tea, was destined for my list of immortals because it's my favorite rose in spite of some annoying growth habits. Personal bias doesn't rule quite so strongly in the remaining 49 selections.

in this chapter—the 50 roses that I consider immortal because they've already stood, or show all likelihood of standing, the test of time. They are, of course, my personal biases, but I'll bet they become yours, too, if you grant them a spot in your garden.

My list is composed of roses from all groups discussed in this book, from species to the current rage. When known, parentage is listed, mothers first.

ALTISSIMO

('Tenor' x unidentified rose)

Altissimo' was hybridized by Delbard-Chabert of France in 1966. After hybridizing 'Tenor' in 1963, he must surely have known he was on track for a fine dark red Climber. 'Tenor' was almost the precise color he sought, and its petals were velvety with substance. Still, the comely seedling wasn't quite what Delbard-Chabert had in mind. Three years later, he mated 'Tenor' with an unrecorded male, and bingo, 'Altissimo'—a hybridizer's dream.

When gardeners tell me that they're in search of a strong-growing, dark red, climbing rose that blooms repeatedly, I ask hopefully if they'd consider a single-petaled rose. If they say yes, I always suggest 'Altissimo'. If they say no, I imagine that the same roadblock stands between them and singles as used to trouble me—that single roses don't last as well as cut flowers or harbor much fragrance. Wrong on both counts. If a fragrant flower that lasts well when cut is the ticket, 'Altissimo' is the rose.

Another of its virtues is a bush so obedient that it behaves precisely as told. If a vigorous climber is called for, 'Altissimo' obliges. If training on a pillar is what one has in mind, 'Altissimo' happily grows straight up, blossoming along its entire height.

Not only is the plant on which 'Altissimo' grows hardy, so is its foliage—large, dark green, and particularly resistant to disease. In addition to all of these qualities, 'Altissimo' is a Modern Rose that grows well on its own roots, rather than depending on rootstock onto which most Modern hybrids are budded (see chapter 14).

Finally, and best of all, blooms of 'Altissimo' are seductive, not only because of their glorious color combination of seven, oversized, blood red petals around a heart of fat golden yellow stamens, but also because of the deliciously scented perfume that surrounds the entire package.

ANGEL FACE

(['Circus' x 'Lavender Pinocchio'] x 'Sterling Silver')

Visitors to my garden are hard pressed to ask a more vexing question than if I grow "the Sterling" rose. What they mean, of course, is whether or not I grow 'Sterling Silver'. I decidedly do not, and I don't like to talk about it. The American Rose Society currently rates 'Sterling Silver' 4.5 on a 10-point scale (roses rated lower than 6.0 are considered to be "of questionable value"). However, 'Angel Face', a descendant of 'Sterling Silver', is rated 8.2 (roses between 8.0 and 8.9 are considered "excellent"). I wholeheartedly endorse the disparity of these two ratings and consider 'Angel Face' the finest mauve rose ever.

Another winner from the clever hybridizing team of southern California's Swim and Weeks, 'Angel Face' was an All-America Rose Selection in 1969, the first mauve rose ever to win this prestigious honor.

It is an exemplary Floribunda. Its blossoms are produced in large sprays with flowers in all stages of development from buds to fully open blooms. Unlike many roses in this color class, 'Angel Face' is clear mauve, not muddied. Although buds are tall and high centered, fully open blossoms are 4 inches wide, are flat, and boast a center of fat golden yellow stamens. Best of all, blooms harbor a strong, enticing fragrance.

Bushes of 'Angel Face' are low growing and tend to spread. Foliage is copper green and reasonably disease resistant.

I've seen bushes of 'Angel Face' in other gardens that are twice the size of mine. In some cases, I write off this dissimilarity to different growing conditions. Secretly, however, I'm certain that my greed has something to do with it. If you, too, are fond of roses as cut flowers, especially intensely fragrant ones, watch out for 'Angel Face'—it's a winner, and an addictive one at that.

usually curl inward at their edges, the total effect is dazzling, especially since petals frame centers of eye-blinking yellow stamens. As a special bonus, branches of 'Austrian Copper' are famous for reverting to their parent plant, so that both pure yellow and bicolored blossoms appear simultaneously on one bush.

Before granting 'Austrian Copper' a spot in your garden, be aware of two important facts. First, it blooms only once each year. Blossoming takes place before most other roses are showing buds, however, and extends over a lengthy period. More important, be forewarned that *R. foetida bicolor*, like its parent, has an affinity for blackspot.

Foliage and wood of 'Austrian Copper' are both distinctive. Although the individual pale green to mid-green leaves are small, they're somehow fitting, particularly in the way they mass themselves nicely and perfectly frame *R. foetida bicolor's* 2½-inch flowers. Wood is mottled chestnut brown, while thorns are even darker, almost black. Because of these colorings, 'Austrian Copper' looks exceptionally fetching when grown against wood, which is just as well, since its towering 5-foot shrubs need support, either with stakes or against walls.

Finally, 'Austrian Copper' puts on quite a show when in full bloom, with blossoms extending along the entire outer reaches of its gracefully arching canes. All in all, 'Austrian Copper' is a thoroughly satisfying rose and a welcome late-spring sight.

AUSTRIAN COPPER
(Ancient sport)

'Austrian Copper', properly known as *R. foetida bicolor*, is a sport (a spontaneous mutation) that has outdone its parent. Not only is its color more unusual, 'Austrian Copper' also smells better than does the species from which it sprang—*R. foe-*

tida, the pure yellow rose from Asia that certainly smells, but not always nicely.

In addition, 'Austrian Copper' is more dramatically colored than is its parent. Instead of yellow throughout, *R. foetida bicolor* is yellow only on the undersides of petals; topsides are copper-red. Because the five petals that constitute the bloom

BARONNE PRÉVOST
(Parentage unrecorded)

Just before the middle of the nineteenth century, the public let rose hybridizers know exactly what they wanted—exhibition-quality blooms. Rose shows had just come into vogue, and competitive rosarians were eager to win ribbons and trophies for their efforts. "Showier blooms, please," they must have said.

In an effort to please greedy exhibitors and with a covetous eye on a trophy from the show table, hybridizers hustled to cross every rose they grew. Since early rose competitions were among blossoms displayed in a box, with no benefit of stem or foliage, the bush of a prizewinner could be anything from a runt to a weak-stemmed skyscraper constantly in need of staking. The form of the blossoms was paramount, the showier the better.

As a result of this attempt to supply the insatiable demand, the Hybrid Perpetual class of roses is famous for its awkward bushes. But there are exceptions—'Baronne Prévost', for instance.

'Baronne Prévost' is a vigorous grower, with mature bushes that are 4 feet all around. Although plants are squat, blossoms are refined.

In keeping with the elegant form of its predecessors, blooms are typically "Old Rose," with petals scrolled so cleverly that they appear hand-stitched by a compulsive seamstress. When blossoms finish quartering into segments, they curl back around a green button eye. Color ranges from pale to mid-pink, and old-fashioned, deep rose fragrance is constant and exceptionally strong.

The Baronne's foliage is nicer than many of its Hybrid Perpetual siblings—it's larger, a more pleasant shade of mid-green, and decidedly stronger at resisting disease.

Like all roses that repeat their bloom over summer, 'Baronne Prévost' responds nicely to regular feeding and deep watering. Although blooms won't recur with the regularity of her modern offspring, 'Baronne Prévost' makes up for modest repeats with stunning results.

BEWITCHED

('Queen Elizabeth' x 'Tawny Gold')

When gardeners ask me to recommend a fragrant pink rose that blooms all season on long cutting stems, I first make sure that they want pure pink, not a blend such as 'First Prize' or 'Color Magic'. If clean fresh pink is what they have in mind, 'Bewitched' is my second-to-none suggestion.

I think more highly of 'Bewitched' than do most members of the American Rose Society, at least those voters who periodically score their roses on a 10-point scale. Fussy rosarians rate 'Bewitched' only 7.0 because the neck just below the buxom bloom is crooked more often that not; I give it a 9.0 because a crooked neck is not a weak neck. Besides, anything this beautiful must have a flaw.

Buds go through a prissy stage when their outsides are brushed with dusky rose and their petals give the first hint that they're about to reflex. Then, as they unfurl, blossoms glow mid- to light pink. Fully open blooms reach dinner-plate size, and fragrance is constant and strong.

Foliage of 'Bewitched' is glossy olive green and moderately resistant to disease. Bushes reach moderate heights.

'Bewitched' has growth habits you should know about. Because they're such workhorses for cut flowers, bushes are vigorous growers. They also like to bloom on new wood, so canes have a relatively short life span, but they're quickly replaced with fresh growth.

If you grow roses for cut flowers, 'Bewitched' is a must. Not only is it a reliable all-season bloomer, but the blooms, in florist's lingo, have extended vase life. Blossoms of 'Bewitched' still look good when their petals roll back without calling it quits. When fully blown, petals frame dense clusters of yellow stamens.

'Bewitched' is a fine arbitrator in the old rose/new rose controversy. To please Heirloom enthusiasts, its blooms reach majestic stages and whimsical form. To satisfy Modern Rose growers, 'Bewitched' is a blooming fool.

BLANC DOUBLE DE COUBERT

(R. rugosa alba x *'Sombreuil')*

I must confess that I first planted 'Blanc Double de Coubert' because someone told me it was Vita Sackville-West's favorite white rose, and I figured that if Vita thought well of it, I was bound to also. Later, I learned that Ms. Sackville-West never made any such claim, but by then it was too late—I had fallen for the fine Rugosa all on my own.

Hybridized by Cochet-Cochet of France and introduced in 1892, 'Blanc Double de Coubert' is supposedly the result of a cross between *R. rugosa alba* and the lovely Tea rose 'Sombreuil'— parentage that many rosarians doubt, since no Tea-rose influence is apparent. In fairness to the skimpy breeding notes of the nineteenth-century hybridizer, however, it should be mentioned that Rugosa roses make such dominant parents that traits of their mates are rarely obvious. In truth, precise heredity isn't terribly important in this case, for 'Blanc Double de Coubert' is among the finest of all Rugosa hybrids, whatever its actual parentage.

First, its growth habits. 'Blanc Double de Coubert' scrambles vigorously to 5 feet, with almost as much girth. Next, its foliage is truly remarkable—dark green and so cleverly corrugated with ridges and folds that leaves resemble finely tooled leather. Finally, the blossoms stand in marvelous contrast to the vigor of the bush and the toughness of the foliage. Not only are they as pure white as any rose, the semidouble blossoms are composed of petals that appear to be made of sheer, slightly crinkled tissue paper. Add to this a center of golden yellow stamens, an intoxicating fragrance, autumnal color along with occasional hips, and it's easy to understand why I fell for that Vita Sackville-West myth.

Several years ago, we needed a rose for landscaping the perimeter of a Victorian belvedere that's used as a focal point for wedding ceremonies in our gardens. Since the structure had been painted blinding white, a similarly colored rose seemed correct. Also, we wanted blooms throughout the wedding season. 'Blanc Double de Coubert' was our choice. We've never regretted the decision, especially after we learned how to deal with such spirited growth habits.

This voracious grower is so determined to flourish that it sends suckers underground to distances yards away from mother plants. Once they resurface, these new bushes can, of course, be dug up and replanted. Be forewarned, however, that, growing on its own roots rather than budded onto well-behaved rootstock, 'Blanc Double de Coubert' claims even more of its rightful share of ground.

BONICA

([R. sempervirens x 'Mlle Marthe Carron'] x 'Picasso')

Before 'Bonica' was proclaimed an All-America Rose Selection in 1987, I planted a large number of its bushes in hopes of harvesting their blossoms for the cut-flower trade. 'Bonica' proved a dud for what I had in mind. The sprays of blossoms were pretty, but they were formed on arching, willowy stems that wouldn't pass muster at market. Besides, the bush was a sprawler and took up more than its rightful share in a cutting field. I decided to give 'Bonica' the heave-ho.

When the last of the 'Bonica' exiles were taken from the ground, one of the bushes tried to speak to me. From its every angle, it seemed to say, "Plant me in the landscape where I belong." So clear was its message that I searched for a good home, and I found one in the hollowed stump of a mighty Monterey cypress tree felled by a windstorm. Although I didn't go to much bother, I added compost, aged manure, and decent garden soil to the hole; put a water emitter near the bush's base; and forgot about it.

When 'Bonica' bloomed during its second year in the stump, I realized that I had forgotten to prune it. I also saw that it didn't need pruning; it clearly had ideas of its own.

It tried to speak again, this time claiming that it wanted to prove that "landscape" roses (as it was being marketed) actually are no-nonsense rose varieties that demand no fuss.

Although I've sometimes had to sit on my shears to keep from taking a whack, in five years I've never touched that bush with pruners, and I've sprayed it only twice, once during a bad attack of downy mildew and one other time when I could no longer stand the sight of a nasty aphid infestation.

My lone 'Bonica' brings traffic to a halt. Each year, during its first flush of bloom it looks like a plump rosy maiden, with bowers of fragrant, soft pink, clustered flowers in all stages of development. Foliage is small, deep green, and admirably disease resistant. Because I don't harvest the last crop of blooms, I reap fine orange-red hips each autumn.

I once talked a rose-growing friend of mine out of 'Bonica' and into a Modern upright Floribunda. She's never forgiven me. To Gerd and 'Bonica', my sincere apologies.

BUFF BEAUTY
(Parentage unrecorded)

As discussed in the section on their family, Hybrid Musk roses were victims of hybridizers notoriously lax in keeping breeding records. Consequently, the precise parentage of 'Buff Beauty' remains a mystery. It is generally agreed, however, that it's one of the finest members of the family and that Pemberton or one of his immediate disciples hybridized it.

Mature bushes reach 6-foot heights with equal girth. Consistent with the size of the bushes on which they grow, leaves are large, too, and also dark green, thick, and abundant. Stems are smooth and tinted brown.

Although it's difficult to proclaim one virtue of 'Buff Beauty' finer than another, its color is a clear plus. Good yellows don't abound among Old garden roses, and 'Buff Beauty' doesn't merely qualify as yellow, its several shades are knockouts. Depending on weather and growing conditions, blossoms range in color from pale primrose to rich apricot-yellow. Tight, cupped buds formed in large trusses open into fully double, flat flowers. Flowering is more or less steady throughout the summer.

If you're fond of fragrance, 'Buff Beauty' is sure to please, unless, of course, you're in search of actual musk perfume. Hybrid Musks, via Noisette roses, are only vaguely related to true Musk roses, although they do carry a whiff of musk in an otherwise sophisticated bouquet. In any case, however you analyze the specific components of its heady perfume, 'Buff Beauty' is richly fragrant.

Finally, assuming you can accommodate its heft, 'Buff Beauty' is a fine landscape rose. Bushes are expansive, but they leave plenty of room underneath their spreading canes for companion plants. Best of all, the majestically colored blossoms of 'Buff Beauty' flatter anything nearby.

CATHERINE MERMET

(Parentage unrecorded)

The Tea family of roses were a hasty lot. Almost as though they sensed their ephemeral stature—a respite on the road to the discovery of the Hybrid Tea—Tea roses came and went soon after their Bourbon and Noisette parents were mated with everblooming stud roses from China. Still, a few have hung on, particularly 'Catherine Mermet'.

When 'Catherine Mermet' was hybridized in 1869 by Guillot Fils (the same firm that introduced 'La France', the world's first Hybrid Tea), it was an instant success as a cut flower, undoubtedly because of its perfectly formed buds and stylish blossoms. Since it was such a hit at flower markets, in England, where Catherine didn't take well to chilly winters, bushes were cultivated in glasshouses.

Besides being winter-tender, the problem with most Tea roses is that their growth is lanky and prone to disease. Although 'Catherine Mermet' is typical of her family when it comes to winter, her bushes, which rarely grow taller than 3 feet, are well behaved and reasonably disease resistant.

'Catherine Mermet' has two especially strong pluses: the color and fragrance of her blossoms. Buds start out blush pink with lilac edges and turn soft beige before they mature. Fragrance is typical of the Tea family, which, according to Britain's heralded rosarian Graham Stuart Thomas, is "exactly like that of a freshly opened packet of China tea."

Like all Tea roses, 'Catherine Mermet' prefers warm, rich, well-drained soil. If blossoming is expected to persist through summer, fertilizers are a must. Unlike their Modern offspring, Tea roses resent severe pruning, preferring only thinning of spindly growth and removal of dead wood.

CÉCILE BRÜNNER

(R. multiflora hybrid x *'Mme de Tartas')*

Although it's alphabetically number 11 on the list of 50 immortal roses mentioned in this chapter, I'm writing about 'Cécile Brünner' last.

I didn't procrastinate because I had problems finding nice things to say about it, I simply hoped I'd get over my resentment toward Madame Brünner. This rose haunts me, not just because it's everywhere I go, but because if people know the name of only one "Old garden rose," it's inevitably 'Cécile Brünner'.

"Oh, you grow Old Roses," they say, "so do I—'Cécile Brünner'," as though it were Antique.

Even so, I think I could handle the rose's fame if it weren't for the size of its blossoms. As I've admitted throughout this text, I'm partial to roses with large blooms—ones I don't have to squint at to make certain I approve of. I'm ambivalent to most Miniature roses for that reason, and although 'Cécile Brünner' is most often lumped with Polyanthas, as far as I'm concerned it might just as well be listed with Miniatures.

Still, I openly admit that I'm in the vast minority when it comes to attitude toward 'Cécile Brünner'. Its fans have some good points.

First, as long as they're small, at least blossoms of 'Cécile Brünner' are wondrously shaped (like a miniature Hybrid Tea) and, second, are lovingly colored (mid-pink centers and pale pink petals). They're also sweetly perfumed.

Like so many fine climbing roses, 'Cécile Brünner' first grew as a bush, in 1881. Thirteen years later, climbing 'Cécile Brünner' was introduced. The climbing version became so popular that most gardeners don't know that it's also available as a bush.

Climbing 'Cécile Brünner' is a piranha among vining roses—easily to 20 feet by 20 feet, in time much larger. Foliage is dark but sparse; wood is low on thorns.

In early summer, 'Cécile Brünner' puts on a flower show that's hard to beat for profusion. Later each season, plants dole out occasional blossoms.

If you're going to grow her, you should learn to pronounce her name properly. The Brünner for whom this rose was named was a lady, so *Cécile* ("say seal") is the correct way.

I'm over my resentment; Cécile is a beauty.

COLOR MAGIC

(Unnamed seedling x *'Spellbinder')*

When a rose wins your heart the way 'Color Magic' has mine, you're in big trouble if that rose isn't well behaved. Keep that in mind as I try to persuade you to grow 'Color Magic' in spite of its faults.

In 1975, William Warriner hybridized 'Spellbinder', a rose that grabbed my attention the first time I saw it. Although I didn't grasp the depth of my affection at the time, I sensed that an ever finer rose was in my near future. Three years later, Warriner crossed 'Spellbinder' with an unknown seedling and produced 'Color Magic'—my favorite rose and an All-America Rose Selection in 1978.

Before I discuss the horrid flaw of this

Hybrid Tea, let me tell you about its merits, most of which are embodied in its blossoms. Fat buds start out dusky pink and reveal paler-colored petals only as they unfurl. By the time blossoms reach dinner-plate dimensions, their centers often turn beige around golden yellow, stamen-clustered centers. Then, as the blooms age, colors deepen again, often to glowing red at the petals' edges. The rose is aptly named—its show of colors is truly magical.

Then, fragrance. 'Color Magic' is as wonderfully perfumed as any rose I know. Not only is perfume intense at all stages, it's clean and crisp.

When the bushes behave, they grow well and are covered in dark green, glossy foliage that's moderately disease resistant. Cutting stems are long and abundant.

Now, the bad news. 'Color Magic' displays a growth habit known as dieback, which means that whole canes, for no apparent reason, begin to turn brown and start dying in a downward direction. No special cultivation techniques or spray materials will stop dieback or even arrest it. Growth must inevitably be sacrificed to a point of healthy wood.

My bushes of 'Color Magic' often die back so severely that I treat the bulk of my plants as annuals and replant each year. I'm embarrassed to admit that, but that's how head over heels I've fallen for this rose. You might, too, if you take a good look. And if you bother to sniff its sweet aroma, you're a goner.

COMMON MOSS
(Origin unknown)

The 'Common Moss' rose, sometimes known as 'Old Pink Moss' or 'Communis', is believed to be the Moss rose from which all others descended. Although the size of bushes and color range of Moss roses were constantly extended after the family's forerunner was discovered, no offspring has surpassed the agreeable growth habits or overall beauty of the blossoms of 'Common Moss'.

Moss roses, as you may recall from the discussion of their family, came about as a sport of *R. centifolia* in the late seventeenth century, when Mother Nature decreed that roses could also have conspicuous glandular, mosslike growth on their stems, calyxes, sepals, leaflets, or the works.

The rose we know today as 'Common Moss' was first spotted in Carcasonne, France, in 1696. For reasons best known to gardeners of the time, more than another century passed before the mossy find was taken seriously. Then, however, Moss roses became the rage of the Victorian gardening world, and hybridizers raced to extend the degree of mossing among their offspring.

Like the rose from which it sported, 'Common Moss' is warm pink and richly fragrant. Among family members, it is said to be "well mossed," meaning that hairlike "mossy" growths are easily visible on sepals, buds, and stems.

Bushes of 'Common Moss' are moderate growers, usually to 4 feet and not quite

as wide. Foliage is mid-green, plentiful, and resistant to disease.

Buds and premature blossoms are rich pink. When fully mature, however, perfectly scrolled, pale pink petals reflex around a green button-eyed center. Fragrance is intense at all stages.

Although roses are still being hybridized with innovative mossing at some spot on a rosebush where none previously existed, the original Moss rose, albeit common, is here to stay.

COMPLICATA

(Parentage unknown)

No one is certain of the origin of 'Complicata'. Some say it's a hybrid of *R. macrantha*, a species that 'Complicata' vaguely resembles. Others claim it's a Gallica hybrid. I say who cares—'Complicata' is a surefire winner. Before tempting you further, however, I must warn you to plan for ample space before digging a hole to accommodate its vigor. Otherwise, you may have an experience similar to mine with this queen of overgrowers.

When I first grew 'Complicata', I read of its robust habits and was told to purchase plants budded onto rootstock or I'd never contain them. I did as I was told, ordered two budded plants, and placed them in a raised bed of old garden shrubs.

The first year, 'Complicata' lived up to expectations and the shrubs remained a manageable size, blending nicely with other varieties. The second season, I realized that my plants were getting somewhat out of hand when they began crowding their neighbors. Still, I thought little of it because I had fallen for the blossoms. "I'll just give them a good pruning," I said to myself, "and get them back to a respectable size."

At pruning time, when I approached the defoliated shrubs, I realized what had gone wrong (or right, depending on one's point of view in these matters)—my plants of 'Complicata' were no longer growing on only the wood onto which they were budded. With determination to flourish, canes arched beyond their allotted space

and rooted themselves everywhere their wood touched ground. I figured that I now had about a dozen plants, and cut them back ruthlessly.

The following season, we decided to plant a row of roses all along the frontage of our rose ranch. When we deliberated the several varieties that would form a suitable hedge, we settled on 'Complicata'. "Before we order any plants," I suggested, "we'd better see how many we already have." You guessed it—more than we needed, all growing on their own roots.

Blossoms of 'Complicata' are single

and pink, hardly a unique combination. What sets this variety apart from other pink singles, however, is a halo of white that forms at the base of the five petals, handsomely framing a boss of sunny yellow stamens. The combination is eye-blinking; the shrub in full blossom is mind-boggling.

'Complicata' isn't particular about the soil in which it grows. Our hedge is planted in riverbed sand and shows all likelihood of soaring to 10 feet if we let it. Plants can also be trained to obey as pillars or climbers.

CRESSIDA

('Conrad Ferdinand Meyer' x 'Chaucer')

In *The Heritage of the Rose*, David Austin says of his 'Cressida': "In the long run I think it will turn out to be better grown as a Climber than a Shrub. Its large, nodding flowers would, I feel, be particularly beautiful when hanging from a wall." The fine British hybridizer penned these words in 1988, only five years after 'Cressida' had been hybridized, so he went out on a limb with his prediction for this English Rose. Time has proved that he could hardly have been more correct; 'Cressida' makes a fine climber indeed. If you've ever seen her mother, you understand why 'Cressida' was destined to tower overhead—'Conrad Ferdinand Meyer', the offspring of a Rugosa hybrid, is a skyscraper, easily to heights of more than 10 feet.

It's not the growth habits of 'Cressida' that have won me over, however, but rather its irresistible blooms. First, the color of its petals—pinky beige with an apricot reverse, a combination that seems

translucent when lighting is favorable. Although the enormous blooms are basically cupped, individual petals are so informally arranged that no two blooms are exactly alike. The clincher is perfume, said by Austin to be of "exceptionally strong myrrh fragrance." In spite of my infatuation with fragrance, I still have never smelled myrrh. If it smells anything like 'Cressida', however, that third Wise Man made a terrific choice.

If you, too, are swept away by the ravishing perfume of 'Cressida' but have no place for a climber, you can, of course, grow it as a bush. Be forewarned, however, that 'Cressida' is a narrow, upright grower, easily to 6 feet, making it somewhat clumsy without proper staking. Foliage is roughly textured, and thorns are large and abundant.

My 12 shrubs of 'Cressida' are planted so that they will eventually cover six iron arches that form a 10-foot walkway between a dozen dwarf apple trees. Although my plants are only three years old, they already cover more than half of the arches' spans. By the time my shrubs leaf out next spring, I hope the archway will be entirely masked.

Almost everyone who visits to view our collection of Austin's English Roses adds 'Cressida' to their order for bareroot bushes the following winter, whether or not they had intended to request a climber. When you see, to say nothing of sniff, 'Cressida' in its glory, you'll understand why. What a fragrance; what a rose!

DAINTY BESS
(*'Ophelia'* x *'K. of K.'*)

I don't recall my precise reasoning for banning pink and single-petaled varieties from my garden when I first began growing roses. As I've mentioned elsewhere, I probably imagined that single-petaled roses didn't last well as cut flowers and pink wasn't a masculine color—foolish reasoning.

Single-handedly, 'Dainty Bess' has changed my mind. First, 'Dainty Bess' makes a fine cut flower, especially when you understand the proper time for removing blossoms from their bushes. As for the pink aversion, well, it helps to know that more great roses are pink or blends thereof than any other color. If pink bothers you, do your best to get over it. 'Dainty Bess', hybridized in 1925, has been the most popular single-petaled Hybrid Tea rose for almost 70 years and is likely to be with us forever. If you wonder how a single rose can qualify as a Hybrid Tea, it's because of the growth habits of its bush: Plants of 'Dainty Bess' look like Hybrid Tea bushes rather than shrubs, and degree of petalage is not a factor in rose classification. Although blossoms of 'Dainty Bess' have only five petals, they're broad and fragrant. They also completely surround a center of maroon stamens. Maroon may not seem like a big deal unless you know that more than 90 percent of rose stamens are yellow. I believe that 'Dainty Bess' would be a winner if its stamens *were* yellow. Maroon makes it a shoo-in.

'Dainty Bess' is officially classified as light pink, but I think of it as dusky pink. Blossoms lighten in the shade, however, so their precise coloring is entirely dependent on where they develop on the bush and the amount of sunlight they're exposed to. They also have an appealing quality of closing at night.

Blossoms of 'Dainty Bess' may appear dainty, but the bush is anything but—upright, tall, and smothered in tough, disease-resistant foliage. Blooms form on long cutting stems and are blessed with an amazing vase life as long as you harvest them when sepals are down and petals first begin to unfurl.

'Dainty Bess' wins my vote for the best single-petaled rose ever.

DOUBLE DELIGHT'

('Granada' x 'Garden Party')

I saw a picture of 'Double Delight' before I saw the rose itself, and I was certain that I was being duped by trick photography. After seeing the rose for myself, I decided that the photographer hadn't done justice to 'Double Delight'—it truly is something else.

Blossoms of 'Double Delight' are a random combination of red and white, no two alike. Depending on the amount of sun and the weather conditions, red sprawls irregularly over the tips and down into the outer reaches of white ruffled petals. The dramatic coloring of the blossoms is surpassed only by their strong spicy fragrance.

Bushes of 'Double Delight' are only moderate growers, but they regularly produce an amazing number of blooms each summer. Foliage is medium green, reasonably disease resistant, and not particularly notable.

If you happen to appreciate show-quality form in Hybrid Tea roses, by all means consider 'Double Delight'. More often than not (particularly if bushes aren't overfertilized), blossoms are picture-perfect in their symmetry and reach their finest stage of beauty somewhere between half to three-quarters open.

Three years after its debut, 'Double Delight' produced an offspring that also won an All-America award—'Mon Chéri', a rose similar to its parent in that it's also a blend, but of red and pink rather than red and white. Otherwise, the family re-

semblance is obvious, including fine fragrance and carbon-copy growth habits.

Finally, 'Double Delight' possesses a charming ability for altering its colors during each growing season. I once took a bucket of mixed roses to a friend and left them on her doorstep. The next day, she called to thank me and to ask the name of the red and yellow rose that looked like a Mexican paper rose.

"Red and yellow?" I asked, confused.

"I don't grow a red and yellow rose."

"Of course you do," she responded, "I'm looking right at it and its fragrance is fabulous."

It was 'Double Delight', of course. I had simply forgotten that at certain times of the year, particularly fall, white is replaced by yellow as the color combined with red. I should have known anyway; 'Double Delight' is usually the first rose asked about in a mixed bouquet.

The reason I'm so adamant in its praise is that 'Duet' is the quintessential rose for cutting. Not only do its blossoms last exceptionally well, the bush is a workhorse. No other Modern Rose I know can touch it when it comes to nonstop blossoming.

'Duet' is officially classified as medium pink. It's actually a pink blend, since the outer petals are considerably darker than those within. Although fragrance isn't overpowering, it's definite.

When 'Duet' made its debut in commerce, it was classed among Grandiflora roses because of its proclivity for forming sprays rather than one-to-a-stem blooms. Later it was reclassified as a Hybrid Tea. I happen to agree with the change, although I don't really care about its categorization as long as I remember to disbud its blossoms for typical Hybrid Tea formation.

Because 'Duet' is so hell-bent toward flowering, foliage isn't typically formed. Individual leaves look as they should, but probably because they develop so quickly, there are often large gaps between neighboring leaflets on a stem. When stems are massed in an arrangement, of course, these gaps are filled in, but they look sparse in a bud vase.

Bushes aren't typical either. Stems often grow in a zigzag pattern or cross the center of the plant. Again, this is undoubtedly a result of this rose's determination to flourish and blossom. When you spot undesirable growth, simply cut it out. More is sure to follow.

DUET
('Fandango' x 'Roundelay')

Because I'm such a staunch fan, I've been accused of being "on the take" for the promotion of this rose. That's untrue, of course, for several reasons, not the least of which is that 'Duet' is no longer under patent protection (patents for rose hybrids last only 17 years, and 'Duet' was introduced in 1961).

EUROPEANA

('Ruth Leuwerik' x 'Rosemary Rose')

No one has ever explained to me why it took 'Europeana' so long to reach America. Hybridized by de Ruiter of Holland in 1963 and an instant hit all over Europe, it took five more years for introduction in the United States. Then the rose made up for lost time, by being selected as All-America in 1968.

When someone trying to understand the classification of roses asks me to name a classic Floribunda, 'Europeana' is my constant answer. Ideally, Floribunda roses produce sprays of blossoms in all stages of development—from buds to fully open flowers—on each stem. 'Europeana' read this dictum and took it to heart.

Gardeners familiar with 'Europeana' can identify its bush even without benefit of blossoms. Plants grow almost as wide as they do tall, and foliage is large, glossy, and strongly tinted mahogany right up to flowering, at which time it turns emerald green. Except for occasional bouts of powdery mildew, bushes are strongly resistive to disease.

Blossoms of 'Europeana' are distinguished for two reasons: first, by a ruby red color that holds without fading from bud stage throughout maturity; and second, by perfectly formed, moderately fragrant, rosette-shaped blooms that look handcrafted.

If you grow Floribundas because of their mighty contribution to the landscape—masses of bloom that often camouflage entire bushes—don't bother to remove any buds while they are forming. If you grow 'Europeana' to enjoy its blossoms indoors, you should remove the central (terminal) bud in each spray as soon as it makes itself obvious by growing larger than all others, after which you may sit back in confident anticipation of a fine spray of blossoms. Either way, you can't lose.

FANTIN-LATOUR
(Origin unknown)

Before telling you about this fabulous rose, let me alert you to the controversy of its origin. Although usually listed with Centifolia roses (as I have in chapter 2), modern-day purists say that 'Fantin-Latour' is actually a Hybrid China, belonging to that family of roses that were hybridized shortly after the China stud roses arrived in Europe in the late eighteenth century. "Its blooms *look* like a Centifolia," they admit, "but its smooth foliage clearly exposes its true China origin." They have a point. Still, I side with Graham Stuart Thomas and other fine English gardeners who place the rose in the Centifolia family. Besides, who has time for such arguments when such a fine rose is at stake?

Named for the nineteenth-century French artist who loved to paint flowers, especially roses, 'Fantin-Latour' is an elegant rose that blossoms only once each season, but it makes up for its brief season with blooms that gardeners live in hopes of.

When flowering commences in late spring/early summer, flowers are so heart-stopping that you, too, might feel an urge to paint. Blossoms start out cupped, but as they age, petals reflex and reveal a button-eyed center. Outer petals are blush pink; inner petals, deeper pink. Fragrance is delicate but ravishing.

Bushes of 'Fantin-Latour' are moderately tall (often to 5-foot heights), not quite so broad, but always shapely. Foliage is large, dark green, and smooth. Disease resistance is so-so.

I know devotees of Modern Roses who admit only a few shrubs of Heirloom Roses to their gardens. When considering varieties that deserve exceptional treatment, even the most adamant of these tunnel-visioned gardeners consider 'Fantin-Latour'. So will you if you ever grant it a trial.

FERDINAND PICHARD
(Parentage unrecorded)

Ever since Gallicas (the first recognized family of roses), striped varieties have been popular among gardeners. 'Ferdinand Pichard' is one of the best striped roses ever. Not only are its cupped, double flowers striped, their colors change majestically as blossoms mature. When blooms first appear, they're clear pink, striped crimson; as they mature, the pink turns blush white and the crimson to purple. Good fragrance is constant. Although flowering is heaviest in spring, repeat blooms occur throughout summer, reliably in fall.

Since Hybrid Perpetual roses were bred with the rose exhibitor in mind, the bushes on which potential prizewinners grew were of little consequence—the bloom was the ticket. Plants of Hybrid Perpetuals are notoriously clumsy. There are, of course, exceptions. 'Ferdinand Pichard' is one.

Mature bushes grow to 5-foot heights (taller if allowed) with light, pointed foliage. Although 'Ferdinand Pichard' is reasonably resistant to mildew, it's no stranger to rust and blackspot. Still, plants respond well to spraying with materials identical to those used to ward off diseases among Modern Roses.

If you cultivate this or any other Hybrid Perpetual rose, it's important to remember that all members of the family grow as though they're more closely related to Modern Roses than to their Heirloom predecessors. Bushes

should be richly planted and pruned severely (to at least half their height each winter). Plants should also be fed regularly and watered copiously if abundant blossoming is expected. The rewards easily outweigh all such attention.

FRAGRANT CLOUD

(Unknown seedling x 'Prima Ballerina')

Even if I didn't love it as I do, I'd grow 'Fragrant Cloud' as a surefire rose to silence those gardeners who moan that Modern Roses aren't fragrant enough. When I encounter one of these naggers, I take him over to my bushes of 'Fragrant Cloud' and suggest he take a whiff. So much for that complaint.

Germany's Tantau hybridized 'Fragrant Cloud' in 1963 and named it 'Duftwolke', which was changed to 'Nuage Parfumé' when the rose was marketed in France. By the time the perfumed beauty hit American shores in 1968, it had been renamed 'Fragrant Cloud'. Considering its ravishing fragrance, any name would probably have worked.

'Fragrant Cloud' is officially classified as orange-red (I call it lipstick red), but I know no other rose this exact color or one quite so changeable, depending on the weather and where it grows on the bush. As sunlight increases, so do orange hues. I've found no one ambivalent to its color; people either love it or hate it. As blooms age, petals take on a silvery sheen that looks terrible under fluorescent light (but then so do most colors).

Although blossoms have only 25 to 30 petals, they're exceptionally well formed, especially considering their large size. Foliage is large, too, but also prone to mildew.

If you like your Hybrid Tea blooms one-to-a-stem, plan on removing side buds early in their formation, leaving only the large center bud to develop.

Blossoms of 'Fragrant Cloud' have what exhibitors call a fault, in that up to three of the outer petals have a characteristic greenish white streak. If you exhibit roses, these petals should be removed. If not, don't bother—as blooms open, outer petals fold back and conceal the streaks. Besides, once you get a whiff of this rose, you'll want every petal possible.

GOLD MEDAL
('Yellow Pages' x 'Shirley Laugharn')

In spite of its being passed over for an All-America Rose award, 'Gold Medal' wins my vote for the best rose of the 1980s. Ever since 'Peace' was hybridized in the early 1940s, rose breeders have been scrambling pollen with aspirations of discovering another great yellow rose. With 'Gold Medal', hybridizer Jack Christensen gave us a doozy.

'Gold Medal' isn't simply yellow, the petals of its blossoms are a dazzling combination of golden yellow with tawny edges. It's difficult to focus on a well-grown spray of blooms because eyes involuntarily dart back and forth from one clear vivid color to another. The overall effect is simultaneously pleasing and cheerful. As if their color weren't enough, blooms are notably fragrant, too.

The bush is also thoroughly satisfactory. It's hardy and nicely shaped, and it won't pout if you prune it low. If you prune it high, which it actually prefers, it will still reward you with bowers of bloom. For this versatility, 'Gold Medal' is a fine landscape rose. Foliage is abundant, large, mid-green, and about as disease resistant as that growing on any Modern Rose bush.

When it comes to blooming, 'Gold Medal' is a particularly obedient Grandiflora—it will do as it's told. If you fancy sprays, you can have them with long cutting stems and multiple blooms. Should you prefer one-to-a-stem blossoms, you can have them, too, as long as you disbud in a timely fashion. With such a well-tempered rose, I can't think of a reason not to have both.

As a final plus, 'Gold Medal' is one of the last roses to blossom each season. That might not seem very important during summer when you have more roses than you know what to do with, but come late fall, it's a blessing.

HERITAGE

(*Unnamed Austin seedling* x [*'Wife of Bath' x 'Iceberg'*])

In *The Heritage of the Rose*, David Austin says simply of his 'Heritage', "I think this is the most beautiful English Rose." Although I don't entirely concur, I believe that 'Heritage' will outlive other English Roses because of the thoroughly appealing color and exquisite form of its blossoms—blush pink petals cleverly arranged into shell-like, precise formation.

Probably because 'Iceberg' is one of its parents, 'Heritage' has lots going for it, not the least of which is a bushy plant that freely breaks new growth to ensure flowering throughout the entire summer. Thanks also to its 'Iceberg' ancestry, 'Heritage' has smooth stems and attractive, pointed, reasonably disease-resistant foliage. You should, however, stay on the prowl for rust.

Although the blossoms of 'Heritage' are only medium-sized, they occur in sprays and carry a strong perfume with an undertone of lemon. They also make good cut flowers and have an extended vase life.

Like most of David Austin's English Roses, 'Heritage' repeats its blooms throughout summer. The biggest flush, though, is always the first, after which blossoms are doled out with satisfactory regularity.

Don't let the appearance of its blossoms fool you into thinking of 'Heritage' as an Old garden rose. Even though blooms are as delicately and cunningly formed as the oldest of roses, the bushes on which they grow should be cultivated as Modern hybrids, including watering, feeding, and, most important, pruning.

I must confess that while I deliberated over which of Austin's varieties should be included in this chapter, I considered several. 'Mary Rose', for instance, has a lot going for it, including its delightful habit of blooming so early. Alas, 'Mary Rose' is short on fragrance. 'Leander', on the other hand, is fruitily fragrant and delightfully colored, but it's stingy in repeating its bloom.

All in all, like its hybridizer, I'm confident in favoring 'Heritage'.

HONOR

(Unnamed seedling x *unnamed seedling)*

In 1980 the fine American hybridizer Bill Warriner made a clean sweep of the All-America Rose Selections by winning in all three categories—Grandiflora, Hybrid Tea, and Floribunda—with 'Love', 'Honor', and 'Cherish'. Personally, I've never taken 'Love' seriously because of its weak necks and puny growth habits. I like the blossoms of 'Cherish', but its bush is too runty to suit me. 'Honor', on the other hand, is a triumph.

Except for the pink lining on the petals' edges (which disappears as blooms mature), 'Honor' is as uncompromisingly white as any Modern hybrid I know. Its other merits include a bush with upright growth habits and a determination to blossom freely.

Besides growing on exceptionally long cutting stems, blossoms are elegantly shaped. Outer petals grow stiffly upright to form an urn-shaped casing for the 20-odd petals they surround. As blooms mature, petals reflex into a well-rounded blossom. Although fragrance isn't strong, it's definite and outstanding for a pure white rose.

The bush is urn-shaped, too, with canes radiating symmetrically around the bud union. Because they're such tall growers, bushes of 'Honor' should be reduced by at least half their height each pruning season. Foliage is large, dark green, and disease resistant.

'Honor' has one peculiar growth habit you should know about. With a headstrong determination to flower, after its first flush of bloom more new growth appears than bushes can possibly support. The only remedy, of course, is to remove some of it—up to half. Keep in mind, however, that bushes of 'Honor' can sustain more growth than can most Modern hybrids. Still, your considerateness at reducing spirited growth will pay off with large, elegantly shaped blossoms on long, sturdy stems. I must say, I wish more Modern Roses had this particular "problem."

ICEBERG
('Robin Hood' x 'Virgo')

If you asked rosarians around the globe to name the best, not necessarily their favorite, rose in the world, 'Iceberg' would probably be the winner. In choosing an all-purpose rose—one that landscapes well, blooms repeatedly, and makes a good cut flower—you can't go wrong with 'Iceberg'.

Bred by the Kordes clan of Holstein, West Germany, 'Iceberg' was introduced in Europe in 1958 as 'Schneewittchen', a name the English-speaking world could never wrap its tongue around. When the Floribunda made its debut in America, it became known as 'Iceberg'.

Blossoms of 'Iceberg' are pure white and appear in large sprays with as many as a dozen flowers per stem. Although buds are perfectly formed and high centered, blooms open flat. Fragrance is definite, sharp, and clean; foliage is small, light green, and glossy.

'Iceberg' is a late bloomer, which at first may seem like a disadvantage. When you grow a sufficient enough number of rose varieties to appreciate staggered crops, however, you'll change your mind, especially when you realize that over an entire season, 'Iceberg' produces as many blossoms as does any Modern Rose.

One of its enduring qualities is that it performs precisely as trained. If you prune its bush low in search of cut flowers, you'll be rewarded with masses of sprays on long cutting stems. If you're after garden display and allow bushes to grow tall, you'll still have copious blooms; they'll simply appear on shorter-stemmed, large bushes.

'Iceberg' is also one of the few Modern Roses that satisfy Old garden rose enthusiasts. First, it doesn't look Modern. Second, 'Iceberg' is notably fragrant, especially for a white rose. Its crowning achievement, however, is an ability to blossom nonstop on a no-nonsense bush.

JACQUES CARTIER
(Parentage unrecorded)

It seems ironic that although Portland roses were the first family to benefit from the repeat-blooming habits of the China roses, only a handful are in commerce today (in 1848 there were 84 varieties growing at Kew Gardens in England). 'Jacques Cartier', however, is with us to stay.

Like other Portlands, 'Jacques Cartier' grows on a compact, erect bush that rarely reaches heights of more than 4 feet. Its light green foliage closely resembles that of its Damask ancestors.

Besides being richly fragrant, blossoms of 'Jacques Cartier' are elegantly formed and fully petaled. They're soft pink, fading to shell pink as they mature, with shapely petals that unfurl around a button-eyed center. It has short stems and foliage tightly packed around its blossoms—what Graham Stuart Thomas calls a "shoulder of leaves."

Some gardeners criticize Portland roses for their lack of grace, which means that they don't form billowing bushes the way many Heirloom Roses do. I, however, consider that a blessing for small gardens. What's more, I find bushes graceful *because* of their compact growth habits.

I was hard pressed to decide whether to sing the praises of 'Jacques Cartier' or of 'Comte de Chambord', a similarly colored Portland. If you're after as many blossoms as possible, 'Comte de Chambord' may be a better choice. If refinement of flowers is your yardstick, however, you can't beat 'Jacques Cartier'.

JUST JOEY

(*Fragrant Cloud*' x '*Dr. A.J. Verhage*')

Having never met anyone who didn't like it, I call 'Just Joey' the "something-for-everyone" rose. Gardeners devoted to Heirloom Roses admire its mature form and grace, while Modern Rose enthusiasts praise 'Just Joey' for churning out classic Hybrid Tea blossoms. No one can resist its powerful fragrance.

Although officially classified as an orange blend, I think of 'Just Joey' as buff-apricot. Color is deepest during bud stage, lightening as blossoms mature. While there are only 30 petals per blossom, they're exceptionally large and perfectly arranged.

Unfortunately, bushes of 'Just Joey' don't live up to its blossoms. Plants look squat compared with those of most Modern hybrids and somewhat lacking in vigor. That appearance is a mere mirage, of course, since bushes of 'Just Joey' are actually bloom factories. When you harvest blossoms, plants look as though they'll never muster strength again for another crop. But they reliably do.

Foliage is distinctive, too. It's large and shiny dark green. As it develops, however, leaves retain a strong mahogany color that lasts right up until blossom time. Plants are admirably resistive to disease. Thorny stems are thin but strong.

'Just Joey' is particularly popular among florists and gardeners interested in good cut flowers with extended vase life. Not only will properly harvested blossoms open fully in a vase, they also mature to dinner-plate size and retain a fragrance second to none.

I asked a florist who's hooked on 'Just Joey' why she likes it so much in spite of its tendency to produce crooked stems. She pointed out that this is precisely why she so admires the rose—because it arranges itself in floral displays.

'Just Joey' is currently rated 8.0 by the voting members of the American Rose Society, placing it among "excellent" roses. I think they should reconsider its score. I give it a 9.0—"outstanding."

MADAME ALFRED CARRIÈRE

(Parentage unrecorded)

While I had difficulty deciding which member of certain families to include in this chapter, there was no problem with the Noisettes—as far as I'm concerned, 'Madame Alfred Carrière' is the most distinguished member of the entire clan. Like most Noisettes, 'Madame Alfred Carrière' is a climber; unlike many of her siblings, she's particularly robust and a faithful rebloomer. Only a handful of white climbing roses dare challenge her overall performance.

Purists complain that blossoms of 'Madame Alfred Carrière' lack refinement because they aren't classically shaped. On the contrary, I believe that this whimsical form adds considerable appeal. These same complainers gripe that plants are rigid, but I contend that such stiffness is all a matter of training. Properly coaxed up a pillar or lattice, plants can be trained to assume any shape you like.

Blossoms, which have a charming habit of nodding for good viewing from below, are creamy white tinged slightly with pink. Due to their unmistakable Tea-rose ancestry, they are exquisitely perfumed as well. Foliage is large, mid-green, reasonably disease resistant, and plentiful.

Some years ago, I planted David Austin's 'Cressida' in the fragrant garden that Bob Galyean and I share. Although I love the blossoms of the rose itself, I

was disappointed in its climbing habits—it had difficulty covering a span of 15-foot arches. I fretted for weeks over whether or not I should move the bushes elsewhere and select another variety to finish the job.

"Why not leave the 'Cressida' where they are," Bob suggested, "and plant 'Madame Alfred Carrière' inside each arch?"

I was embarrassed not to have had the idea myself. I'm delighted with the results, however. What a pair!

MADAME HARDY

(Parentage unrecorded)

Named for the wife of the head gardener to Empress Josephine at her Château Malmaison near Paris, 'Madame Hardy' is hailed as a classic Old Rose. And although 'Madame Hardy' is conventionally considered a Damask rose, her blossoms manifest clear relationship to the Centifolia family. As usual, however, I part ways here with genealogists who quibble over precise heritage. In the case of 'Madame Hardy', I couldn't care less who her ancestors were—she's the item.

Bushes of 'Madame Hardy' are robust but graceful growers that reach 5-foot heights. Pointed foliage is abundant, light green, and moderately disease resistant. Plants work well into the landscape individually, but they're particularly effective when massed in groups of three so that billowing round mounds are formed.

Although blossoms are smallish, they form in large clusters, and they're wonderfully fragrant with an undertone of lemon to an otherwise classic rose perfume. Blooms start out cupped, then flatten and reflex their petals around a green button-eyed center. Buds and immature flowers carry a pink blush, but mature blossoms are glistening white.

'Madame Zöetmans', first cousin to 'Madame Hardy', is another fine Damask, with flowers that are similarly sized, colored, and perfumed. Bushes of 'Madame Zöetmans' are smaller, though, and the blossoms are not as profuse as those of 'Madame Hardy'. Like all members of the Damask family, blooms appear only in late spring/early summer. Their abundance, however, handily compensates for their infrequency. As the very name of their family suggests, fragrance is never disappointing. Both Damasks also make surprisingly good cut flowers, especially if harvested before blooms are fully mature. Properly conditioned, they obligingly conclude their majestic show in a vase.

MADAME ISAAC PEREIRE
(Parentage unrecorded)

If some cruel-hearted person declared that I could grow but one Bourbon rose, 'Madame Isaac Pereire' would be my uncompromising choice. Bred by Garçon of France and introduced in 1881, 'Madame Isaac Pereire' embodies the finest characteristics of the Bourbon family—she grows on a vigorous plant that reaches 7 feet as a shrub (even more as a climber),

produces scads of intensely fragrant blossoms during each flush, and repeats bloom cycles throughout the year, especially during autumn. If that weren't enough to make her a star, her foliage is nice, too—thick, dark green, and as disease resistant as that of any family member.

More than the enviable growth habits, however, it's the individual flowers this sumptuous beauty spews forth that has won me over. Deep-pink-shaded-

magenta blooms that will reach 6-inch spans start out cupped, then reflex their petals, and eventually quarter themselves into majestic floral splendor just before they reveal a charming button-eyed center. As flowers mature further, they fade at the edge of their petals, becoming two-tone hot pink. Perfume is ravishing all the while. In fact, many gardeners believe that 'Madame Isaac Pereire' is the most fragrant rose ever hybridized.

After observing how well Bourbons grow when trained along horizontal supports (and after noting the smashing addition their dried whole blossoms make to potpourri), I selected three Bourbons that would add color variation to the fence *and* blend well together: 'Madame Isaac Pereire'; her pale pink sport, 'Madame Ernest Calvat'; and the madly striped 'Variegata di Bologna'. My experiment in fence decor only confirmed my prejudices: although the latter two varieties perform well enough, they can't touch the bounty or ravishing perfume of 'Madame Isaac Pereire'.

One last note: The reason that Bourbon roses such as these are so well suited for training on fences, pergolas, or pillars is that they reliably produce more blossoms than freestanding bushes can possibly support. Even when canes are tied down horizontally, branches mass themselves with blossoms along the upper third of their reaches, then gracefully nod to the ground. Visually, they're nearly impossible to resist; if you bother to sniff them, you haven't a chance.

MAIDEN'S BLUSH
(Parentage unknown)

Although no one is certain of its precise age, those devoted to rose lore agree that 'Maiden's Blush' definitely predates the sixteenth century. The number of names by which it is known would support this theory. In France, 'Maiden's Blush' is called 'Cuisse de Nymphe' because its color is said to resemble that of the thigh of an aroused nymph (!). Elsewhere, 'Maiden's Blush' is commonly known as 'Incarnata', 'La Royale', 'La Séduisante', and 'Virginale'. No matter what it's called, 'Maiden's Blush' is a provocative beauty and the pride of the Alba family.

Blossoms are loosely double and blush pink. Although individual blooms are only medium-sized, their overall flowering effect is large because they mass themselves in sprays. Individual stems are short, but entire sprays can be cut on long stems. As they mature, petals reflex and pale in color, especially at the edges. Fragrance is delicate yet pungent.

The bushes on which these sensually colored flowers grow are large (to 5 feet) but graceful with arching branches and good overall form. Foliage is typically Alba—gray-green and plentiful. But don't let the fragile appearance of its blossoms fool you into imagining that the bush is tender. It's anything but. Not only is it easy to grow, it will thrive in awkward garden locations where other roses perish. In fact, when considering where to plant its bushes, remember that 'Maiden's Blush', like other members of the Alba family, is tolerant of more shade than are most roses. Remember, too, that bushes massed together make effective hedges. Alas, you must also bear in mind that flowering is but once a year—over an extended, albeit solitary, period.

MEDALLION

('South Seas' x *'King's Ransom')*

Apricot has always been a popular color for roses, but it took hybridizers a while to include it in their palette of colors for Modern hybrids. Once they did, a whole new strain of roses emerged. Of these, I think 'Medallion' leads the pack.

An All-America Rose Selection in 1973, 'Medallion' is a fine Hybrid Tea rose, particularly if you like somewhat oversized blossoms. An appreciation for long cutting stems would help, too.

Buds of 'Medallion' are exceptionally elongated and pointed; they're also stiff with substance. Outer petals are often heavily brushed dark rosy apricot, and while mature blossoms fade to light apricot, the moderately strong fragrance of 'Medallion' won't fade a bit.

Bushes are especially stately, possessing a tendency to spread in a classic urn pattern. This means, however, that they need proper treatment at pruning time. (Because they grow so tall, it's easy to imagine that they want to be left tall after pruning. They don't.) I reduce the height by at least half each year. Before blooms appear, stems often reach 3-foot lengths; flowering is nonstop until late fall. As for the foliage, it's dense, mid-green, and—perhaps the only serious fault with this rose—slightly prone to mildew.

Although the general rule of thumb for timing the harvest of roses centers around when sepals turn downward, 'Medallion' is an exception. Not only must 'Medallion' drop its sepals, its first row of petals should clearly separate from inner rows before blossoms are cut. Only then can they be expected to conclude their majestic display in a vase. Properly timed, however, blooms reach enormous proportions, never lose form, and never disappoint.

MINNIE PEARL
(['Little Darling' x 'Tiki'] x 'Party Girl')

I've never made a concerted effort to conceal my ambivalence toward Miniature roses. It's not a matter of my not liking them altogether, but simply a strong preference for their larger-flowered kinfolk. 'Minnie Pearl' is a notable exception.

Officially color-classed among pink blends, Minnie's overall color is light pink, but petals have a darker pink reverse. Her abundant high-centered blossoms are wondrously formed and as shapely as those of many Hybrid Teas. Although sometimes one-to-a-stem, they more often appear in large sprays. Catalogs will tell you that she's fragrant, but my nose says otherwise.

It's quite possible that one of the reasons I'm partial to this Miniature rose is that I don't have to squat on the ground to tend its bushes or to harvest its blossoms. 'Minnie Pearl' is tall among Minis; she's also swathed in dark to medium green, semiglossy foliage that's not impervious, but is resistive, to mildew nevertheless.

A plus for all Miniature roses is their ability to last as cut flowers. 'Minnie Pearl' is no exception. Properly conditioned blossoms hold their form for a seeming eternity. When mixed in a floral arrangement, 'Minnie Pearl' often outlives all else.

If you decide to cultivate Miniature roses, keep in mind that just because they're short, they're not immune to infestations of spider mites. In fact, the

microscopic creatures have a particular affection for diminutive bushes and love to congregate at their bases. Also, foliage on many Miniature roses ('Minnie Pearl' included) grows smack down to the ground, providing easy access for spider mites and other gnawing insects. Should you have an aversion to chemical sprays, at least keep bushes well misted with water (spider mites detest being wet) to rid them of tiny pests.

Although Miniature roses may never thrill me, 'Minnie Pearl' will always please me.

MISTER LINCOLN

('Chrysler Imperial' x 'Charles Mallerin')

In 1964 hybridizers around the world who searched for a showstopping dark red fragrant rose were busily scrambling pollen from two fine red roses of the day—'Chrysler Imperial' and 'Charles Mallerin'. Although Meilland of France enjoyed moderate success when his efforts resulted in 'Papa Meilland', the American team of Swim and Weeks hit the jackpot when their crosses resulted in two fine offspring—'Mister Lincoln' and 'Oklahoma'. Of this trio of entries to rosedom, only 'Mister Lincoln' has staunchly stood the test of time.

'Mister Lincoln' is the world's favorite red Hybrid Tea rose and is likely to remain so for some time. After it won an All-America award in 1965, it took almost two decades for another red Hybrid Tea to win that honor—'Olympiad', in 1984. While 'Olympiad' is a fine rose, it hasn't a whiff of fragrance. 'Mister Lincoln', on the other hand, is sinfully perfumed.

Besides ravishing fragrance, 'Mister Lincoln' has other fine attributes. First, its bush, which almost naturally grows into a classic upright urn cloaked in large, matte, mid-green foliage. Second, as though 'Mister Lincoln' knows that's how it's loveliest, its blossoms usually occur one-to-a-stem. When side buds do appear, they're easily disbudded. Finally, 'Mister Lincoln' is a robust grower and a faithful bloomer.

When people ask me to recommend a deep red rose, I unhesitatingly suggest 'Mister Lincoln'. Its buds are as dark velvety red as those of any Modern Rose I know, so dark that they often appear black. As blossoms develop, color lightens to cherry red, however. Fragrance is outstanding at all stages.

If 'Mister Lincoln' has a fault, it's that blossoms tend to "blue" as they age. Still, that doesn't occur until the very last stage of an exceptional vase life. Otherwise, 'Mister Lincoln' is yet *the* modern dark red Hybrid Tea to beat.

MUTABILIS
(Parentage unknown)

'Mutabilis' is so ancient that many people claim that it's a species. Although I agree that it's probably of species age, I'm certain that 'Mutabilis' is actually a naturally hybridized China rose. In any case, 'Mutabilis' is irresistible.

I love to walk visitors over to a bush of 'Mutabilis' in full bloom and wait for their response. "Is that one bush, or have you grafted several together?" they often ask. 'Mutabilis' displays three different distinctly colored blossoms at the same time. Better yet, they look terrific together.

Buds start out copper-yellow, then fade to pink as they open and enlarge. As they reach maturity, petals turn crimson. Fully open blossoms are so dainty that 'Mutabilis' is sometimes called the butterfly rose because plants in full bloom look like pit stops for packs of vividly colored butterflies.

Bushes are healthy and notably easy to grow, and they sport dense, dainty foliage that's admirably disease resistant.

Although it's adaptable to most conditions, 'Mutabilis' is happiest when growing next to a wall or dense plants toward its northern exposure. Properly warmed, bushes grow to twice the size of chilly siblings.

When you look at a bush of 'Mutabilis', there's no question that you're gazing at an Old Rose. Foliage is distinctly of China heritage, and growth is whimsical compared with that of Modern hybrids. Once you observe its blooming habits, however, there's no question of how to tend bushes of 'Mutabilis'—like a Modern Rose granted copious waterings and steady meals, particularly if you expect to enjoy those mad multicolored blossoms all season long.

NEVADA

(Precise parentage unrecorded)

In the mid-1920s, Pedro Dot of Spain crossed the vigorous Hybrid Tea 'La Giralda' with a form of *R. moyesii* and hit pay dirt when he discovered 'Nevada' among the seedlings borne from his marriage. It made its debut in 1927 and has been a favorite Modern Shrub rose ever since, more so in Europe than in America, for reasons I've never understood.

I have only three plants of 'Nevada' and they're merely four years old, but this last spring they put on quite a show at one end of a pergola of wisteria. First, my shrubs of

'Nevada' reached the prime of their bloom just as the wisteria was on its way out—almost purposefully it seemed, as if they intended to challenge the vines of wisteria to a game of one-upmanship in floriculture. Next, blooms smothered the arching canes from base to tip. Then, of course, there was the color—rich creamy white petals surrounding dense stamens of butter yellow.

Almost everyone who strolled by the 'Nevada' show without knowing what was taking place said the same thing: "Look at that, is that a rose? The flowers look like dogwood blooms." Then visitors would ask how I trained the plants to look

the way they do—with beautifully arching canes radiating symmetrically from their roots. My reply was a steady "Nothing," since I've never urged those plants in the slightest direction; they simply grow as though they perfectly understand how to look most irresistibly graceful.

Well-grown shrubs of 'Nevada' reach heights of 8 feet, with almost as much horizontal spread. Because my plants receive considerable shade, not only from the dense wisteria nearby but also from a Japanese pagoda tree towering above, I doubt that they'll reach these proportions, but they're sure to climb both the pergola and that pagoda tree.

Although 'Nevada' blossoms sporadically throughout summer and sometimes stages a modest fall show, the most spectacular bloom of the year takes place in early summer, when flowers nearly camouflage the small but plentiful, light green foliage. Stems are a handsome shade of mahogany, complementing both leaves and blossoms.

Since we never spray plants in the fragrant garden, where 'Nevada' grows, these shrubs have never known chemical fungicides; neither have they mildewed or developed rust. I'm told that 'Nevada' has an affinity for blackspot, but I've never seen it.

Twenty years after 'Nevada' was introduced, a sport was discovered that was a carbon copy of its parent except for the color of its flowers. Gardeners who fancy deep pink may prefer 'Marguerite Hilling'. I'll stick with creamy 'Nevada'.

NEW DAWN
('Dr. W. Van Fleet' sport)

It's always struck me as ironic that the first rose ever patented in America is a sport, a spontaneous mutation of an existing rose. 'Dr. W. Van Fleet', a rampant Climber bred from the species *R. wichuraiana* and the charming old Tea rose 'Safrano', blossomed only once each year. As if in shame of his greed, shortly before 1930 the good doctor decided to produce an everblooming rose similarly colored to his own—'New Dawn', which has ruled the roost of robust Climbers for more than 50 years.

'New Dawn' isn't simply vigorous, it's hardy, too. Glossy foliage is abundant, dark green, and notably disease resistant. Although plants are aggressive, they're easily trained—up a pillar, over a pergola, or smothering a wall. When content, bushes reach 20-foot heights.

Semidouble blossoms are loosely but appealingly formed from petals that begin apple-blossom pink, then pale to a shade of pink so soft that it's actually off-white. Fragrance is fruity and strong.

I planted 'New Dawn' as one of six rose varieties on a long pergola. I've noticed that its foliage appears earlier than that of adjacent Climbing roses and that its buds also form early. Blossoming, however, is markedly delayed—to a good six weeks after the first Climbing rose appears. Then, however, 'New Dawn' makes up for lost time with a breathtaking display of fluffy pink blossoms. Although subsequent flushes of bloom are never as

dramatic as the first, they're reliable. I've never walked that pergola without at least one lovely blossom in sight.

Remember that you, too, may find a sport. Given loving care, rosebushes are known to present their caretakers with occasional rewards by developing a new rose all on their own.

We should all be so lucky as to discover a 'New Dawn'.

Part of the endearing charm of this fine rose is that no two blossoms are exactly alike. Although the basic color of each bloom is yellow, 'Peace' is officially classed as a yellow blend, since the petals of each blossom look as though they've been dipped in a darker color. To add further drama to these chameleonlike qualities, blooms also change their primary color during the year, depending on the strength of sunlight and heat. In spring and fall, base petals are deep clear yellow and edges are sometimes coral-orange. In midsummer, the combination may be off-white and light pink. Although the blooms of many Modern Hybrid Teas are prettiest just after their bud stage, 'Peace' reaches its glory when it is half to three-quarters open.

Bushes of 'Peace' are moderate growers, often as wide as they are tall. Foliage is leathery, dark green, and shiny.

I used to complain vigorously over the lack of fragrance, and I'd argue with those who claim that 'Peace' actually harbors perfume. Once, a knowledgeable rosarian assured me that I was smelling at the wrong time.

"Never hope for fragrance from 'Peace' while it's on the bush," he said, "or when it's less than half open."

Although this advice made not a lick of sense to me, I took it anyway. I was delighted to be proved wrong, although I still can't explain why, especially the "on the bush" part.

'Peace' will be with us forever, and not from sentiment alone.

PEACE

(['George Dickson' x 'Souvenir de Claudius Pernet'] x ['Joanna Hill' x 'Charles P. Kilham'] x 'Margaret McGredy')

'Peace' is hands-down the most famous rose in the world, and not from merits of the rose alone. Besides being the ultimate accomplishment of Francis Meilland (of the illustrious hybridizing family in Cap d'Antibes, France), 'Peace' is famous because of its notorious origins. Budwood of 'Peace' was spirited onto the last plane leaving France before its occupation during World War II, and the rose itself went on to become the floral symbol of the United Nations' formation in San Francisco in 1946 and the All-America Rose Selection that same year.

PLAYBOY
('City of Leeds' x ['Chanelle' x 'Picadilly'])

I've never been crazy over orange roses and think even less of orange blends. Still, I believe that 'Playboy' is one of the most smashing roses ever hybridized; it's also particularly well named because it's single, flashy, and seductively fragrant.

'Playboy' is a madly colored rose. Burgundy-tinged-bronze buds quickly mature into large blossoms whose petals are randomly splashed orange, yellow, and scarlet. Although its blooms actually contain 7 to 10 petals, everyone thinks of 'Playboy' as a single rose because it can't wait to show off its yellow-eyed center framing golden yellow stamens. 'Playboy' is fragrant, too, with a perfume that some liken to sweet apples.

The bush faced a tough challenge in living up to its sassy blossoms. Still, it managed—with disease-resistant foliage that's as glossy green as that of any rose in commerce. Plants are aggressive growers but usually top off at medium heights.

Healthy plants freely produce large sprays of blooms on long cutting stems. If you worry that blossoms such as those of 'Playboy' don't last well because of their low petal count, get over it; this Floribunda produces flowers that outlive those of most Hybrid Teas—in a vase or on the bush.

I have a planting of 'Playboy' in an area where roses serve the landscape rather than my greedy shears. I deadhead their flowers during summer, but I always leave the last crop on the bush. In return I'm rewarded with a fine crop of hips each winter.

After taking 'Angel Face' as a lover, when he was only 10 years old, 'Playboy' parented an offspring. 'Playgirl' is sassy, too—hot pink and yellow centered. I admire the easygoing disposition of her bushes, but give me 'Playboy' any day.

POPCORN

('Katharina Zeimet' x 'Diamond Jewel')

I long ago declared that 'Popcorn' would be my choice if I could grow but one Miniature rose. That's still true.

'Popcorn' is a perky thing, with spray after spray of single blossoms showing off hearts of golden yellow. When the whole plant is in bloom, it looks as though someone tossed a batch of freshly popped corn all over an upright little rosebush. Individual blossoms are semidouble (13 petals) and small (1 inch). Some people tout the flowers as scented of honey, but I wouldn't hyperventilate in search of proof if I were you. Bushes are short but upright, and foliage is glossy and disease resistant.

'Popcorn' isn't seen as widely as it should be, for the strange reason that single roses weren't very popular in 1973, the year northern California's champion horticulturist Dennison Morey hybridized the clever fellow. Fifteen years later, southern California's formidable rose grower and exhibitor Louis Desamero found a sport of 'Popcorn' that's making up for lost time.

'Gourmet Popcorn', the spontaneous mutation that Desamero discovered in his garden, is similar to 'Popcorn' except that its blossoms have a few more petals (up to 20) and its bush is considerably larger (easily to 2 feet). Plants are well shaped, with an attractive cascading habit, and are exceptionally free flowering. Blossoms form massive sprays, and their com-

plementary foliage is both handsome and plentiful. All in all, it's easy to see why 'Gourmet Popcorn' has become the most popular Miniature rose in America.

Both 'Popcorn' and its sport are terrific choices for the landscape, whether planted in masses or in rows. The two varieties are nice side by side, too.

PRISTINE

(*'White Masterpiece'* x *'First Prize'*)

Although 'Pristine' isn't my favorite of the many fine roses hybridized by Jackson & Perkins's indefatigable William Warriner, I predict that it will go down in history as his single greatest triumph. It's definitely *the* rose of the 1970s.

The bush is about as rough-looking as that of any modern Hybrid Tea rose. It's tall, spreading, vigorous, heavily thorned, and smothered in tough leathery foliage that starts out mahogany red but turns dark emerald green before blossoms appear.

Paradoxically, 'Pristine' blossoms look fragile. The arrangement of 25 to 30 large petals is unique among Hybrid Teas in that, collectively, they resemble a gardenia whose petals have been dipped in lavender–rose-pink. Good cutting stems are exceptionally long; fragrance is mild but definite.

Although I'm generally in favor of disbudding all Hybrid Tea roses for one-to-a-stem blooms, in the case of 'Pristine' I sometimes make an exception. Sturdy new canes often appear that almost speak their desire to bloom in a cluster. If the large centermost bud is removed from these dense clusters, deferring all energy to side buds, the result is a sight to behold.

You should not only allow 'Pristine' more growing space than you grant most Hybrid Teas, you should also plan to prune its bush ruthlessly, unless, of course, you're in search of a mighty statement in your garden's landscape. If so, 'Pristine' is the rose for you.

Gardeners to whom I've recommended 'Pristine' often complain that they don't like it as a cut flower. "It blows too quickly," they lament. My response is consistent: "You're not cutting its bloom early enough." 'Pristine', like 'Mister Lincoln' and other Hybrid Teas that lower their sepals early, can be taken from its bush in tight bud. It agreeably concludes its lovely show in a vase.

QUATRE SAISONS
(Origin unknown)

If roses of great antiquity appeal to you, 'Quatre Saisons' (also known as 'Rose of the Four Seasons' and *R. damascena*

bifera) must flourish in your garden—it's a rose antiquarian's dream.

Although it may not have been the precise variety known now as 'Quatre Saisons', a nearly identical rose grew on

the Greek island of Samos near the end of the tenth century B.C., where it was used in the worship of Aphrodite. It was later introduced in mainland Greece, where it paid homage to Venus. During the first century B.C., Virgil spoke of a rose that bloomed more than once each year—surely it was the Autumn Damask we now call 'Quatre Saisons' and the only repeat-blooming rose known to Europeans until the China roses were introduced in the late eighteenth century.

One doesn't cultivate 'Quatre Saisons' for the appearance of its shrubs; they're rather gawky and also notably prickly. Foliage is gray-green and plentiful (right up to the neck of blossoms).

Because of their loose, somewhat unsophisticated form, blossoms are also unconventional, but they're packed with true Damask fragrance, which was a key ingredient for many ancient recipes for potpourri. Blooms form in clusters while they unravel their crumpled but silky, clear pink petals.

Bushes may reach 5-foot heights each growing season. At pruning time, however, remember that this rose, although ancient, repeats its blossoms and should be pruned more severely than most Old garden roses.

As for how often blooms appear, don't count on four separate flushes. Spring's abundance is certain; so is a good repeat in fall. No matter how frequently periodic blossoms occur in between, they're always a welcome sight and a mighty treat for the nose.

QUEEN ELIZABETH

('Charlotte Armstrong' x 'Floradora')

What a stir 'Queen Elizabeth' caused when it was presented to the rose world as an All-America Rose Selection in 1955. No one had ever seen a rose quite like it. In anticipation of similar hybrids sure to follow, in America a whole new category was created for the Queen—Grandiflora. Alas, no Grandiflora ever bred has quite matched the many virtues of 'Queen Elizabeth'.

First, its size. 'Queen Elizabeth' is a skyscraper. In a single season, its bushes grow taller than any other Modern Rose. And it will do you no good to attempt to change her habits—'Queen Elizabeth' is a stately grower and pouts if pruned too low, spending a large part of each season reaching a height at which she blooms comfortably.

Second, disease resistance. Planted with good air circulation in mind, bushes of 'Queen Elizabeth' aren't simply easy to grow, they're tough, with large, leathery, deep green foliage that looks and feels impervious to pests or fungi. For the most part, it is.

Finally, the Queen's floral display. Panicles of rose and dawn pink blooms of 37 to 40 petals each occur mostly in clusters. Properly disbudded, the sprays are showstoppers and form on exceptionally long cutting stems (to 3 feet on established bushes). Fragrance is no stronger than mild, but give the Queen a break— she's otherwise thoroughly royal.

The voting members of the American Rose Society currently give 'Queen Elizabeth' a score of 9.2 (ratings from 9.0 to 9.9 denote "outstanding" roses, with 10.0 reserved for "perfect"). Even though 'Queen Elizabeth' has been with us for more than 35 years, I predict that her score will go higher yet, as rosarians realize just how fine a rose she is. As for bettering her, I pray for that day but don't see it in sight—'Queen Elizabeth' is an enduring beauty.

R. BANKSIAE LUTEA

(Origin unknown)

The Banksian family, as we noted in the section on Ramblers, is centuries older than the date of their discovery. *R. banksiae banksiae*, the first member of the royal family to be introduced, didn't make its debut until 1807, after a special expedition to China. *R. banksiae lutea*, my pick of the entire clan, came along 17 years later.

Like its predecessor, *R. banksiae lutea* scrambles to heights in excess of 25 feet, produces scads of rosette-shaped flowers once each year, and is winter-tender. Unlike *R. banksiae banksiae*, blossoms are pale to deep yellow (rather than white) and not as strongly perfumed. And as with all members of the family, wood is almost thornless, while foliage is long, light green, and shiny.

Whenever reading about Ramblers, one often reads that certain varieties are house eaters capable of gobbling up entire pergolas, fences, and live trees. Such claims commonly prove to be exaggerations, but not where *R. banksiae lutea* is concerned. In its case, believe every story you hear. *R. banksiae lutea* is so vigorous that it can hold its own with wisteria. (Not only will these two hungry vines grow alongside each other, they bloom at the same time.)

At the risk of overstressing this point, be forewarned that *R. banksiae lutea* can grow out of control. I've seen whole sheds collapse under the weight of a mature plant in full bloom and live trees choked by its overpowering growth. On the other hand, *R. banksiae lutea* is a dandy solution to dead trees that aren't in danger of toppling or to other garden eyesores that need covering.

Finally, like other Ramblers that bloom only once each year, *R. banksiae lutea* makes up for nonrecurrence with a staggering abundance of bloom over a six-week period each late spring/early summer.

ROSA MUNDI
(Ancient sport)

Rarely does a spontaneous mutation become more famous than its parent, but 'Rosa Mundi' has. Also like its parent, *R. gallica officinalis* (the apothecary rose), 'Rosa Mundi' has a rich history. The sport, officially known as *R. gallica versicolor*, was named after Rosamond Clifford, mistress to Henry II. Redouté immortalized the variety in his *Les Roses* and refers to it as "Fair Rosamond's Rose."

'Rosa Mundi' makes a compact shrub that grows exactly as wide as it does tall (to 4 feet). Foliage is plentiful, coarse in texture, and grayish green.

The enormous appeal of 'Rosa Mundi' is in the dramatic semidouble blossoms that are blush white striped randomly with crimson, pink, and light purple, no two alike. Blooms are carried in handsome sprays that nicely arrange themselves to mask entire plants. Occasionally, 'Rosa Mundi' reverts to its parent, in which case striped as well as solid light crimson flowers blossom. As with other fine Old garden shrubs of this age, flowering occurs only once each year.

In Britain, 'Rosa Mundi' is treasured as the quintessential border rose. Because of their compactness and obedience to training, shrubs make a fine low-growing hedge. Rows of 'Rosa Mundi' look particularly fetching when shrubs are alternately planted with its parent.

If you choose your roses because you want to dry their petals for potpourri after you've enjoyed them fresh, 'Rosa Mundi' is a splendid selection. Blossoms not only retain intricate striping, they also preserve as much rose fragrance as does any variety.

SALLY HOLMES
(*'Ivory Fashion'* x *'Ballerina'*)

While I'll try to exercise restraint in singing its praises, I must admit that I'm besotted by this rose. The only reason 'Sally Holmes' isn't generally considered to be one of the finest Shrub roses ever hybridized is that it was bred by an amateur in England and never aggressively marketed. Americans are about to be given a chance to make up for lost time.

When bushes of 'Sally Holmes' are in bloom, from a distance they look like rhododendrons. Although individual flowers are only semidouble in petalage, they're packed together in crowded heads, the sum total of which is abundance.

Buds start out light apricot, spend most of their life creamy white, and then fade to pure white before petals drop. Fragrance is mild but pleasant. Foliage is dark green, shiny, and notably disease resistant. Stems are long and smooth, except for widely spaced, sharp thorns.

Bushes of 'Sally Holmes' are voracious, quickly forming large mounds up to 5 feet in height with nodding branches reaching as wide. I've seen Sally cultivated as a climber, yet also obligingly sprawling along a fence. However she's grown, 'Sally Holmes' blossoms repeatedly from early summer well into fall.

Until recently, plants of 'Sally Holmes' were available only from a few small American and Canadian growers. Now Weeks Roses of Upland, California, has added Ms. Holmes to their line, which

should give the rose a considerable boost.

When people ask why I bother to plant grade 2 roses (see chapter 8 for a discussion of grading), I take them to my patch of 'Sally Holmes', plants that were no larger than my thumbs when I planted them (they were the largest I could get my hands on at the time). Not only did they reach full maturity in less than two years, I now have to prune ruthlessly to keep

them in bounds. Sally's not simply obedient to all such training, she rewards it with the damnedest display of blossoms I've ever seen.

Finally, if you worry that 'Sally Holmes' isn't a satisfactory cut flower because other roses like her aren't, you have a surprise in store. Just wait till you see how she takes to vase life—Sally's an all-around winner!

SEA PEARL

('Kordes' Perfecta' x *'Montezuma')*

As gardeners who travel will attest, certain roses grow better in certain parts of the world than elsewhere. I live in 'Sea Pearl' country.

When Britain's fine hybridizer Patrick Dickson graced rosedom with 'Sea Pearl' in 1964, he presented a classic Floribunda—a rose that would rather bloom in sprays of flowers than one-to-a-stem. The bush is another matter.

Part of the enduring charm of 'Sea Pearl' is the lustrous shades of peach-pink and buff-yellow, no two blooms exactly alike. Fragrance is clean and of moderate strength.

Technically, a spray of roses is a group of florets on one stem. The pattern that these individual flowers form is called the inflorescence, which may be circular, oval, or any geometric form that pleases the eye. 'Sea Pearl' is determined to please, with large, usually circular sprays of blossoms on particularly long cutting stems. If you take the trouble to remove the terminal bud in each spray (the largest of any) soon after it develops, you'll be rewarded with a mass of flowers in all stages from tight buds to fully open blossoms—the reason 'Sea Pearl' breathes fire in rose exhibitions.

Unlike most spray roses marketed as Floribundas in the United States, 'Sea Pearl' is a lofty grower, and it will do you no good to try to change its habits by pruning low. Bushes are upright, densely caned, and almost naturally urn-shaped. Foliage is rather undistinguished, except that it's a handsome shade of dark green and decidedly disease resistant.

As if its many merits weren't enough to make 'Sea Pearl' a pet of mine, it was M.F.K. Fisher's favorite and a reason we became friends. Many thanks, 'Sea Pearl'.

SHOT SILK

('Hugh Dickson' seedling x *'Sunstar')*

I often complain about poor choices for roses' names. 'Precious Platinum', for instance, is a vivid red Hybrid Tea, and the Floribunda 'Little Darling' is much too big a girl to be called anything diminutive. 'Shot Silk' is aptly named, not only for the silky texture of its petals but also for their coloring—salmon-pink with streaks of lemon yellow. And as if its form and color weren't enough, 'Shot Silk' is deeply fragrant.

With only 25 or so petals per blossom, 'Shot Silk' is in that never-never land between single and double roses, which means that the only time its flowers are traditionally shaped is while they're in bud. Once blossoms open, they assume a whimsical appearance all their own. Fully open blossoms are irresistible in form; in fact, I can't imagine a more comely arrangement of this many petals around a golden center of fat stamens.

Foliage is abundant, dark green, and slightly crinkled. Wood turns a handsome shade of rosy brown during winter, then greens again each spring.

In spite of its unique coloring, 'Shot Silk' mixes happily in a pergola or colonnade of climbing roses. Not only does its color blend with every other pink rose nearby, its charming growth habits fill in spaces left by thoughtless neighboring climbers. (The problem with most climbing roses that first grew as conventional bushes is that they're awkward. Not 'Shot Silk'; the climbing version, which oc-

curred seven years after the rose had been hybridized as a bush, puts its forerunner to shame.) Finally, 'Shot Silk' has an endearing habit of scrambling to the top of what it's expected to cover so that it wastes no time smiling down with roses.

If the beguiling blossoms alone don't grab you, take a whiff.

SOMBREUIL
('Gigantesque' seedling)

When people tell me that they love Old garden roses because of their precision form and rich fragrance and in spite of their inability to repeat their blossoms, I lead them to 'Sombreuil'—a rose for all ages. Since it came from a cross between the Hybrid Perpetual 'Gigantesque' and an unidentified co-parent (probably a Tea), 'Sombreuil' is technically a Hybrid Tea. As such, it blooms all season long. Some years after its introduction as a bush, 'Sombreuil' began growing as a climber, where it reached its finest glory.

Plants of climbing 'Sombreuil' arch their growth to 12-foot heights. Its canes are pliable, easily trained, and naturally graceful, and if the foliage is unremarkable (and widely spaced), the plants are hardy.

Blossoms of 'Sombreuil' are breathtaking, not just because of their creamy white, flesh-tinted, deliciously perfumed petals but also for their precise arrangement. Flat, quartered blooms are so re fined in their placement that one gawks in admiration. I've often studied blossoms to find a spot where I could improve on petal placement. It's impossible.

Besides the enviable habit of blossoming along their entire lengths, plants of climbing 'Sombreuil' make terrific hosts for companions, particularly clematis—the refined color of 'Sombreuil' flatters any other nearby.

Don't let the old-fashioned appearance of its blossoms fool you into thinking of 'Sombreuil' as an Old garden rose that requires serious feeding only in spring. 'Sombreuil' blooms repeatedly and requires deep drinks of water, nutritional fertilizer, and vigilant deadheading of spent blooms. In case that seems like a tough bill to fill each summer, just wait until you see its fall line of blooms!

SPARRIESHOOP

(['Baby Château' x 'Else Poulsen']
x 'Magnifica')

Almost everyone who sees 'Sparrieshoop' for the first time asks the same question: "What's that wonderful Old Rose that looks like a huge apple blossom?" They err only in assuming that it's old, for 'Sparrieshoop' was hybridized in 1953 by the Kordes family of West Germany. After 'Iceberg', considered by many rosarians to be the finest rose in the world, I think 'Sparrieshoop' may go down as the most important contribution the Kordes clan ever made to rosedom.

'Sparrieshoop' is a true shrub, so if you're looking for a bush, read on. Well planted and maintained, 'Sparrieshoop' grows to the size of a small car, or, trained properly, to enormous climbers or pillars.

Blossoms of 'Sparrieshoop' are composed of bright, clear pink, wavy petals that surround large centers of brilliant yellow stamens. The fragrant blooms are produced on long cutting stems that last well, on or off the plant.

I've planted my shrubs of 'Sparrieshoop' alternately with the blood red 'Altissimo' (another immortal; see entry in this chapter) on a tall fence just at the entrance to our ranch's field of garden roses. From mid-April until late October, the shrubs are rarely out of bloom and visitors never fail to ask about them.

Because I intend to cut their blossoms to sell, I train my plants upright. Recently, however, I visited a garden in the nearby Napa Valley where bushes of

'Sparrieshoop' are grown simply as shrubs. Left on their own, with ample space to develop, these specimens are the largest I've ever seen, except for ravenous climbers. I tried to count the blossoms on one gargantuan shrub but lost track somewhere in the hundreds. Don't worry, though—if you plant 'Sparrieshoop' to enjoy its blossoms indoors, you'll know just where they are and when to harvest their blooms so you won't miss a single glorious spray.

EIGHT

Buying

*I*f you intend to follow my many suggestions for proper rose culture, it only makes sense to begin with quality rosebushes, which means buying from growers who specialize in roses. Also, you must decide when you're going to purchase—

during "bareroot" season, when roses are naturally dormant, or later, when bushes are potted up into containers. Before telling you what's available after dormant season, let me try to persuade you to shop at the right time.

GLORIOUS BAREROOTS

I bought no bareroot bushes the first year I grew roses. First, there weren't many choices left among varieties by the time I went shopping, but more important, I worried that bareroot plants would never amount to much.

"Looks like a fistful of sticks to me," I'd say as I walked past bareroot roses in nursery bins. "Give me a plant in a proper pot any day—look, there are some rosebushes in biodegradable containers." Sold.

All-America Roses, which are chosen through the auspices of All-America Rose Selections, Incorporated, are the best indicator I know for good roses that are headed down the pike. In 1980, America's indefatigable hybridizer Bill Warriner made a clean sweep of the All-America Rose Selections by winning with his entries **'Love'**, **'Honor'**, *and* **'Cherish'**.

By the next buying season, I had become seriously smitten with rose fever, and the rosarians I liked to pal around with took me aside to assure me that I had to get over this aversion to naked bushes. "Get real," they urged, "bareroot plants are the way to go." Having taken their advice, I can only say that I'm so pleased that I conquered my fear of leafless plants. You will be, too, if you give bareroots a try. Here's why:

First, aiming at your practical side, bareroot plants are cheaper than those already potted up, not just due to the cost of the pot and soil but also because of the labor of proper planting.

Second, vigorous roses get planted in containers too small to accommodate their roots, which get crammed inside. Bareroot bushes, on the other hand, slip into holes especially dug for them, which allows you the luxury of spreading their roots precisely where they want to settle.

Finally, roses planted from containers need time to readjust to the soil in their new home after they have been removed from their cans or to grow through biodegradable containers. In contrast, bareroot plants start life in homes with soil prepared just for them.

As I freely admit in the next chapter, containerized roses are nothing to sneer at, particularly once dormant season passes and growers have no choice but to pot up their bareroot bushes. Still, given the choice, bareroot is the way to go. Once you witness the miracle of how these

When local rose specialists carry bareroot bushes, they often feature them for six weeks in raised beds filled with sawdust. If possible, buy them then; otherwise, bareroot bushes are potted up and sold for higher prices. Besides, select varieties will have been picked over.

"fistfuls of sticks" mature, you'll never buy roses any other way.

GRADING

Rosebushes marketed by professional growers must be graded according to specific standards. Usually you should consider buying nothing but grade 1, which, for Modern varieties, means that bushes of two-year, field-grown roses must have at least three vigorous canes (main stems), each of a specific length. Grade 1½ denotes fewer canes, but it may be satisfactory when no grade 1's are available. Steer clear of grade 2 and those wax-coated, packaged rose plants sold at supermarkets (it takes a blowtorch to remove the wax).

An important note about grading: Standards apply only to roses that have been budded onto rootstock. Roses growing on their own roots or custom-budded

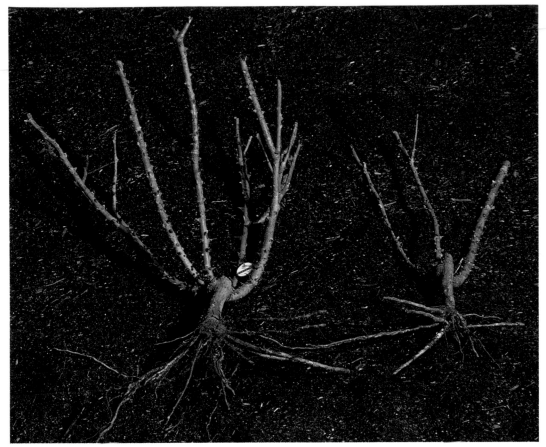

Bareroot roses are graded according to specific standards of number of canes of specific lengths. When possible, buy grade 1, like that on the left. Grade 1½, like the plant on the right, is also acceptable, but steer clear of grade 2.

truly aspires. More often, however, photos are pitifully unjust and either rob the variety of its true color or fail to capture actual form.

While reading catalogs, learn to read between the lines. Above all, learn catalog lingo. When someone admits that a variety is "tender," you can bet it will either freeze in winter or wither in summer. If a catalog confesses that a plant is "disease-prone," prepare for it to crumple before every ailment known to your area. You can depend on smelling blossoms said to be "powerfully fragrant," but you'll need a bloodhound's nose to sniff perfume from blooms that are only "lightly scented."

Nevertheless, I strongly urge you to shop for your bushes through catalogs, and I've included a list of current American and Canadian suppliers with whom I've dealt in the Sources.

Antique varieties aren't required to meet such standards. In these cases, you must depend entirely on the reputation of the grower.

SUPPLIERS AND CATALOGS

Rose growers who sell from catalogs have lots going for them. First, they list broad scopes of selections. Second, they use efficient shipping methods for delivering healthy plants, timely in their arrival. Finally, reputable suppliers replace plants without question when delivery is unduly delayed or when stock is below expectations.

The catalogs themselves are another matter. Although I wouldn't care to endure a winter without my rose catalogs to peruse, I don't take them as gospel. Catalog writers get carried away when describing roses, especially when photographers have supplied them with glorified transparencies. Color photos can make a variety look better than it is in real life or lend a hue to which it never

ALL-AMERICA ROSES

Although one must judge the merits of Heirloom Roses for oneself, with Modern Roses help is available through the All-America Rose Selection process. If you're intrigued with rose varieties hot off the hybridizing floor, by all means check them out.

For years I was an outspoken critic of certain All-America Rose Selections. I understood why beauties such as 'Duet', 'Peace', 'Queen Elizabeth', 'Medallion' and a host of other stellar roses carried the prestigious honor, but I cursed those judges who let stinkers such as 'Oregold', 'Bing

Crosby', 'Love', and 'Sundowner' walk away with the award.

"Why not stop bellyaching and become a judge yourself?" I asked. Now I operate one of 25 official All-America Rose Selection test gardens in the United States. I also appreciate that what is All-America in Petaluma, California, may only piddle around in Ames, Iowa, or fall flat in Wauwatosa, Wisconsin (two other test sites), and vice versa.

What makes a rose "All-America"? All-America Rose Selections, Incorporated, is a nonprofit research corporation founded in 1938 for the purpose of evaluating new rose varieties worthy of a special stamp of approval. Hybridizers who believe that they've come up with potential winners must submit four bushes of each variety to every official garden for a two-year trial. Usually 40 to 50 varieties are tested each year.

The judges are instructed to "give roses under test commonsense care," including planting in well-prepared soil, regular spraying, feeding, irrigation, mulching, pruning, and reasonable winter protection.

Currently, five types of rosebushes may be entered for consideration: Hybrid Teas, Floribundas, Grandifloras, Miniatures, and, the latest group, Landscape roses. Each entry's performance is scored twice a year, no later than the first of July and again by the first of November to make sure that roses are evaluated at their peak bloom cycles. Entries are scored on a five-point scale for 15 attri-

butes: novelty; form, buds; form, flowers; color, buds; color, open blooms; aging quality; flowering effect; fragrance; stem/cluster; plant habit; vigor; foliage; disease resistance; repeat bloom; and personal opinion.

Following each judging session, scores are forwarded to the AARS executive director, who conducts a secret ballot of the test-garden voting members each January. Winners aren't announced until the following year so that growers have time to bud extra plants of a surefire commercial winner.

In order to become the judge of an official garden, one must first operate a "demonstration" garden for two years. During that time the judge under consideration raises the same roses as do official judges under the same rules, including biannual scoring. Although the scores from demonstration-garden judges don't count in final ballots, they're benchmarks for making certain that prospective judges know the difference between great, good, mediocre, and worthless roses.

The first time I judged the entries from my demonstration garden, I agonized for weeks over their final scores. A month later, to my great shock, I learned that the varieties I had rated first, second, and third were ranked ninth, fourteenth, and twenty-third by the judges.

I discussed the matter with a judge who has been at the game for years. "Don't worry about it," she said. "Just don't let your color biases carry too much weight."

Since no flowers accompany bareroot bushes, suppliers sell plants with pictures of what the rose will look like when it blossoms. Don't bank on what you see; sometimes sunlight will have bleached an accurate depiction.

I realized that that was just what was wrong. The roses leading the trials from that first scoring were shades of vivid orange or red—not my pet colors, especially if no fragrance is attached.

I've since learned to keep sheer opinion to myself. If I don't happen to like a rose being considered because of its hue, I pretend it's another shade. I've even considered wearing rose-colored glasses while scoring entries for form, substance, or flowering effect.

As my garden progressed through its two-year demonstration status, so did the proximity of my scores to those of the big guys. Last year, all the roses that won were in my top 10, too, though not necessarily at the top. In fact, the rose that grabbed my heart won't even be declared All-America, although it will be introduced to commerce. That's the American process, for you.

Whatever else they are, All-America Roses are the triumphant winners from the majority of test gardens across the country and worthy of consideration. For the record, here's a list of winners since the award began:

1940 Dicksons Red, Flash, The Chief, World's Fair

1941 Apricot Queen, California, Charlotte Armstrong

1942 Heart's Desire

1943 Grande Duchesse Charlotte, Mary Margaret McBride

1944 Fred Edmunds, Katherine T. Marshall, Lowell Thomas, Mme Chiang Kai-shek, Mme Marie Curie

1945 Floradora, Horace McFarland, Mirandy

1946 Peace

1947 Rubaiyat

1948 Diamond Jubilee, High Noon, Nocturne, Pinkie, San Fernando, Taffeta

1949 Forty-niner, Tallyho

1950 Capistrano, Fashion Sutter's Gold, Mission Bells

1951 No selection

1952 Fred Howard, Helen Traubel, Vogue

1953 Chrysler Imperial, Ma Perkins

1954 Lilibet, Mojave

1955 Jiminy Cricket, Queen Elizabeth, Tiffany

1956 Circus

1957 Golden Showers, White Bouquet

1958 Fusilier, Gold Cup, White Knight

1959 Ivory Fashion, Starfire

1960 Fire King, Garden Party, Sarabande

1961 Duet, Pink Parfait

1962 Christian Dior, Golden Slippers, John S. Armstrong, King's Ransom

1963 Royal Highness, Tropicana

1964 Granada, Saratoga

1965 Camelot, Mister Lincoln

1966 American Heritage, Apricot Nectar, Matterhorn

1967 Bewitched, Gay Princess, Lucky Lady, Roman Holiday

1968 Europeana, Miss All-American Beauty, Scarlet Knight

1969 Angel Face, Comanche, Gene Boerner, Pascali

1970 First Prize

1971 Aquarius, Command Performance, Redgold

1972 Apollo, Portrait

1973 Electron, Gypsy, Medallion

1974 Bahia, Bon Bon, Perfume Delight

1975 Arizona, Oregold, Rose Parade

1976 America, Cathedral, Seashell, Yankee Doodle

1977 Double Delight, First Edition, Prominent

1978 Charisma, Color Magic

1979 Friendship, Paradise, Sundowner

1980 Love, Honor, Cherish

1981 Bing Crosby, Marina, White Lightnin'

1982 Brandy, French Lace, Mon Chéri, Shreveport

1983 Sun Flare, Sweet Surrender

1984 Impatient, Intrigue, Olympiad

1985 Showbiz

1986 Broadway, Touch of Class, Voo Doo

1987 Bonica, New Year, Sheer Bliss

1988 Amber Queen, Mikado, Prima Donna

1989 Class Act, Debut, Tournament of Roses, New Beginning

1990 Pleasure

1991 Carefree Wonder, Perfect Moment, Sheer Elegance, Shining Hour

1992 Brigadoon, Pride 'n' Joy, All That Jazz

1993 Rio Samba, Sweet Inspiration, Solitude, Child's Play

1994 Midas Touch, Secret, Caribbean

1995 Brass Band, Singin' in the Rain

1996 Carefree Delight, Livin' Easy, Mt. Hood, St. Patrick

1997 Artistry, Scentimental, Timeless

1998 Fame!, First Light, Opening Night, Sunset Celebration

1999 Betty Boop, Candelabra, Fourth of July, Kaleidoscope

$\mathcal{P}$lanting

$\mathcal{A}$lthough roses can now be purchased for planting year-round, as mentioned in the previous chapter, bareroot is the preferred season for planting because select varieties are available then. Also, planting roses bareroot affords

gardeners the opportunity to prepare a home that is bound to thrill the plants. Besides, bareroot bushes are so much easier to handle.

Your own bareroot season depends on where you garden. In my northern California climate, for instance, I plant bareroot bushes during December and January (later, only if suppliers can't ship earlier because of frozen ground). Gardeners in New England may have to wait until mid-March to plant. Generally speaking, roses can be planted as soon as hard frosts are over.

CHOOSING A SITE

I have always advocated giving roses as much sun as possible. Lately, I've bent my rules.

The bulk of my rosebushes are planted in an open field where they receive sunlight from daybreak until dusk. Along one perimeter of the field is a grove of native willow trees that

When rosebushes arrive from specialists, they're usually bundled in lots of 10. Leave them as they are until you're ready to plant them, otherwise they become tangled in each other's thorny canes.

Immediately before planting bareroot rose-bushes, soak them in tubs of water to which household bleach has been added. The water will plump out any canes that have dried out during storage, and the bleach will clean up unwanted bacteria. A good root stimulant would help, too.

Just before planting them, clean up bareroot plants by trimming their roots of any broken wood. With the same sharp shears, many rosarians nick the tips of all stems to encourage rapid growth, which seems like a good idea.

While you're handling bareroot bushes that seem like nothing more than a fistful of sticks, try to dwell on how pretty their blooms will be. Plant bushes in well-prepared holes that have a cone of soil rising from their middles, over which roots can be comfortably draped.

came with the property. I've always blessed that thicket of willows because it serves as an effective windbreak. I've noticed, however, that the bushes planted nearest to the trees have blossoms with deeper colors on longer stems—due, I believe, to those two hours (approximately) of late afternoon shade.

I've observed similar differences among some Bourbon roses that are planted on a 225-foot fence along another end of the rose field. Magnolia trees growing at both ends of the fence afford nearby roses partial shade, which they appear to appreciate.

Certain rose families tolerate considerable shade, and some varieties thrive even in dense shade (these are noted throughout the text). Still, I concur with those experts who recommend that rose-bushes receive at least five hours of sun each day—the earlier the better.

Where summers are especially hot, gardeners have no choice but to consider providing some degree of shading, because most roses can't stand up to heat over 100 degrees F. When deciding whether to grant morning or afternoon shade, choose afternoon—roses prefer morning sun.

Water is as important as sunlight for roses. Always select sites in proximity to reliable water sources.

Roses despise wind because it damages both their blooms and their foliage. Plant close to, but not smack against, fences and garden walls (south-facing walls are best, of course, because they're the sunniest and therefore the warmest).

Don't plant roses too close to trees or large bushes that compete for root space and nutrients. Rosebushes are persistently hungry and don't like sharing their food with neighbors.

Finally, drainage should be as close to

perfect as possible. If you worry that a hole you've prepared doesn't drain well enough to suit a rose, fill it with water. If the hole hasn't drained in an hour, dig 6 inches deeper and fill the extended depth with a layer of coarse gravel.

READYING THE BUSH

Bareroot rosebushes purchased from reliable nurseries or shippers should arrive in good condition, but if inclement weather has delayed planting, bushes may have dried out. To replenish moisture and plump out dried wood, simply submerge bushes in a bucket of water until all roots are covered and leave them to soak for up to 24 hours. It's also a good idea to add some household bleach (about $\frac{1}{8}$ cup per 5-gallon soaking tub), thereby cleaning up whatever unwanted bacteria might be hanging around. While you're at it, you might also add a shot of all-purpose fertilizer or vitamin B_1 .

Because they're havens for disease, broken stems and roots must have their damaged sections cut out. Using sharp shears, make a clean cut into healthy growth $\frac{1}{4}$ inch from each break. Many gardeners also believe that all root tips should be nipped to stimulate new growth, which is probably a good idea, but certainly not mandatory.

Next, turn your attention to the almighty hole.

THE ALMIGHTY HOLE

Of all the fine horticulturists I wish I'd met, I most long for the person who said, "I'd rather plant a two-bit rose in a four-bit hole" than vice versa. Nothing you ever do for a rose is as vital as preparing the hole that receives its bush. When you consider that most rosebushes outlive the gardeners who plant them, it makes sense to give special attention to preparing their permanent homes.

After experimenting with an array of dimensions, I've decided that the ideal hole for a rosebush is 2 feet wide by 18 inches deep. This may seem shallow, but remember that roses don't have taproots. In fact, the large roots that come with mature bareroot rosebushes won't grow much longer or thicker than they already are. Instead, feeder roots develop that provide bushes with the bulk of their nourishment. These feeder roots—masses of hairlike mats growing within a 2-foot radius around each bush—begin developing immediately after bushes are planted. For them to develop properly, the soil in which these feeder roots grow must be friable (easily crumbled).

Examine carefully the soil obtained from digging a hole 18 inches deep by 2 feet wide, and plan to find a new home for half of it—all of it if the soil is poor, heavily compacted, or claylike. Instead of reusing soil that's already spent, buy packaged all-purpose gardening soil. To half of the soil needed to refill the hole, mix equal parts of aged manure and organic materials.

Most nurseries carry only cow and steer manures, but if you can get your garden spade on aged chicken, turkey, or rabbit manure, your roses will bless you. Whichever you choose, *never* use fresh manure, because the heat it generates during early decomposition will burn those treasured feeder roots.

Organic materials are available from a number of satisfactory sources. First, of course, is peat moss, although it's probably the most expensive of all choices (and also acidic). Cheaper sources include redwood shavings, fir bark, and other shredded wood. If you decide on a wood derivative, keep in mind that it should be in compost form. Raw sawdust, while correctly textured, requires its own source of nitrogen in order to break down. If you don't provide additional nitrogen for this purpose, raw sawdust will rob rosebushes of nitrogen intended for their enjoyment. To my good fortune, I garden near a sawmill that provides "nitralized sawdust"—fine wood shavings to which nitrogen has been added. My roses love this product, and I bless it for how easily it mixes with soil and other organic materials.

Ask local agricultural agents about nearby sources for compost. You may be lucky enough, for instance, to live near a mushroom farm, in which case you can purchase mushroom compost—a medium in which mushrooms are grown for one crop, after which it's spent as far as more mushrooms are concerned, but pure gold for roses.

Mix well the soil you saved (or purchased), the aged manure, and organic material; fill half of the almighty hole,

Planting affords an excellent opportunity for adding dry fertilizers, which should be scratched into the soil all around the extension of the bareroot plants' feeder roots. Everything should then be thoroughly soaked with water before the remaining space is filled with soil.

How deep you plant bareroot bushes depends on the relationship of the bud union to the ground. To accurately gauge that distance, put a shovel across the almighty hole and set a bush in place. Choose the final resting height according to how much mulch you intend to add.

If you plant roses in the fall, you might begin planting while your other bushes are still in bloom. No matter when you plant, be sure to mound bushes after you've sunk them into the ground. Any mulch material will suffice as long as you mound it over at least half the bush.

and water well. While waiting for the hole to drain, refresh your memory on the anatomy of a bareroot rosebush.

THE ANATOMY OF A ROSEBUSH

Except for those specifically grown on their own roots, most rosebushes in commerce are actually a grafted combination of two separate rose varieties. The rootstock, the part underground, comes from specific varieties known not for their blooms (which are usually insignificant, sometimes unattractive) but rather for their ability to form good roots. The vari-

ety desired for its blooming habits is grafted onto this rootstock to grow above ground: the hybrid. Where the graft of these two varieties is made, a bulbous growth develops that forever bears testament to the marriage: the bud union.

If rosebushes had hearts, they would beat within the bud union. It is from this globule that new growth spurts when growing conditions signal that it's time to do so. More important, for now, the bud union is the landmark for measuring planting depth, depending on the climate zone in which you garden—the warmer your

climate, the higher above ground level the bud union is placed. Where I garden, for instance, I place the bud union 2 inches above soil level (planning to add 2 inches of mulch to the soil), because winters are never sufficiently cruel to freeze rosebushes. Many rosarians can't afford this luxury and must plant their bud unions at (or below) ground level (see chapter 15; also, local consultants can tell you the proper height of bud-union placement for where you live). In any case, you must first create a cone of mounded soil over which the bareroot bush is placed.

A sturdy cone is best formed by gradually placing handfuls of planting mixtures and patting them down to eliminate large air pockets. Think of the cone as a tepee of soil and form it bit by bit.

Check the right height for the bud union by laying a shovel handle or stick on the ground and across the hole. When the cone is at the right height, formed and compacted, the almighty hole is ready to receive its bush.

PLACING THE BUSH

The only decision left after a cone has been properly formed is which direction the bud union should face—a matter of considerable controversy. Some rosarians believe that the bud union should face the direction of the strongest source of light; others avow that lopsided portions should be planted to the north. Once, when I had nothing better to do, I experimented with a wide array of bud-union placements and found not a hoot of difference.

Set the bush directly onto the tip of the cone, carefully spreading the roots outward and downward. Then, holding the bush in place, begin filling in the rest of the hole, pressing the soil mixture down firmly enough to eliminate air pockets but carefully enough so that fragile roots aren't broken in the process. Use your hands, *not* your feet, to tamp down the soil. When half of the filling is completed, water to soak thoroughly.

If you plan to use dry fertilizers, now is the time to apply them.

I have mixed feelings about dry chemical fertilizers, particularly the timed-release ones designed to break down over extended periods. Although I approve of these extended-release fertilizers in theory, I've found that they require more heat than my soil can provide to break down entirely in one growing season. Instead of timed-release formulations, I employ the help of water-soluble granulated fertilizer in a balanced ratio such as 15-15-15 and apply ½ cup to each hole. These granules begin breaking down as soon as they're wet and continue to do so with each watering thereafter.

I have no reservations whatsoever in regard to dry organic fertilizers, and I use them every time I plant a new bush. Although numerous organic fertilizers do the job, I prefer hoof and horn (14-0-0) and bone meal (0.5-30-0) at the rate of 2 cups each per hole. If you have trouble finding these, fish meal in a satisfactory substitute for hoof and horn, and superphosphate works about as well as bone meal.

The dry fertilizers of choice should be applied and watered in while the hole is half full. Then the remaining soil mixture should be put into the hole, carefully tamped down (again, with hands, not feet), and watered thoroughly.

MOUNDING BUSHES

I'm so sold on the wisdom of this next step that friends have accused me of harping on the subject. Nevertheless, I'm convinced that if newly planted bareroot bushes aren't mounded, all previous efforts may have been in vain when cold winter winds inevitably parch their canes (see chapter 15 for more on winter protection).

Any of the materials used for preparation of the planting hole can be used; a combination is ideal. Mix leftover soil with any of the suggested organic materials and heap the combination over the bush until *at least* half of the plant is covered. Water everything down, not away, and turn your back to a well-planted rosebush.

CONTAINERIZED BUSHES

Already-planted rosebushes come in either rigid containers that must be removed or biodegradable ones that are planted intact. If you buy a bush in a rigid container and don't have a can cutter of your own, be certain to have the container cut before you take the bush home. *Never* pull bushes from uncut containers, because you'll damage their roots.

If soil around bushes from rigid containers is loose, try to get it all into the hole with as little disturbance as possible. If the soil is compressed, rub and loosen it so that roots can be aimed in the right direction.

Although cones aren't formed for containerized plants, planting techniques are identical to those for bareroot bushes, as is fertilizing and bud-union placement. If plants have already developed leafy growth, they shouldn't be mounded; otherwise, they should.

Bushes purchased in biodegradable containers may be planted intact (after holes are punched in the bottom and sides), but use the bud union, *not* the lip of the container, as the landmark for deciding planting depth. If the bush has sunk into the container, either cut off the unsightly lip or resolve to live with it until it disintegrates (be forewarned, however, that it may take an entire growing season to break down on its own).

TRANSPLANTING ROSES

I once attended a demonstration given by a consulting rosarian on the proper transplanting of rosebushes. The purpose, of course, was to show how to move bushes during the growing season; otherwise, everyone knew that dormant season is the preferred time for transplanting roses.

My most vivid memory of that experience is my vow never to move a bush in full foliage. It was backbreaking work and involved more than one shovel and several sacks of burlap.

I have a friend who had written into the escrow instructions for the sale of her house that she had rights to return in January and remove her rosebushes. Very sensible. Transplant roses only during bareroot season; sometimes not even then.

I've been thought ungrateful when refusing to transplant certain rosebushes to my garden.

"Why, it must be twenty years old," people have bragged about a mature shrub of the fine Gallica rose 'Madame Hardy'.

"You're welcome to the whole thing."

I don't want the whole thing. Hefty mature rosebushes are a terror to transplant, and without the help of a sturdy back (better yet, a backhoe), you'll never move an intact rootball no matter how careful you are. An alternative, of course, is to prune the bush severely and hope that the roots you drag along are adequate to get the plant going again. Take my word, if you can get your hands on a young grade 1 bareroot bush, plant it instead. In three years, you won't be able to tell the difference between it and a 20-year-old specimen (unless, of course, the transplanted specimen is still waiting for its roots to take hold, in which case it pales in comparison to junior).

OWN-ROOT ROSES

Roses growing on their own roots (see chapter 14) have no bud union. Determining the correct planting depth for these rosebushes is no problem, however, because of decided swellings that form where roots join aboveground growth. Also, there is considerable leeway for what is absolutely proper.

Remember, too, that own-root roses are sold bareroot during dormancy periods, and, like budded roses, plants need to be mounded after planting to keep their canes from drying out. These rosebushes should also be given the same carefully prepared holes and fertilizer afforded their budded cousins.

Speaking of care in planting (more important, of attention to detail), keep in mind that the planting instructions offered in this chapter are vital for all rose varieties that repeat their bloom cycles during a single growing season. As for those varieties that blossom only once each year, planting rules are considerably less stringent. Species roses, for instance, as well as those I label Antique (Gallicas, Damasks, Albas, Centifolias, and Mosses), are fuss-free compared with those roses that follow them historically. For these ancient diehards, many rosarians go to no special bother at all, planting bushes where they are expected to grow, without benefit of special soil preparation or fertilizers.

I'm somewhere in the middle when it comes to such "grow or die" approaches to rose culture. When I plant a new (to me) species or Antique variety, I forget almighty holes and special chemical fertilizers. I do, however, grant them organic fertilizers such as bone meal and hoof and horn. They seem to appreciate it. On the other hand, when I'm comfortable that I have a hell-bent-for-survival rose that demands no coddling whatsoever, I do little more than stick it in the ground. 'Complicata', as I mention while discussing its immortality in chapter 7, is a classic example of a rose that expects no special favors.

Once rosebushes have been planted, they should be left alone except for keeping them just on the wet side of moist. If it doesn't rain periodically, water the plants yourself and get ready for a glorious eruption.

TEN

Maintaining

$\mathcal{A}$lthough rose varieties actually exist that require little in the way of maintenance, they're the exception. Most roses, indeed all but species and Antique varieties, expect substantial help in order to reach their full potential. A

rule of thumb for remembering how much care roses demand centers around how often they bloom—the more often a variety blossoms, the more pampering it requires.

UNMOUNDING

Assuming you've just followed the instructions in the previous chapter for planting roses bareroot, the first step is to unmound them. The time to do so is after leaflet sets begin appearing on exposed wood and the danger of frost is past.

Lots more than those leaves has been developing on prop-

erly mounded bushes and it's not all visible. In order to protect these tender concealed developments, mounding materials must be removed carefully. The best technique is to use the slow trickle from a water wand or garden hose to coax clumps of mulch off canes. Should water not be available, use your fingers (not your hands or a garden implement) to flake mulch away.

With certain roses, it's important to declare a preference for blossoms one-to-a-stem or in clusters. Depending upon which you choose, you must disbud accordingly.

MULCHING

Because I'm so sold on the compatibility of mulch and roses, I quickly lose interest in problems that plague gardeners who don't bother to mulch their bushes. Mulching is nothing more than layering organic materials over soil, yet in spite of the simplicity of the process, nothing is more beneficial to rosebushes and the beds in which they grow.

Mulching makes three important contributions to good rose culture. First, water flows over and through mulch each time you irrigate, releasing some of the mulch's nutrients each time. The fact that mulch is organic means that it contains valuable nutrients that aren't available all at once. Instead, they break down steadily over summer, usually reducing their bulk by half in one season.

Second, mulch not only provides a blanket of protection from the hard rays of summer sun, it also conserves water. Since the irrigation method I hope to persuade you to try calls for watering infrequently but deeply, mulch will keep water under the soil surface.

Finally, God bless it, mulch retards weeds. If mulch is thick enough, weeds have trouble growing through it. And even if they do, they're not difficult to remove because the underlying soil is kept so friable that weeds can't stubbornly anchor themselves.

Unmounding affords the perfect beginning for mulching, since the materials used to mound a newly planted bush are precisely the same as those you want for

Rosarians live in hopes of new growth from the bud union. When basal breaks appear, they are usually red and bursting with vigor. Sometimes bushes grow with such determination to flourish that they produce unwieldy growth. If you know what to look for, you can nip such problems in the bud.

mulch. Once you begin mulching, adding dry organic materials each spring becomes easier as mulch becomes looser and more amenable to additives. In well-mulched beds, it's easy to rake circles around bushes, work in dry fertilizers, and cover the whole area with fresh materials for the coming season.

No mulch material is more beneficial than manure, but keep in mind that just as in planting, manure must be aged to keep from burning the bud union and the delicate hairlike feeder roots just below the soil surface. Although gardeners bless aged manure for its nutritional value, an even greater plus is the heat that mulch generates as it decomposes, which warms soil and accelerates bacterial reactions.

Another mulch material I'm sold on is alfalfa, although I hesitate to recommend it after what happened the first time I suggested using two 2-pound coffee cans full of it scattered around each garden rosebush. One reader decided that if two cans were good, four would be better, and removed the top layer of soil from the pots in which she grew her roses and refilled her containers with alfalfa pellets.

After watering in her overkill, she wrote to me to say that the meal swelled to the point that it was rising up the canes on the bush. She reported further that her alfalfa treatment had turned so hard that it was shedding water, then asked if she should send pictures.

The only thing I hated more than the thought of pictorial proof of how this grower had misinterpreted my advice was that she didn't give me her phone number so that I could have called to tell her to begin undoing her wrong. I wrote to her immediately and mailed my response the same day, but the ghastly experience still gave me nightmares.

At the risk of similar misinterpretation, I again assert that alfalfa is a goldmine addition to mulch for roses. Not only is alfalfa readily available (if not in feed stores, in pet shops), it's inexpensive and easy to use. It makes no difference whether you use the meal or pelleted form as long as you make certain that no additives such as sugar have been included.

I still use two 2-pound coffee cans full per bush for roses grown in the ground and about half that per 15-gallon container for roses in pots. Please don't try more than these amounts, but if you do, for goodness sake don't offer me pictures.

You should also be forewarned that alfalfa turns khaki green after it's watered and that it looks foreign against other mulch materials, most of which are dark brown. If that color contrast is likely to bother you, simply spread the alfalfa as the first mulch material and heap others on top. However it's applied, alfalfa should be scattered widely around the base of each rosebush.

The reason alfalfa is such a boon to roses, by the way, is that as it disintegrates, it yields an alcohol called tricontanol, to which roses take a particular shine. When tricontanol reaches their roots, roses act as though they've been longing for just such a stiff drink.

Any organic material that decays into humus serves as mulch: compost, aged bark, leaf mold, rice hulls, or peat moss. As mentioned earlier, wood shavings and sawdust also provide excellent bulk for mulch except for the fact that they require their own source of nitrogen in order to break down; if it isn't provided, they will usurp bushes of the nitrogen meant specifically for them. If you can obtain "nitralized sawdust," it's ideal, since nitrogen has already been added.

While lawn clippings and pine needles are also good additions to mulch, they're problematical because they tend to mat down if they aren't blended in well, causing water runoff that inevitably interferes with irrigation.

Scads of other good mulch materials exist. As already mentioned, I'm in cahoots with a nearby mushroom farm and buy truckloads of their spent compost. Grape grower's pomace is also a rich source for mulch, as are buckwheat hulls, bagasse, and ground corncobs. Look for sources close to home.

Finally, if for reasons I can't fathom, you refuse to mulch your rose beds, you must devise some other scheme each spring before fertilizing your bushes. Soil with no blanket of mulch becomes hard and compacted, and fertilizers can't be scratched in. Compressed soil also inhibits the development of feeder roots.

RAISED BEDS

Any gardener cursed with soil that doesn't drain well or smitten by plants for which drainage is never too perfect knows the advantages of raised beds. The technique I use for creating raised beds is somewhat unconventional, but it works.

I plant and mound rosebushes directly into the ground, whatever its terrain. After unmounding, I begin adding mulch to a height that demands something to hold it in. Then I lay lengths of pressure-treated 2 x 6 wood on edge and toenail them together to frame beds, supporting them every 5 feet with stakes. When the frames are completed, there is a 5-inch (1 inch of wood is underground, in a narrow trench) border around each bed, which can be filled with mulch that won't drain away with successive waterings. I like to use 4 inches of mulch, not only for the nutrients it provides but also to discourage weeds that would otherwise establish themselves.

WATER

Roses are insatiable drinkers, but they prefer long drinks to skimpy shots. Feeder roots develop on rosebushes no matter how they're watered, but long roots develop only if forced to search deep for water.

The watering method roses prefer—flooding—is facilitated with raised beds, which when flooded spread nutrients throughout the mulch. With proper drainage, water also reaches levels well below the soil surface, encouraging long roots (roses don't have taproots) to find it.

Water wands are useful garden gadgets for irrigating roses because they gently break up the flow of water passing through them. Hard spurts from an open hose disturb mulch and can expose the fragile feeder roots.

Except on mornings of guaranteed warm days when you want to rid bushes of dust or spray residues, never water rosebushes from overhead. Wet foliage beckons diseases such as mildew.

When I tell people that I water my roses only once each week, they give me an "Oh, sure you do" look, as though they're positive I water more frequently but don't care to admit it. I remind these doubters that my rosebushes are planted in raised beds with veritable carpets of mulch, which ensures that bushes have plenty of moisture to last more than a week between waterings. When hot spells come along or bushes demonstrate signs of drying out (usually by drooping growth at the tops of bushes), I water more often.

How often you should water depends not only on how much mulch you use but also on where you garden. Generalities don't apply when days are exceptionally warm or wind so persistent that it robs bushes of moisture. When in doubt, especially if drainage is good, water.

FERTILIZER

The only thing roses love more than water is food. When properly fed, roses reward you with abundant bloom.

I've confessed more than once that I like to put dry fertilizers into the hole of newly planted bushes, then use dry fertilizers again once each year thereafter, as early in spring as sets of leaves appear.

For established bushes, fertilizers should be applied in a trench raked around the drip line—that imaginary circle beneath the outer reaches of the tips of a pruned rosebush. Rake soil back over the trench after applying fertilizers and water well.

I've accepted the fact that I'm complimented more often on my rose-feeding program than on any other aspect of rose cultivation—unglamorous, perhaps, but appreciated. I feed my roses heavily (especially those expected to bloom repeatedly) with liquid fertilizers (usually one strong dose at least once a month throughout their season of bloom). The Modern Roses I grow for the sale of their blossoms are fertilized twice each month during their entire blooming season, and rarely with identical chemical formulations. Before you can hope to become savvy in fertilizer lingo, however, it's important that you understand three letters.

N, P, K

All fertilizers, whether organic or chemical, are rated with numbers reflecting their content of nitrogen (N), phosphorus (P), and potassium (K). Fertilizer blends said to be "balanced," such as 15-15-15, carry equal amounts of these three elements. If a blend of fertilizer is stronger in one element than another, that weighting will be noted. For instance, a fertilizer whose label reads 10-5-0 has twice as much nitrogen as phosphorus and no potassium whatsoever.

Nitrogen is vital at the start of each growing season to get plants off and

The materials you use for mounding newly planted bushes should be the same ones you employ for mulch. When possible, use organic materials from close to where you garden. My local favorites are nitralized sawdust and mushroom compost.

growing, whereas potassium is important at season's end when new growth shouldn't be encouraged. Phosphorus is critical throughout seasons of bloom.

PH

It will do you no good, however, to worry about which fertilizer to use when unless you understand the makeup of the soil in which your roses grow. For that, you must get acquainted with two more letters— little p, big H.

I heard about pH long before I knew what it meant.

"Oh, I grow mostly camellias," savvy gardeners would say. "My soil is acidic, you know."

Although I realized that I should memorize the pH of my own soil, I dragged my feet because I secretly feared that exposing my soil's pH was more than I was prepared to bargain for, in terms of doing something about it.

Later, when I started gardening seriously and was forced to read up on those plants I yearned to cultivate, I found that I couldn't escape pH—it was everywhere I read. Lower this, increase that, references would tell me. Once I started paying attention, I discovered that pH isn't nearly so mysterious as it seems.

The pH scale runs from 0 to 14 to distinguish the relative degrees of acidity or alkalinity of a soil. The lower the pH, the more acidic the soil; high numbers signify alkaline conditions. Soils with a pH of 7.0 are neutral, precisely where most agricultural crops like to grow. Roses thrive in such soils, too, although they actually prefer slightly acidic soil between 6.5 and 7.0.

Once I'd finally decided to get acquainted with my soil's pH, I thought I should test it myself. I bought two kits—one with a tiny gauge and another with fibrous papers on which I spooned bits of moist soil, then watched for color clues. I got different gauge readings every time I sampled the same soil, and my test papers never turned identical colors.

I turned to the Yellow Pages.

Experts who test soil samples are listed under "Laboratories—Testing." They send foolproof instructions for collecting samples. To get an idea of a garden's overall pH, soil is gathered from several sites, then mixed inside a plastic storage bag and mailed for testing.

Reports from soil laboratories don't merely assign numerical pH values, they tell you what to do about them. If, for instance, that site you've set your eyes on for roses proves to be so acidic that only rhododendrons or azaleas would be happy growing there, you might be told to add limestone to make it more alkaline. Conversely, if the site of your rose dreams is too alkaline, you might be instructed to give it an acidic boost of soil sulfur.

Besides revealing pH, soil analyses tell about soil salinity (whether you're under- or overfertilizing), soil fertility (whether nutrients are available), and how to correct for any deficiencies. If you fertilize with an irrigation system, a soil report taken from several areas will reveal whether your garden is being watered evenly or only in pinpoint spots.

Once you've corrected the pH of the soil in which your roses grow (which you should do annually), fertilize accordingly. When you begin and end, of course, will vary with where you garden. In southern California, for instance, where roses blossom from early April until as late as Christmas, fertilizers are applied over a longer period than they are, say, in New England, where blossoming may not commence until June and conclude in October. If you request your local soil laboratory to suggest a feeding program for your roses, including when you should begin and end it, they will.

One fertilizer I'm sold on is Epsom salts, properly known as magnesium sulfate and available even from your corner grocer. I scatter $1/2$ cup of Epsom salts around the drip line of rosebushes twice a year—at the beginning of and midway through each season. Magnesium sulfate is more than a trace element; it promotes basal breaks—those desirable growths that spring from bud unions to form the major canes on rosebushes.

FINGER PRUNING

Rosebushes that are properly planted, mulched, and fertilized go bananas in spring by throwing out more growth than they can realistically support. The remedy, "nipping in the bud," requires no equipment other than your fingers; new growth is so supple that it can be rubbed off with your thumbs.

Check bud unions first. Those red swellings you see are just what you desire, of course, but healthy bushes often sprout too many. Ten or twelve new canes appearing on a bush you just pruned to six may be more than the bush can ultimately support.

First, rub off any buds that are growing in the middle of the bush. Next, try to anticipate whether those you leave will interfere with others as they grow. If you worry that everything can't coexist, rub some off.

In chapter 13 I recommend making "knobby cuts" when you're not certain where else to properly prune. The places where these cuts are made harbor lots of dormant eyes—too many, in fact, for all to remain. When three sprouts form in close proximity, try rubbing the middle one out and hope that the other two will grow away from each other. If even more are massed in one spot, rub off half.

The advantages of finger pruning might not sound like welcome news to those of you in search of as many roses as your garden can produce, but remember that contented rosebushes have aspirations they can't always sustain and that the laterals on which stems grow must support all the growth you leave. If you're in search of medium to large blossoms on stems strong enough to support them, you must eliminate surplus growth.

BLIND GROWTH

In spite of loving care, every now and then growth develops that looks as if it's going

When roses start to grow in spring, they literally have at it. When you see stems with more new growth than they can realistically support, you must rub some of it off (finger-prune), after which you'll be rewarded with good cutting roses whose stems don't rub against each other.

A novice rose grower gave me nightmares once when she told me that she cut off her first rose growth because "it was red, not green." That's how roses are—spring's growth looks like it belongs in autumn. As blossoming approaches, as if on cue, foliage turns from mahogany red to emerald green.

to result in a bloom but doesn't. Such growths are called "blind" because they continue to develop without producing buds.

The problem is satisfying yourself when growth is indeed blind. Certain rose varieties are tricky and reveal their buds late in the development of their stems, while others produce buds at odd angles or at spots where you're not used to scrutinizing.

The best way of determining whether or not growth is indeed blind is to compare it with growth you know isn't. When a budless stem develops that is distinctly longer than all the other stems on a bush that already have buds, pinch it back to a set of leaflets pointing away from the center of the bush. Never decide that growth is blind by comparing a budless stem on one bush to that on another variety. Rosebushes are strictly individual when it comes to how they display bud formation.

DISBUDDING

Disbudding is nothing more than deciding whether you want one-to-a-stem blooms or sprays of blossoms on a single stem, depending on your own preference or on what is generally considered most beautiful for each rose variety you grow.

One-to-a-stem disbudding is meant mostly for Modern Hybrid Teas, many of which produce only one bud per stem anyway, as if they already know that that's how they're prettiest. Others produce one large bud at the end of a stem and smaller buds, usually two, just beneath.

The large bud, properly called the terminal bud, is the one you want to leave. Side buds should be removed when they get to be about $1/4$ inch long, when they

With roses that bloom in sprays, like 'Love', you should snap out the center bud to help all others open at the same time. If you forget, and spot something like this, just pluck it out with its stem something shorter than an inch and put it in a low-necked, opaque container (be sure to keep the stem in water).

Some roses, such as 'Electron', seem unaware that their blooms are prettiest one-to-a-stem. If you think they are, just snap off a side bud with your fingers as soon as you notice it forming. Otherwise, it will drain energy from the main bud. On the other hand, if you like it, leave it. Just don't hope too hard that it will ever open.

When you go to prune your rosebushes, you'll find some wood with practically no thorns at all. With other bushes, it's difficult to find a cranny that doesn't harbor a vicious thorn. Degree of thorniness has no bearing on a bush's growth habits or the quality, color, or fragrance of its bloom.

can be grasped at the base and snapped off close to the stem without leaving a stub. When making these snaps, be certain to hold on to the terminal bud so that you don't end up with it in the palm of your hand.

Side buds can be left, of course, to develop into blooms themselves. They'll always defer to the terminal bud, however, and open only after it has finished blooming. If you imagine that side buds will open in a vase after the terminal bud has finished blossoming, forget it; they won't. If you like the looks of side buds anyway, leave them.

Disbudding for sprays is the exact opposite of disbudding for one-to-a-stem blooms. For sprays of blossoms, terminal buds are removed and side buds are left to develop. Terminal buds left in sprays will develop fully and open before side buds have a chance at maturity. If varieties look better in sprays, remove terminal buds and channel energy into the spray formation. What's more, do it early so that no scar is left.

Please don't imagine that disbudding is necessary; it isn't. Gardeners disbud only if they plan to exhibit their blossoms for competition or if they plan to enjoy

blooms as cut flowers without unsightly scars from bud removal. Otherwise, many rose varieties could drive you mad if you intended to keep up with their disbudding needs. Finally, if you decide to cut a spray of blossoms whose terminal bud should have been removed as soon as it was spotted, maturing side buds will eventually camouflage the scar of its removal.

UNWANTED GROWTH

Although the majority of growth appearing on rosebushes will thrill you, some of it can drive you to despair. As soon as you know it's undesirable, get rid of it.

Rose foliage comes in sets of three, five, seven, and higher odd numbers of leaflets. Although you'll treasure them all, the leaflet sets to which you'll eventually pay the most attention have five leaves each.

No unwanted growth is more vexing than dieback, particularly since no one is certain of its cause. Classically, dieback occurs when any rose wood is cut at the wrong place, after which stems start to die in a downward direction and keep dying until the spot is reached where a proper cut should have been made in the first place. Unfortunately, dieback doesn't always stop there, sometimes progressing instead all the way down to the bud union.

The key to proper eradication of dieback is to cut it out as soon as you spot it. Not only should dieback be removed in a timely fashion, successive cuts should be made as long as you spot brown rings within the pith of the wood you cut away. If you see brown, keep cutting. When you reach the point of healthy greenish white pith with no brown rings, dieback has been arrested.

You should also rid your bushes of yellow foliage as soon as you're convinced it's permanently yellowed. Green leaves turn yellow either from age or to signal a bush's need, usually for iron or nitrogen. Once yellowed, leaves are of little use to plants, which will only waste time trying to make them well. Remove them.

The first leaves to yellow on rosebushes are generally those at the bottoms of bushes. You can kill two birds with one stone by removing them, since you'll simultaneously discourage spider mites, which get their start on leaves close to the ground. Many rosarians advocate "summer pruning," the removal of all yellowed leaves and spindly growth on the bottom quarter of rosebushes. Not only will air circulation be improved, sprays of water during normal irrigation will discourage insects.

Unfortunately, no amount of good maintenance will control certain insects or fungal diseases. For those problems, you have no choice but to consider spraying.

ELEVEN

Spraying

Although all gardeners I know pray for the day when they no longer have to spray their rosebushes for diseases and insects, that day has not yet arrived, and roses continue to have more specific diseases named for them than for any other flower. Before dealing with the nitty-gritty, however, it's important to understand the diseases and insects most closely associated with rosedom.

FUNGAL DISEASES

Roses are potentially threatened by so many diseases that whole books have been devoted to the subject, such as the comprehensive *Compendium of Rose Diseases.* Chances are, however, you'll never be plagued with anything but mildew, rust, and blackspot. If you learn to control these "big three," you've got it made. How severely any of these nuisances will affect your rosebushes depends on where you garden.

Powdery mildew is so integrally associated with fungus among roses that it transcends locale. The first signs of powdery mildew are leaves that hold their color but begin to crinkle. Then small patches of mold appear that develop into spore-bearing fungal filaments on foliage, stems, thorns, or the works.

When leaves begin to crinkle without changing colors, stay on the lookout for small patches of mold—the earlier mildew is arrested, the better. Roses mildew because of certain weather patterns, crowded plantings, or water deprivation.

Classically, powdery mildew is caused by warm days and cool nights; it also occurs in overcrowded plantings and in damp shady gardens where air circulation is poor. Rosebushes stressed from a thirst for water are also prime targets for a powdery mildew infestation.

Rust looks just like it sounds—reddish orange pustules that resemble warts on the undersides of leaves. Left unchecked, rust works its way to the top sides of leaves, eventually defoliating entire rosebushes. In order for rust spores to germinate, leaf surfaces must remain wet for four hours, as they will during periods of winter rains, summer fogs, or extended periods of heavy dew. Insects, wind, and rain spread disease spores, especially if fallen leaves are left on the ground to dampen.

Blackspot develops during humid weather, particularly where summer rainfalls are abundant or watering is excessive. The fungus manifests itself with black then yellow-fringed rings on both sides of leaves that enlarge as they develop. As blackspot infestations worsen, whole leaves turn from green to yellow.

INSECTS

Although they don't exhaust the list, three insects are roses' worst enemies: aphids, thrips, and mites. It's a toss-up as to which is most disgusting.

Aphids are tiny, soft-bodied, sucking creatures that appear in congested numbers on tender rose growth, particularly buds. Although they're usually green (of-

Thrips are microscopic flying insects with a color preference for white and off-white blossoms. The distressing sign of a thrips infestation is a blossom just on the brink of beauty suddenly developing brown flecks on outer petals. The rest is unappealingly downhill.

ten the identical shade as the growth they're sucking dry), some aphids are reddish brown. Whatever their color, aphids are abundant in early spring.

If you haven't noticed aphids, but you've seen ants on your bushes, look closely: ants maintain a symbiotic relationship with aphids, protecting them from other predators while they feed off a honeylike substance secreted by the aphids.

Thrips are heat-loving, flying insects with a partiality for white and pastel roses. Because they're practically microscopic, to see thrips at all you must break open a bloom and shake its petals over a white cloth while looking for quick, tiny movements.

Mites are actually spiders. Like thrips, spider mites are microscopic and leave a telltale calling card—in this case, a web underneath leaves at the bottom of rosebushes. Although most spider mites are red, some are green or yellow; they all suck leaf juices and render the leaves dry. Spider mites are known to thrive in hot, humid weather and also where air circulation is poor.

I wish I could tell you that the trios of fungal diseases and insects just discussed are all you must ever worry about, but

At first, mildew is confined to foliage. As it spreads, wood becomes infected, too; even thorns. Whether you attack mildew with organic fungicides or with chemicals, do something about it when you see it; left unchecked, mildew is an ugly sight.

Rust is one of the best-named diseases in all of horticulture because it looks precisely as it sounds. If rusty warts on the undersides of leaves aren't controlled, they can defoliate whole plants. Rust occurs most frequently during periods of excess moisture.

The time to respond to blackspot is the moment you spot it. Here, only telltale black spots are visible, which, left unchecked, would develop yellow fringes and eventually rob leaves of all green. Some geographical areas are climatically conducive to blackspot. Thankfully, certain nearby rosarians know how to combat it.

they're not. You must also stay on the prowl for exotic diseases such as crown gall, cane canker, and downy mildew (which has nothing whatsoever to do with either down or powdery mildew), and insects such as diabrotica, rose midge, whitefly, and the ever-unpopular Japanese beetle.

The real question is how to deal with whatever scourges plague your roses. You have two choices: chemicals or organics. While I secretly long to march with the organic approach, I long ago gave up on such "safe" treatments. Although I'm politically correct whenever possible, I've bent my rules in the garden. I have no intention of handing over my precious roses to a fungus destined to blight my bushes or to any insect with a terminal case of the munchies.

CHEMICALS

Chemical sprays have developed such a nasty reputation among gardeners that they're discussed in hushed tones as the "C word." Before you, too, banish the C word from your gardening vocabulary, be certain that you fully understand the warnings printed on the labels of chemical sprays. If directions are followed to the letter, many products aren't nearly as dangerous as you may imagine.

As part of their pesticide registration regulations, most states require manufacturers of chemical materials to clearly label their products in one of three toxicity categories, depending on their LD50—a term you must understand if you have any intention of employing garden chemicals.

LD50, usually listed as oral (the amount that must be swallowed) but sometimes quoted as dermal (the amount that must be absorbed by the skin), is an expression of the lethal dose in milligrams

Downy mildew is a horrible horticultural mis-nomer—the fungal disease has nothing what-soever to do with down. Disfiguring purple blotches appear anywhere on rosebushes, from canes to sepals. The very best preventive is a dormant spray with a heavy concentration of zinc or copper.

Aphids are about as ugly as insects get, both in appearance and in action. To make matters worse, the devious creatures are often the very color of the buds they suck dry. I know garden-ers who pluck them off by hand. I spray.

Don't even look for spider mites—they're mi-croscopic. If you suspect that these dreads of summer are visiting your garden, inspect the undersides of leaves for webs. Fortunately for organic gardeners, spider mites leave after the first spray of water. They also return.

per kilogram of body weight that kills 50 percent of laboratory test animals.

Chemicals with an LD50 between 0 and 49 are classified as Toxicity Category I, with labels marked "danger" or "poi-son" (normally accompanied by a skull and crossbones). I believe that these chem-icals have no place in the garden, ever.

Toxic chemicals in Category II have an LD50 somewhere between 50 and 499 and are considered moderately toxic, hence the "warning" label. The probable lethal dose for a 150-pound man is be-tween 1 teaspoon and 1 ounce.

Chemicals in Category III have "cau-tion" printed on their labels because LD50

rates between 500 and 1,999 mean that the average man's lethal dose is between 1 ounce and 1 pint.

For perspective on the relative toxic-ity of common items, you should know some LD50 ratings (the lower the LD50, the more toxic the chemical). Nicotine is 53; caffeine, 192; aspirin, 1,240; table salt, 3,320.

Understand also that the probable lethal dosages of garden chemicals refer only to concentrations of the active ingre-dient of the product, not the commer-cially available diluted form—to croak, you'd have to drink even more of that. Still, you don't want even a headache,

so if you decide to admit moderate- to low-toxicity chemicals to your garden, take precautions.

First, to avoid any possibility of irri-tation, cover all body parts and wear goggles and rubber gloves, including when mixing spray materials. Never use a solu-tion stronger than the manufacturer sug-gests, don't remove chemicals from the labeled containers, and keep materials stored far from any child's reach. Finally, when you must spray, use the safest ma-terial for the job.

It will do me no good to recommend precise fungicides, insecticides, or miti-cides, because they're sure to be yanked

The manner in which you spray rosebushes is more vital than the spray materials themselves. To cover plants properly, begin spraying from their bases upward. Although the undersides of leaves will be covered first, drifts of spray will cover the upper sides, too. When you have only a few plants to spray, backpack sprayers work well. No matter which type of sprayer you use, be sure to cover all body parts and wear goggles while employing chemical formulations.

from commerce or replaced by improved formulations before these words go to print. Besides, what's known by one name in certain states is marketed under another name elsewhere. For treating whatever ails your roses, check with either your local agricultural agents or consult rosarians nearest your garden.

While I can't be explicit in recommending chemicals, I want to be *exact* in recommending proper spray technique. The manner in which rosebushes are sprayed is as important as the spray materials themselves.

Rosebushes should be misted with spray materials. Fortunately, all com-mercial sprayers, from hand-held to commercial models, are capable of emitting fine mists. Proper technique requires first spraying the undersides of leaves, where disease begins, starting at the bottom of the bush and working toward the top. Since mists of spray are being directed upward, a constant fallout drifts down and covers the tops of leaves. When the top of the bush is reached, most foliage surfaces will already be covered. Those that aren't can be finished with a single downward shot of spray.

Unless you spray for something such as thrips that attack blooms, don't spray rose blossoms; chemical sprays discolor them. Be forewarned, however, that it's almost impossible to keep all spray materials off flowers.

Certain spray materials spread un-evenly. If you learn that you must use one of these noncovering formulas, you must first add a "spreader sticker" to the liquid spray to ensure complete foliar coverage. You can buy commercial spreader stickers, but mild household detergent at the rate of 3 to 4 drops per gallon of spray material works perfectly well.

You'll bless your effective spray program when you harvest healthy rose blossoms accompanied by attractive foliage. At last the fun begins.

$\mathcal{P}runing$

$\mathcal{N}$othing about horticulture frightens novice gardeners more than pruning. "You expect me to cut it off *where*?" they ask incredulously. "Nothing will be left," they grumble. "Where will this year's blossoms come from?"

In spite of such protestations, rosebushes must be pruned for two reasons: (1) to eliminate nonproductive (or damaged) growth, thereby encouraging new, and (2) to shape plants.

Dormant rosebushes aren't certain which way you want them to grow unless you prune to budding eyes pointed in the right direction. Unless aimed correctly, rambling and climbing roses don't know whether to scramble this way or that. Without an annual thinning, shrub roses become thorny tangles of insignificant flowers on spindly stems. Face it—we rosarians have no choice but to prune.

WHEN TO PRUNE

Gardeners get fidgety soon after their roses have stopped blossoming. Overcome from the joys of maintaining bushes and harvesting their blossoms, rosarians sense an irresistible urge to do *something*. Although I'm quick to advocate attention to roses almost any time of the year, this is a time to relax. After bushes have served duty for an entire season, they need time to collect starches and sugars in preparation for their next season. Give them a break.

Ideal times for pruning roses vary by which roses they are,

In just one year in the ground, garden roses become a tangle of thorny wood that must be unraveled with pruning shears. Don't even consider the job until you have removed all foliage and given bushes a chance to sprout new growth that signals where strategic cuts should be made.

but more about that later. For now, let's discuss repeat-blooming varieties.

Debates over the proper time to prune remontant roses focus on winter versus spring pruning. Wintertime pruners point out that rosebushes pruned early would just as soon rid themselves of useless wood as soon as possible. Spring pruners live in fear of unseasonal frosts capable of nipping new growth in the bud. Before deciding what's right for you, read what my zonal rosebuddies have to say in chapter 15 about when they prune.

I've erred in both directions. One year, when those people who throw darts at weather maps predicted an exceptionally mild winter, I pruned too early and lived to regret it when a biting cold snap damaged early growth. Another year, I procrastinated because the "forecasters" assured me that winter would linger. It didn't, and my roses blossomed two weeks later than they would have if I had gone ahead and pruned when I sensed it was right.

There's no foolproof answer for when to prune, unless, of course, you're sure that dormancy is broken and there's no threat of another hard freeze. If so, prune as soon as you can.

PRE-PRUNING

Nothing facilitates pruning more than stripping bushes of their foliage about two weeks before you plan to prune. When rosebushes are defoliated, Mother Nature sends an urgent message for foliar rejuvenation. In response, bushes begin swelling where new growth is to appear. These "eyes"—junctures of leaf formations on the stems on which they grow—signal precisely where judicious pruning cuts should be made. The dormant eyes were present all along, of course; they simply weren't visible to the human eye until stripping stimulated them to swell, turn red, and become obvious.

Foliage should be cut, not ripped, off. If you tear leaves off, you risk damaging bark tissue at the exact points of dormant eyes, thereby stunting their development.

Whether or not you worry that rosebushes are harboring disease spores from the previous year's growing season, seize the opportunity afforded by their stripped state for spraying plants with dormant sprays. These special materials are formulated to clean up any diseases that might be lying about and to provide a healthy environment for new growth.

Even rosarians who resist spraying in general are supportive of dormant sprays—they're safe and extremely effective. Many dormant sprays have a sulfur base, although the precise formulation doesn't seem to matter much. I seem to purchase a different dormant spray every year and have noticed no real differences among them, but consistent effectiveness.

Downy mildew, a disease new to American gardeners, has become a mighty threat to rose growers. The very best treatment for downy mildew is prevention, which is best achieved with applications of a zinc- or copper-based dormant spray material.

While spraying dormant bushes, spray the ground around them, too. Fallen leaves and cuttings may harbor disease spores, and dormant sprays will eliminate the danger of diseases wintering over.

TOOLS

Just as for maintaining rosebushes, no tool is more important for pruning than shears. If you've purchased good heavy-duty shears, as I encouraged you to do in chapter 12, you can use the same ones; you'll simply have to sharpen them more often because pruning dulls shears more quickly than does harvesting blossoms. Sharpen shears well before you begin pruning and again each time you feel them compromise a clean cut.

Rosebushes grown for longer than one year develop canes too thick to cut with shears; these must be cut with loppers or a saw. Loppers have cutting blades not much larger than those of shears, but their long handles afford the leverage required for making thick cuts.

Canes growing from the bud union often develop so close to each other that there is no convenient entry for shears or loppers. Pruning saws designed specifically for these situations are ideal, and so are those saws called keyhole.

Before approaching rosebushes at pruning time, arm yourself with the right equipment. Sharp shears are a must, as are loppers (for oversized wood). Because thorns have been whittled sharp by winter winds, gloves are mandatory.

Gloves are a must, preferably leather ones. The thorns of many roses are vicious, particularly at pruning time when they have hardened and winter winds have whittled them sharp. While pruning, you must hold on to the canes being cut to keep them from falling into the bush (worse yet, on you).

Proper rose-pruning techniques depend on the type of rosebushes being pruned. Because Modern varieties are the most demanding, let's begin with them.

MODERN ROSES

Before grabbing pruners and heading toward a Modern rosebush, fix in your mind's eye what a properly pruned bush should look like. Ideally, Modern rosebushes should form a classic urn shape, with canes radiating from the bud union, arching outward and upward around a free center. The centers of rosebushes don't need to be opened simply for appearance but, more important, so that light can reach their interior growth, thereby aiding the metabolic process for chlorophyll production. Also, rosebushes free of growth in their centers have better air circulation, which helps prevent fungal diseases such as mildew. Blossoms appearing in the center of rosebushes are

This is my idea of a properly pruned Floribunda rosebush. Most Floribundas grow lower to the ground than Hybrid Teas do and must be pruned shorter. Also, the framework for urn-shaped bushes must be fashioned with pruning shears.

Pruning rules are made to be broken, such as the number of canes left on a well-pruned bush. If varieties prove that they're capable of sustaining more than an average number of canes, leave them. This particular Hybrid Tea rosebush likes to be pruned low; by midsummer, blooms will be at eye level.

wasted anyway, because they inevitably tear from being rubbed against other unwanted growth.

WHAT TO CUT

Before agonizing over difficult pruning decisions, start with easy ones. All twiggy growth must come off, as should unhealthy or dead wood and canes that cross the center of the bush.

Rose wood on a single bush varies in color depending on its age. Young canes are often red or some shade of healthy-looking green; older wood is darker, often scaly. Some rosebushes facilitate pruning by color-coding their canes; others produce wood of the same color, regardless of age, making pith examination mandatory.

Pith is soft wood within bark. Creamy white or green pith without brown flecks is healthy; brown or blackened wood is either old or already dead. Besides visual inspection, you'll learn to judge the age of rose wood by how easily you can cut into it—the younger, the easier.

Once flimsy wood has been cut away and centers cleared, stand back from a bush and decide how much more wood you want to leave. I never leave fewer than four canes on healthy bushes, more usually, six (up to ten on vigorous growers that have proved to me that they can accommodate them).

Severity of pruning is determined either by where you garden or by the general effect you seek. *Light* pruning requires a minimum of cutting, with bushes left tall, after only twiggy, wrong, or dead wood is removed. Next season's blooms will be short-stemmed but profuse. *Moderate* pruning leaves five to ten, 1- to 4-foot canes per bush, depending on the vigor of the variety. Generally, half of each cane should be pruned off. Moderate

Certain rose varieties pout if their bushes are pruned too low, and they then spend the summer growing to the height at which they're comfortable blooming. It will do you no good to try to change their ways.

Some rosebushes assist you at pruning time by color-coding their canes. The canes you most want to keep are the red ones that are still bursting with vigor. The green ones are more than a year old, but they still have plenty of life in them. Commence pruning by cutting out canes that are gray or a dead shade of brown—they're too old to harbor blossoms.

pruning produces not only a fine garden display but also some long-stemmed roses. *Severe* pruning, which often leaves only four canes per bush cut lower than 1 foot tall, is either for gardeners who live in cruel winter climates where winter protection is mandatory or for those bloom fanciers in search of the longest-stemmed roses possible.

Keep in mind that severity of pruning (assuming that you don't *have* to be severe due to climate) is determined in part by the rose varieties you grow. It will do

you no good, for instance, to try to change the growth habits of a lofty grower such as the Grandiflora 'Queen Elizabeth', which, if pruned too low, will refuse to bloom until it reaches the height at which it prefers to flower.

While there are no cardinal rules where pruning is concerned, certain generalities help. For example, try to leave no wood on a rosebush less thick than a pencil (unless, of course, you're pruning a Miniature rosebush or a diminutive Floribunda whose canes never reach such

dimensions). Or, if a bush has proved itself to be a hardy grower and bloomer, leave more than the customary number of canes. If the best wood comes from the center and crosses the middle of the bush, leave it alone and prune around it. If you grow more than one bush of a variety, try pruning them differently to see for yourself what suits you best.

If you're a novice at pruning rosebushes, I recommend that you leave all wood on rosebushes that you're not sure should come out; it can always be taken out later when the growth it develops clarifies whether or not it should remain. As you gain confidence in pruning techniques, I recommend the opposite—when you have doubts about the wood's worth, cut it out.

Often the healthiest canes on a rosebush are growing too close to each other and you'll yearn to spread them apart. You can. Decide, within reason, how far apart you'd like to spread them and cut a section that length from a cane you've already pruned (from that bush or any other). Insert the ends of your spreader into thorns on the two canes you're separating, and don't worry if you can't find it again after foliage develops. No harm will come if the prop lingers until you prune

again the following year, by which time the canes will be permanently spread apart and it can be removed.

WHERE TO CUT

If you've followed the advice at the beginning of this chapter and stripped your rosebushes of their foliage at least two weeks before you intend to prune them, you'll have no difficulty spotting dormant eyes—they will have swollen and turned red. Look for dormant eyes facing *outward* from the center of the bush and make pruning cuts $1/4$ inch above them.

When I first grew roses, and for many years thereafter, I was assured that proper cuts should be made precisely at 45-

degree angles, with the downward slope toward the bush's center. I've since learned that this is nothing more than needless busywork. I'm still careful not to make cuts so close to the budding eye that I might damage it, and I generally avoid flat cuts where water could collect, but I've long since abandoned the 45-degree-angle requirement.

Often the precise spot at which you yearn to prune has no budding eye pointed in the right direction. You have two choices for how to treat this aggravating situation. First, cut higher than you'd like to, planning to cut lower later after additional eyes swell. Or, make what rosarians call "knobby" cuts, which leave $1/4$-inch stubs on last year's stems. Dormant eyes abound just under the junctures of stems and the canes on which they grow. Knobby stubs aren't as attractive as clean cuts above a budding eye, but they'll do the job and impending foliar growth will soon disguise them anyway.

When whole canes need to be removed from a bush, they must be cut off at the bud union. Here, too, rosarians quibble over precisely how these cuts should be made. Hard-nosers say that cuts should be made flush with the bud union to keep it looking respectable. Gardeners in search of as much bloom as possible recommend leaving a $1/4$-inch stub under which dormant eyes abound. Although I'm not a fence-sitter in matters such as these, I find myself subscribing to both schools. When a bush is so vigorous that it produces more canes than I can keep up with anyway, I

Test rose wood for health by cutting into canes and examining the pith within. As long as you see brown, keep cutting. Healthy wood capable of producing good flowers is reached when pith is evenly colored light green.

Light pruning demands only the removal of twiggy and dead wood. Although the blossoms that follow will be short-stemmed, they'll be profuse.

Moderate pruning requires that five to ten canes be left on bushes. Depending on the severity of winter where you garden, canes may be up to 4 feet long or shorter than 1 foot.

Severe pruning leaves fewer canes per bush, often cut down to 1-foot lengths. Gardeners who prune severely expect either trophies at rose shows or a cruel winter.

cut flush with the bud union. With less vigorous varieties, I leave that stub and hope that my fellow greedy bloom-seekers are correct (they are more often than not).

POST-PRUNING

Should pruning cuts be sealed with orange shellac, rose paste, tree-wound paint, or aerosol sprays designed for such purposes? It depends on whether or not you live where caneborers exist. If local agricultural agents say not, don't bother.

As for sealing pruning "wounds," that shouldn't be necessary either if you prune at the right time. If, on the other hand, you learn that sealing is required for where you garden, seal only cuts larger than $1/2$ inch in diameter; the rest will seal themselves.

Cleanups, however, are vital no matter where you garden. Cuttings, foliage, and twigs that inevitably fall to the ground during pruning are setups for disease. Remove them all and throw them away (never mulch them).

SPECIES AND ANTIQUE ROSES

Species and once-blooming roses existed long before man learned about the neces-

sities for pruning or had tools for the job. Moreover, many of these rosebushes mature into gargantuan shapes that won't respond to general rules for shaping anyway. Besides, gardeners often choose these house-eaters because only such monsters fill large spaces, and pruning may lessen expectations.

Most experts say that if roses in these categories are pruned at all, cuts should be made right after plants flower, so that new growth will be encouraged on which next season's crop will blossom. I agree, but only to a point.

First, I don't prune these roses at all

When two canes you want to leave on a pruned rosebush grow too closely together, separate them with a cutting anchored into thorns and don't worry about removing your stretcher until the next pruning season, by which time the canes will have grown forever apart.

The only way to make judicious pruning cuts is to strip bushes of all foliage and wait two weeks for budding eyes to develop. Then, with the help of sharp, heavy-duty shears, pruning slices can be made at strategic points.

for the first three years I grow them; with some, not until they've been in the ground for five years. The only exception to this seemingly neglectful attitude involves cutting out dead or twiggy growth any time I spot it, regardless of season.

After these Heirloom Roses have grown to the approximate sizes I'm looking for, I begin pruning just after they've finished flowering each season. Although I'm still not fixed on general shaping just yet, I remove all wood that either has proved itself unproductive or looks as though it's about to become so. Then I grant only general garden care for the balance of the season and strip foliage late in winter, two weeks before I intend to consider any further pruning.

I realize that this approach is unconventional, that purists would say that all pruning should be completed when flowering is over, but I've found that the abundance of foliage confuses me. Remember that just because these bushes quit flowering, they don't stop growing, and their abundant foliage camouflages those spots where judicious pruning cuts should be made.

Two weeks after foliage has been stripped, dormant eyes swell, turn red, and show me where to properly place my shears. Only then do I seriously prune for shape and size.

CLIMBING ROSES

Climbers repeat their blossoms during each season and should be pruned late in winter. Climbers should also be stripped of foliage before getting pruned, not just to encourage dormant eyes to swell but also because naked canes are easier to shape into classic climbing form.

For their first several years of growth, Climbing roses require little pruning except for the removal of dead or spindly

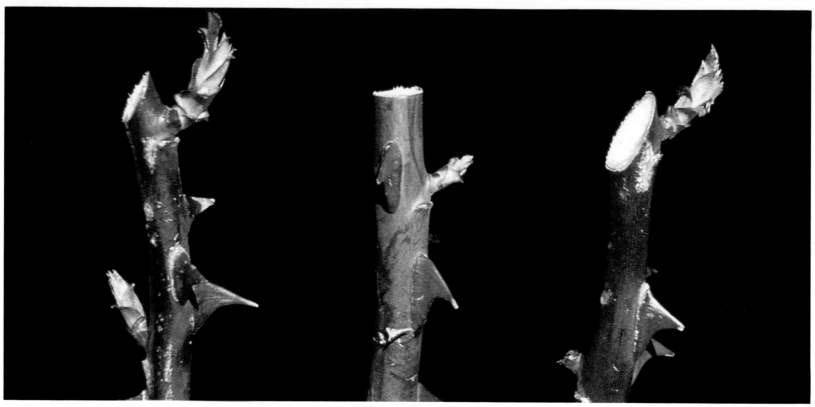

Before you approach your rosebushes with shears, memorize the perfect cut—the one on the left. Make your cuts on 45-degree (approximately) slants, about ¹/₄ inch above a swelling bud eye. The cut in the middle is too stubby and too far removed from its new eye, and the one on the right cuts too sharply into new growth.

wood. Then, as vigorous varieties mature, more wood (including entire canes) must be sacrificed if plants are expected to remain within bounds.

The controversy over proper pruning for Climbers has nothing to do with main canes or strong laterals growing from them—those should simply be shaped into place with their tips pointed downward to ensure that sap flows throughout their lengths. Argument, however, exists for how to handle the stems that grow from these canes and laterals. They are, after all, the wood from which blossoms are produced. Many experts advocate cutting back all these side shoots to 3-inch lengths. Several rosarians devoted to Climbing roses, however, maintain that side shoots should be cut back to a mere stub on the heftier wood from which they sprout. The rationale behind this latter theory is that abundant dormant eyes exist where stems meet canes and laterals and that leaving short side stems will only encourage weak stems. Again, I side partially with both camps, depending on whether I grow certain Climbers for general garden display or in hopes of producing blossoms for cutting on strong stems—the stronger my quest for sturdy cut flowers, the harder I prune.

RAMBLING ROSES

Rambling roses demand even less pruning than Climbers do, mainly because Ramblers blossom only once each season and their overall shape is generally informal. Because ramblers are usually rampant growers, however, more of their basal growth must be cut out each season to make room for new. Ramblers that are *R. multiflora* hybrids, for instance, are so vigorous that new basal growth is often choked out unless older wood is first sacrificed.

If you've been told that caneborers live near where you garden, you might have to seal pruning wounds with orange shellac or a special paint. Before you go to the trouble, check with a local agricultural agent; you may find that large cuts need sealing, but small ones seal themselves.

Guide wires are a must if roses are expected to cling close to brick walls. Also, climbing roses require special pruning techniques to increase the flow of sap all along flowering wood.

When you go to prune your rosebushes, you may discover canes in shapes you never imagined possible. Once bushes are masked in spring foliage, miraculous growth patterns develop during summer, especially in the center of bushes. If a cane is in the way, prune it out, but remember that crooked wood isn't necessarily weak wood.

On the opposite extreme, Banksian roses are generally left unpruned altogether, as are certain other specific varieties such as the voracious 'Kiftsgate' and the evergreen 'Félicité et Perpétue'. Just as with Modern Roses, it's important to know the pruning preferences of individual Rambling roses.

STANDARDS

Roses grown as standards should be pruned when and how their bush counterparts are, except that they must never be allowed to grow as large, else they become top-heavy. Pruning to outward-facing eyes is paramount, since the head of the standard must always be kept in shape and plants must not become lopsided.

If you like weeping roses grown as standards, go easy on pruning, especially of long weeping stems; otherwise, plants become too bushy. With many weeping varieties, only thinning and nipping back of tips is necessary.

After experimenting with a number of pruning techniques, I've learned that I have considerable latitude for what I consider proper pruning and that many varieties are far less demanding than I previously thought. I've never taken shears to my shrubs of 'Nevada', for instance, probably because they're growing in considerable shade, but also because they seem to know how much space they should take up. Similarly, I've not pruned my Modern landscape rose 'Bonica' simply because I'm experimenting with how long I can avoid the issue (the end doesn't seem in sight). As discussed in chapter 18, I bend all rules when it comes to Miniature roses. As for my Modern rosebushes, however, I follow to the letter every suggestion mentioned in this chapter.

$\mathcal{P}$ropagating

osebushes are propagated either by grafting onto rootstock or from cuttings. There are advantages to both methods. Grafted roses mature quickly because they grow atop rootstocks known for their ability to quickly form massive roots. Roses growing on their own roots from cuttings develop slowly but are reputed to be free of virus and winter-hardy.

GRAFTED ROSES

Rootstocks, as you recall from chapter 9, are known not for their flowers (which are insignificant, even ugly) but rather for their ability to form sturdy root systems so that hybrids grafted onto them develop as swiftly as possible. Although there are theoretically multiple numbers of roses capable of serving as rootstock, in the United States seven principal varieties have been used and an eighth one is on the rise.

R. canina, commonly known as the dog rose because a distillation of its roots was a reputed treatment for combating rabies, has always been a favored rootstock in Europe but has never been successful in America, probably because hybrids grow slowly when grafted onto it. Advocates point out, however,

'Ragged Robin', properly known as R. chinensis, *is from old French stock, but it grows well in California and produces the nicest flower I know of any variety of rootstock. While other rootstocks may develop deeper roots faster, the blooms from most are downright ugly.*

that plants grafted onto *R. canina* are long-lived. *R. canina* is particularly thorny and prone to suckering.

R. chinensis, commonly known as 'Gloire des Rosomanes' or 'Ragged Robin', comes from old French stock. It caught on in California because it withstands heat and dry conditions and also because it is resistant to nematodes. *R. chinensis* is a steady grower and willingly accepts grafts over an extended season.

R. 'Dr. Huey' is currently the most commonly used rootstock in America, not only because it stores well but also because its bark is thin (allowing for successful budding over an extended season), its exceptional vigor seems to stimulate even weak hybrids, and it adapts well to irrigation and alkaline soils. Drawbacks to 'Dr. Huey' include poor tolerance to sub-zero temperatures and susceptibility to blackspot and mildew.

R. multiflora is available in several "strains," some virtually thornless. Selected forms are widely adaptable to soils and climates across the United States, except in the South. Cuttings root well, grow vigorously, resist nematodes, and rarely sucker. The bark of *R. multiflora*, however, sometimes becomes so thick in late summer that budding is impossible.

R. x *noisettiana* 'Manettii' is a favorite rootstock for greenhouse and Miniature roses. 'Manettii' is also easily propagated, reasonably vigorous, and adaptable to sandy soils. Although 'Manettii' is rarely used for roses grown outdoors, it is said to produce blossoms of superior quality.

R. odorata is rarely used for outdoor varieties because it is not cold-hardy. It is, however, a favorite among greenhouse growers who appreciate its quickly forming, massive root system and its ability to adapt to both dry and wet growing conditions.

R. rugosa is a rootstock with mixed blessings. Although it produces shallow fibrous roots that sucker freely, plants budded onto it are reputed to be exceptionally long-lived. *R. rugosa* is also adamantly resistive to cold and a favorite for producing the upright stems used in standard (tree) roses.

The rootstock on the rise among American rose propagators is *R. fortuniana*. Although known for years to grow well in hot, sandy soils, *R. fortuniana* has recently been reported to perform better in Florida than any other rootstock variety, both because it adapts well to native soil and because it can be budded "high," for planting several inches above ground level.

OWN-ROOT ROSES

Roses on their own roots grow from cuttings. Although it takes longer to grow rosebushes from cuttings, advocates of own-root roses believe that such rosebushes are worth the wait. First, assuming that cuttings are taken from healthy plants, roses growing on their own roots are virus-free. Rose propagators have been plagued for years with rootstock infected with virus impossible to eradicate except with heat so intense that entire plants are sacrificed. If present, virus in rootstock is eventually transmitted to the hybrid, rendering it unsightly.

Second, because they grow on their own roots, roses taken from cuttings don't develop suckers. Finally, own-root roses are said to be more winter-hardy and to enjoy a longer life than do budded roses.

I've rooted only one rose myself. Years ago, when I first saw 'Sally Holmes' and coveted it on sight, I had no choice but to root it myself—it wasn't for sale anywhere in the United States.

A rose-growing friend sent me a plastic bag filled with cuttings and a note assuring me that I couldn't go wrong. "Sally will grow in any friendly soil," the note said. Sure enough, more than half my cuttings took—and my thumbs aren't entirely green in matters such as these.

When Rick Weeks opened his nursery at our ranch, he told me of his intentions to grow roses on their own roots. "You have a wonderful collection here," Rick said, "with several varieties no longer for sale. I want to experiment with rooting them." I wished him the best of luck and lent him all the references I had on the subject. His results are admirable, and the suggestions I offer for growing roses on their own roots are based on his experiences.

If you want to try rooting your own

roses, first select varieties from which you can realistically expect success. Almost all roses known as "Old garden rose" root well, particularly members of the Gallica, Damask, and Rugosa families.

Next, take cuttings from established rosebushes during either spring or fall, when plant cells within rose wood are most active. Supple stems terminating in buds just beginning to show color should be harvested from their bushes with at least four budding eyes, the swellings that signal new growth. Remove all but the uppermost set of leaflets.

A good rooting medium is composed equally of sand, peat moss, and perlite. Tips of cuttings should be dipped in a rooting stimulant (liquid seems better than powder) and inserted into the rooting soil with two eyes below and two above. Cuttings should then be placed in an area of 50 percent shade and kept moist with frequent misting.

If you've fallen in love with a rose that's no longer in commerce, try rooting it yourself. It's also wise to take more cuttings than you intend to plant, thereby increasing your chances that at least one of them will form a sturdy root system.

Among Modern Roses, the more vig-

The vast majority of rosebushes sold in the United States are propagated near Wasco, California, where immense growing fields are sights to behold during early summer and fall. To meet specific grading standards, field-grown roses must reach certain proportions by bare-root season.

Budding roses is the process of removing budwood from one stem and grafting it onto another. Here, a bud is extracted (along with a thin layer of outer tissue) from the stem of the hybrid rose on the left and placed on the stem of rootstock on the right. Special rubber bands hold the bud in place until it sprouts. Note that a portion of the leaf axil just below the bud is retained for ease of handling.

orous the hybrid, the greater are its chances for growing on its own roots. The majestic Grandiflora 'Queen Elizabeth', for instance, grows well on her own roots, whereas the relatively puny 'White Lightnin'' Grandiflora won't budge unless grafted onto vigorous rootstock. Similarly, the aggressive Floribunda 'Sea Pearl' has a better chance of growing on its own roots than does the diminutive 'Angel Face'.

Try rooting any Modern hybrid you like, but remember that roses are protected under patent for 17 years. If you intend to enjoy a rosebush you root yourself, then have a go at it, but *never* try to peddle it.

If the thermometer in your garden dips to 20 degrees F for five consecutive nights, you must afford rosebushes winter protection. Marsh hay is effective, especially when surrounded by Mother Nature's insulator—snow.

At the Boerner Botanical Garden in Wisconsin, research is conducted each year on new methods for winter protection of rosebushes. Plants must have insulation by late autumn if they're expected to survive sub-zero winters.

A popular method for protecting roses calls for tying bushes together at their tips, then forming a cylinder of quarter-inch mesh hardware cloth around each bush that can be filled with soil. Executed too soon, bushes won't go dormant.

The Bonnetts prune their roses no sooner than the second week of March (ideally during the last week of March) and resolve to complete pruning before the second weekend in April. Old garden roses enjoy their first peak of bloom shortly after mid-May and Modern Roses near the first weekend of June. Bloom cycles for remontant varieties are about every five to seven weeks, although there is considerable slowing in July and August. "The last decent rose of summer will be seen during the first week of October."

The ubiquitous 'Dr. Huey' seems to be the favored rootstock for desert areas because "it seems to have the strength to push deep into heavy clay soil and provide plants with good root systems." The Bonnetts recommend planting bushes with bud unions even with ground level and pruning them for the conventional one-third to one-half removal of each season's growth.

THE MIDWEST

When roses are expected to flourish in USDA Zone 5, winter protection becomes mandatory. Steve Rulo, who grows roses in Palos Park, Illinois, used to protect his roses the way most of his neighbors do; now he's constructed a structure to enclose his entire rose garden.

Conventional winter protection in this area calls for tying dormant canes together, mounding bushes with soil 10 inches above the ground, covering the mounds with cones into which ventilation holes have been punched, and weighing down the winter home with bricks. Even in such a cozy environment, bushes must first be planted with their bud unions at least 2 inches underground.

Although there were problems with this method (including the removal of soil each spring), Rulo followed these procedures in his early rose gardens and achieved good results. Now, in his new formal rectangular rose garden, Rulo has constructed temporary "houses" from 2 x 4 lumber, $^3/_8$-inch plywood side walls,

Although rosebushes may be mounded just as they are, frameworks are necessary around tree roses. Here, chicken wire is used to fashion a frame into which hay is stuffed. When winter is just around the corner, a canvas cover should be added.

When winter temperatures plummet to the degree that blankets of hay won't keep tree roses from freezing, standards are tipped into the ground and a wooden framework is constructed for holding additional soil in place. Snow will soon afford additional insulation.

Styrofoam cones are commercially available with removable lids. When temperatures are above 20 degrees F, lids are removed. Tips of canes must be cut to fit under the lid, then tied together so that they don't touch the sides of the cone.

and a 2-inch Styrofoam roof with permanent ventilation holes.

Because he believes that planting bushes with bud unions below soil level softens wood and retards the development of basal breaks, Rulo now plants bud unions at ground level; he mounds them religiously, however, no later than October 31 each year—the same date by which he puts the side walls of the winter houses into place. Since the roofs can be secured in a few hours' time, they're added only after dormant season is certain.

Although each spring differs, rosarians in this area prune between mid-April and May 1. Severity of pruning is dictated by the amount of healthy wood that survived the previous winter (hopefully, at least 6 inches). Rulo agrees with local rosarians who do their best to prune before significant new growth appears; otherwise, bushes suffer when pruning cuts are made below leafy developments. Blossoms appear in significant numbers by mid-June and repeat their cycles until almost the last week of October.

Rulo agrees with other rosarians in the Chicago area who state that rose petals' substance (the density of their starches) is more crucial than the number of petals per blossom. Among Modern Roses, 'Gold Medal', 'Olympiad', and 'Touch of Class' fill the bill.

THE DEEP FREEZE

Gardeners in USDA Zone 4, where average minimal winter temperatures plummet from −20 to −30 degrees F, have great difficulty overwintering roses. For the most part, gardeners in these chilly regions plant only the oldest of garden rose varieties (Gallica, Damask, Alba, Portland, and Moss), plus certain shrubs known for their hardiness, especially members of the Rugosa family. Few Modern Roses survive these winters even when given winter protection like that described for Zone 5. In many areas of Vermont, for instance, Modern Roses are treated like annuals and replanted each year.

Roses in the Garden

In *Garden Open Today*, Beverly Nichols, that silver-tongued British plants-man who minced no words where his opinions toward gardening were concerned, suggested that all gardens should be cut in half: "Even in stately homes of many acres the magic lies not so much in a grand parade of terraces or a noble sweep of lawns as in the faint gleam of silver from a distant lake, half hidden by the trees. It is to such a prospect that the eye dances in delight, demanding more."

Mr. Nichols went on to explain that dividing a garden in half affords gardeners the possibility of a secret garden—one not visible at first and all the more appealing for its seclusion.

Where roses are concerned, I heartily agree with Nichols, but not for identical reasons. I think that the ideal garden incorporates both a landscape section that includes roses among other flora and another plot devoted strictly to cutting. This means that bushes belong in one place and shrubs in another.

BUSHES

As much as I love Modern Roses, I reluctantly admit that I don't care to gaze at their bushes. Compared with shrubs of Heirloom Roses, most Modern rosebushes are awkward—an

*Good companion plants support each other in the landscape. Here, the sprawling Hybrid Perpetual **'Archiduchesse Élisabeth d'Autriche'** benefits from the sturdy growth habits of linaria and peonies but especially from the staunchly upright Moss rose **'Madame de la Roche-Lambert'**, growing just behind.*

insignificant fact when you consider that these varieties are grown not for the appearance of their plants but rather for their blossoms.

As long as Modern rosebushes are to be treated like bloom factories, I think they should be planted as such—in raised beds arranged in rows with paths in between that allow for easy access for maintenance and harvesting. How close together they're planted depends on the size of their mature bushes, which means that most Grandifloras and Hybrid Teas should be planted 3 feet apart from each other. Plants of Miniature roses and diminutive Floribundas can be placed more compactly, of course, but rarely closer together than 2 feet apart. Aggressive Floribundas such as 'Sea Pearl' should be treated like Grandifloras and Hybrid Teas and planted at 3-foot intervals.

Attention to color in cutting gardens need not be as studied as in the landscape, but you'll be happier if you devote certain thought to color compatibility. At least at the outset, try to keep color groups together. In time, of course, rules must be bent, especially when you run out of space and the planting of any new bush necessitates the removal of another. For instance, when you fall in love with a new mauve variety but the only spot you can bear creating it is where an orange rose presently grows, the new pairing is bound to displease you.

SHRUBS

While I believe that cutting gardens devoted exclusively to roses make sense, I think that landscapes devoted only to roses are dull. Roses are exalted in beauty when complemented by other flowers, especially by companions that grow lower than rosebushes do or by plants that blossom in colors roses don't, namely blue. Although most gardeners consider herbaceous borders sacred for what flourishes within them (restricting their choices to fleshy- rather than woody-stemmed plants) roses make fine additions to herbaceous borders, especially those varieties that mature into graceful shrubs.

When choosing a rose to fit in the landscape, after deciding which color you want, pay close attention to its reputed performance in areas near where you garden—not simply to how often it blooms but, more important, to the size it assumes at maturity. Although I offer general guidelines throughout this text regarding sizes to be expected from specific varieties, nothing beats local advice. While certain roses may disappoint you by not assuming the heft you dream of, nothing is more heartbreaking than a shrub that surpasses your expectations to the point that it must be removed. Judicious pruning helps, of course, but it's not the last word.

Remember, too, that not all roses are everblooming. If you spot a rose in late spring/early summer that wins your

When looking for a rose to border a gate, be sure to consider Ramblers like **'Goldfinch'**, *which doesn't have the gargantuan habits most Rambling roses do. Here, it's perfectly in scale.*

heart and decide that it must flourish in your garden, make certain that you ask about its bloom habits. If it's a one-timer, no amount of tender loving care will change that fact.

MONSTERS

Although several hybrid roses discussed in this text grow to be huge, their sizes pale in comparison to the dimensions attained by species roses. While there are numerous exceptions, the majority of species roses grow into monsters and become discontent if gardeners try to stifle their lofty aspirations.

Listen to what Graham Stuart Thomas says in *Shrub Roses of Today* about the appropriateness of species roses in the garden at large:

Species can easily predominate in a country garden of large size, but I feel they are not happily placed near the house. Putting it simply, I like a slight sense of orderliness and prefer my Hybrid Teas, my Floribundas, or my Old Roses fairly near the house; they are man-made and assort well with seats and paths, vegetable plots, formal lawns, and flower beds. At the other end of the scale are the species roses, breathing of fresh air and freedom and the wild countryside; appealing but not perhaps showy; of a beauty which needs other natural things around it in herbaceous or woody plants.

Above: Certain rose varieties not only make good standards, they also gracefully weep. In the lovely gardens of the Roseraie de l'Hay, the Rambling rose 'Excelsa' is used to perfection. Other roses that grow as modest ramblers or ground covers also weep naturally when grown as standards.

Left: Birch trees make fine garden backdrops, and because tree roses also tower above the ground, space is wide open for companion plants. Here, a hedge of R. ophiolepis attractively sets off standards of 'Cherish', a good Floribunda.

STANDARDS

As you'll recall, most commercially available rosebushes are actually two separate varieties grafted together at the bud union. The rootstock is the portion underground, and the hybrid is the portion growing above the bud union. In standards, a third variety is introduced between the two—a cane of rose wood along whose length nothing is intended to grow. Its sole purpose is to provide height for the hybrid growing on top.

Standards, which are often called tree roses, can be any height from 18 inches to 3 feet tall, even taller if custom budded. Standards are a landscaper's dream, especially as a means of squeezing in additional roses. Since their major growth will be carried so high, tree roses can be planted smack between mature bushes. Standards are also popular for lining walkways and paths, particularly when handsome, low-growing companions are planted at their feet.

Be careful when choosing rose varieties to grow as standards. Although theoretically any rose can be grown as a standard, aggressive varieties are ultimately disappointing—they become top-heavy, and overstaking looks crude. Roses that have a natural weeping growth habit, such as 'Excelsa' and 'Nozomi', are ideal, as are Miniatures and several Floribundas. Certain Hybrid Teas and Old garden roses also grow well as standards, particularly those that have compact growth habits. Keep in mind that any rose that towers

as a bush will behave in precisely the same manner as a standard.

COMPANION PLANTING

I've always admired people who have a natural design sense in the garden, because I don't.

Usually I choose companion plantings that weren't my idea but rather my version of what I saw and liked in someone else's garden. For instance, I've never visited Sissinghurst, the horticultural triumph of Vita Sackville-West (a British gardening daredevil who had an unerring flair for combining plants), without returning home with intentions of duplicating a tiny piece of that fabulous place.

Until 10 years ago, I had observed such talent only from afar. Then I began gardening with Robert Galyean and saw flair in action.

After establishing my rose ranch (which is nothing more than a glorified cutting garden), I finally turned my attention to landscaping with Heirloom Roses and asked Bob to help. Selecting the dowager roses was my responsibility; finding suitable companions for them was Bob's.

When he decided to feature orna-

Here at Garden Valley Ranch, Oenothera (commonly called Mexican evening primrose) is a workhorse of a companion plant for roses. Both the white and pink forms compete with shrub and climbing roses for floral profusion all summer long.

In Europe, clematises are irrevocably associated with roses. Good potential combinations are endless, but make sure the respective colors please you.

You don't have to have a garden the size of Sissinghurst if you want a section devoted to a color scheme. This diminutive white garden saluting Vita Sackville-West features the icy white 'Iceberg', Digitalis alba, and white dianthus and violas.

Roses are sitting ducks for comely companions. With 'Président de Sèze', a fine old Gallica, it's hard to go wrong. Although any flower ranging in shade from violet to silver-gray would work, it's difficult to imagine improving on this selection—Salvia pratensis.

Few climbing plants can match the vigor of R. banksia lutea, but wisteria can; what's more, it blooms at the same time. Keep in mind that they are both voracious growers.

Certain arrays of color look nice encircling shrub roses. Here, a pink beauty is nicely complemented by white lychnis and also by pink and purple linaria.

Well-chosen companions to roses sometimes tone down the latter's bright color. Here, the pink and carmine 'Magna Carta' benefits from plantings of campanula and lavender.

mental grasses among the shrubs of roses, I told him he was crazy. I remembered German gardens with a few grasses near roses, but grasses as a feature? Somehow I doubted that roses and grasses belonged together any more than wisteria and pineapples do. Besides, how could I allow 'Gold Band' pampas grass to grow behind my sophisticated butter-yellow English Rose 'Graham Thomas', or New Zealand flax at its feet?

Finally, I admitted that just because I had never seen roses and grasses flour-ishing side by side didn't mean that I wouldn't like the combination, and Bob planted what he knew was right all along. Now, of course, I could kick myself for not thinking of the golden pairing myself.

When our Antique Roses blossom, which most of them do only once each year, no one wonders what's planted beneath or beside them—all eyes fix on roses. Then, after about six weeks of glory, excitement subsides and people begin noticing that those rosebushes have leggy bottoms and foliage unwor-thy of scrutiny all summer. That's when ornamental grasses take over.

Because most ornamental grasses should be sheared to the ground in late winter (just before spring forces them to rise again), they're still short when once-blooming roses blossom. When the roses subside, as if on cue, grasses begin to stretch outward and upward, sending their shoots into openings among neigh-boring plants, often with complemen-tary effects.

Shrubs weren't the only roses that Bob introduced to companions like a

born matchmaker. We built a colonnade through the center of the garden with spaces for 42 climbing roses. I agonized for months over which roses they should be and finally decided to mix only six varieties—two deep pinks, two soft pinks, and two near-whites. Safe choices.

It was soon obvious that the limits I had placed on the number of rose varieties didn't faze Bob's number of accompanying clematises—he couldn't get his clematis selection below 20 varieties.

The number didn't bother me, but the range of colors did. How could it be correct to have the hot pink, deliciously perfumed Bourbon 'Zéphirine Drouhin' paired with the translucent white clematis 'John Huxtable' on one column and with the violet-blue 'Gypsy Queen' on another? The thought of star-shaped clematis blossoms next to informal blossoms of the buff-white Noisette rose 'Madame Alfred Carrière' was appealing, but wine red? I remembered the grasses and kept faith. You should see that colonnade in bloom!

The most beautiful display of roses and common plants I've ever seen is in Mottisfont Abbey, near Romsey in England's Hampshire County. Not only does the garden house the private rose collection of Graham Stuart Thomas, it's home to a breathtaking array of favored companions, such as campanula, daylily, iris, artemisia, and a host of salvias. In fact, in my opinion, the companions outshine the roses.

The specific plants you choose to companion your garden roses is, of course, a matter of taste. The assortment of choices is endless. Besides selecting plants in complementary colors and flattering heights, make certain that you investigate their preferences for water, remembering that roses are persistently thirsty. This constant need for irrigation poses real problems where herbs are concerned. Not only do herbs need less irrigation than roses do, if overwatered they won't bloom at all and their growth becomes rank or woody.

The irrigation pitfall is easy to avoid. If you encircle rosebushes with a band of flexible metal, you create a moist, fertile blanket from which water will not spread. Bands of aluminum sheet metal work well, especially those that are 6 inches wide. Form the rings equal to the drip lines, and then insert half of each ring's width underground. The 3 inches remaining aboveground provides a boundary from which moistened mulch will not leach. The most satisfactory herbs to cultivate outside the fertile field, as far as companions to roses are concerned, are lavender, rosemary, and salvia.

No matter how much you love them, certain plants should never grow right next to roses. Ground covers such as sweet woodruff could never tolerate so much sun, and shrubs such as azaleas and rhododendrons crave soil too acid for roses.

ROSES IN CONTAINERS

Roses adapt well to container culture as long as you keep in mind that the pots or boxes they grow in must be large enough to accommodate their roots and that containerized roses demand water more often than do those grown in the garden. Miniature roses, of course, are ideal because they're so compact, but so are the smaller members of most rose families from Gallicas to Hybrid Teas.

Climbing Roses

Roses don't climb naturally the way ivies and honeysuckles do, because they have no tendrils or air roots for attaching themselves to what they grow on. While evolutionists assure us that roses developed thorns not simply to ward off

predators but also to attach their branches onto tree limbs, these prickles don't suffice for security. So, before digging a hole to accommodate any rose that climbs, resolve that you must train it, at least during its formative years.

RAMBLERS, CLIMBERS, AND PILLARS

As already agreed, Rambling roses are those varieties that bloom only once each season. Ramblers have other distinguishing features, including pliable stems, vigorous growth, and the production of trusses of small flowers.

Climbers are distinguished from Ramblers by their ability to bloom repeatedly each season and also by more-rigid stems. Although there are exceptions, most Climbers are more modest than Ramblers in their growth habits, usually topping off at 10 feet. Several climbing roses produce one-to-a-stem blossoms as impressive as those of bush forms.

"Never plant a red rose next to a brick wall," many gardeners pledge. I happen to agree, believing that brick walls should be used to flatter yellow, white, or pastel climbing roses. In fact, I'd add pink to that axiom. Here, pretty as it is, this hybrid of the 'Anemone Rose' would look better against another color.

Wooden pergolas make fine hosts for climbing roses because canes train to wrap around both upright and horizontal wood. Depending on how you arch their limbs, climbing roses can be encouraged to bloom over an extended season.

Pillar roses are distinguished from Ramblers and Climbers simply by the manner in which they are trained—straight up. Although certain rose varieties seem as though they were hybridized specifically for vertical growth, several Rambling and Climbing roses are successfully grown as pillars.

SUPPORTS

If you've never tried cultivating climbing roses, begin with simple support structures such as tepees, tripods, and pyramids. All are easily constructed and durable, especially when fashioned from metal or pressure-treated wood set properly in the ground. Another advantage of these simple supports is that they can be placed anywhere in the garden—at the rear of flower borders or as specimens anywhere in a lawn.

A tepee is made from three supports anchored in the ground and tied together at the top. A tripod is a tepee that has been reinforced with crossbars. A pyramid is made from four reinforced poles.

Existing fences also provide convenient supports for experimenting with climbing roses. Although generally unsightly, chain-link fences are setups for training vining roses. Wooden fences work well, too, although it's a good idea to choose sturdy ones with a reasonable life expectancy (removing a contented mature climbing rose from a fence in

Nothing is more durable for roses to climb on than metal. Depending on whether you want one fabulous flush of bloom or several more modest ones, choose carefully among varieties. Once plants are mature, it will break your heart and back to remove happy climbers.

Many Antique rambling roses can be trained to engulf full archways; several varieties will do so in less than two years. Choose colors carefully, depending on the mood you want to create under your walkway. Here, hot-colored roses beckon visitors to a cool gray refuge.

*French gardeners are masters of garden architecture. Here, in the Roseraie d l'Hay, two colors of the dowager Rambler **'Dorothy Perkins'** festoon a towering monolith. In the background, **'Alexander Girault'** concludes his weighty show on intricate latticework.*

need of repair is a nasty experience). It's also wise to bear in mind that a mature climbing rose, especially one in full bloom, is weighty.

Walls also provide good support for climbing roses as long as they can support not only the weight of an established plant but also the metal hooks and eyes required for its training. If there are no convenient places for securing training wires, remember that an entire trellis can be con-

structed to fit against an existing wall.

While contemplating walls for supporting climbers, be certain to consider their color. Red brick walls, for instance, are poor choices for climbing red roses. Also, try to determine when a painted wall will next require repainting; the only job more aggravating than removing an established climber is trying to paint around it.

Finally, arches and pergolas are ideal supports for climbing roses, but

they, too, must be solidly constructed. Wooden pergolas and archways should be built with pressure-treated materials long enough to allow for 18-inch concrete footings.

No support for climbing roses intended for walking under should be shorter than 8 feet, and not simply for aesthetic reasons. Once they reach the top of their supports, climbing roses like to nod their blossoms. Walkways must also be sufficiently wide—at least 5 feet

Rambling roses blossom only once each season, but they flower over an extended period. This arbor of ramblers was all blossom three weeks earlier. Still, it's a blooming delight to walk under, and it will remain so for at least another month.

for strollers walking side by side among mature plants.

TRAINING

Except for tepees, tripods, and pyramids (inside which plants are centered), in order to allow for proper root development, climbing roses should be planted at least 16 inches from their support structures. Training should commence immediately after planting.

Never tie young growth with wire; it will inevitably cut the wood of expanding growth. Although I still despise its looks, I prefer green plastic tape. Not only will pending growth camouflage its presence, plastic tape expands as growth does. Also, in time—once growth is steadfast—training tape can be cut out entirely. Gardeners who refuse to employ unsightly plastic ties use twine or raffia, accepting that these materials don't stretch and require occasional loosening to prevent girdling rose canes.

When training a rose on a tepee, tripod, pyramid, trellis, or wire fence, ties can be made directly onto the structure. Fixing climbing plants to solid surfaces, however, requires providing something to tie to. Wires are ideal, but they should be stretched about 4 inches away from any flat surface to allow for air circulation, reducing diseases such as mildew. Guide wires should be strung at 12- to 18-inch intervals through eye hooks screwed into vertical supports.

In St. Albans, the headquarters for England's Royal National Rose Society, climbing roses are featured on pergolas with sturdy brick supports. In some cases, roses completely conceal the brick columns, blooming straight upward from their bases. Several varieties are accompanied by clematises, which rival and complement the roses.

Except for roses grown into vertical pillars, the goal in training climbing roses is to encourage as much horizontal growth as possible. If climbing rose shoots are allowed to grow straight up, a chemical inhibitor within plants prevents side buds from breaking into flowering shoots. Young stems bent sideways, on the other hand, produce fan-shaped growth patterns that produce bloom-bearing shoots along the entire length of stems.

Even roses grown as pillars benefit from lateral training. If, for instance, canes can be angled around a post (rather than tied staunchly upright), bloom potential is heightened. In fact, abundant blossoming on a pillar is best ensured by alternately braiding canes clockwise then counterclockwise around a vertical support. Alternatively, canes can be wound in only one direction, like a barber's pole.

ROSES IN TREES

If you've never seen a rose scrambling into a tree, you have quite a treat in store when you see a Rambling or Climbing rose in full bloom. Certain trees make better hosts than others, namely those that are sparsely foliated. Being deciduous helps, too, which is why apple trees are favorites. Never plant a climbing rose in an evergreen tree if you have any intentions of managing its growth at pruning time.

Because apples and roses are first cousins, apple trees appreciate cultural practices identical to those afforded rose-bushes, including water and fertilizer. Always keep in mind, however, that if you use noxious chemical sprays on your roses, you must treat the apples as Adam was instructed—forbidden fruit.

If you decide to plant a rose to grow up a tree, plant its bush at least 3 feet from the tree trunk to reduce root competition for water and nutrients. Early training must include sturdy training toward the tree trunk, including tying growth directly onto the tree trunk or along wooden stakes angled toward the tree. Once climbing roses reach lower tree branches, they'll train themselves as they climb ever upward in search of light. Then early staking ties can be removed. I have a collection of climbing China roses (Chinas accept considerable shade) planted in a grove of deciduous, native California willow trees. Because there is no longer evidence of tying, it appears that they were never trained. Early on, of course, they were.

One final tip: If your garden has a prevailing wind, plant climbing roses on that side of the tree in order to capitalize on breezes blowing new growth into, rather than away from, branches.

Roses are wonderful in trees, and not just when they reach the tops. This plant of the fabulous Noisette rose **'Alister Stella Gray'** *is just beginning its second year in the ground and has made it only one third of the way to the top of its host tree. Even so, it has no intentions of waiting any longer to blossom.*

EIGHTEEN

Roses Headed Down the Pike

Although I haven't yet got around to hybridizing, I'm intensely interested in the development of new roses for several reasons. First, I oversee an All-America Rose Selection test garden. As the official judge, I like to walk visitors through the test grounds and listen to what they have to say about varieties under trial. Although the final vote is mine, where this garden is concerned I can't help being swayed by their often savvy opinions. Second, I sell rose blossoms to the public and have learned the hard way that what I like isn't necessarily the answer to increased sales. Colors in roses come in and out of vogue the same way color phases in and out of decor. When I first began my rose venture, for instance, mauve and orange roses were hot; now I can't give them away. Finally, I'm ever on the lookout for roses that are foolproof to grow. When a new rose hits the market that doesn't contract diseases the way its similarly colored predecessors do, loyalty flies out the window.

As for trends in the world of new roses, I couldn't be happier—some terrific varieties are headed down the pike.

The rose named for the famous film actor and passionate rosarian, 'James Mason', looks for all the world like an ancient Gallica rose rather than the Modern Shrub rose it is. Rose breeders are hard at work mixing rose lineage to create roses for every taste—and, thankfully, smell.

*'**All That Jazz**', another landscape trophy winner, is vividly colored. Not only are petals bright coral, they seem even brighter because they surround thick clusters of golden yellow stamens. Plants are free-bloomers, and bushes are easy to prune into mounded shrubs or stylized borders.*

LANDSCAPE ROSES

I can't abide the thought of another person telling me that he or she doesn't grow roses because "they're too much trouble." I grew up with a mother who stated time and again that she had "no intention whatsoever of growing something that has more ailments named for it than any other flower."

For those of you as ornery as my mother, I have good news: Hybridizers are hard at work creating everblooming rose varieties that are not only revolutionary in their resistance to disease but also require only occasional pruning (some varieties not at all).

Rosedom is so thrilled over the development of these new beauties that no one has decreed what they should be called. Some people refer to them as Modern shrub roses—a name that probably won't stick because it's too easily confused with Heritage shrub roses. More likely, and my personal vote, these breakthroughs will be labeled "landscape roses."

The first landscape rose that made the gardening world take notice was 'Bonica', which I list among the immortal roses discussed in chapter 7. Four years after its debut, another landscape rose, 'Carefree Wonder', won the All-America title. It's more rounded than

'Bonica', decidedly disease resistant, and blessed with shocking pink blossoms whose petals have a creamy reverse. Now yet another landscape rose has made the All-America Selections list—'All That Jazz', which produces single, coral, fully petaled blossoms with golden yellow stamens.

Not all landscape roses are All-America, of course. Those in the Meidiland series, from the French House of Meilland (the same hybridizing clan that gave the world the 'Peace' rose), weren't even entered in the All-America trials, so eager were the hybridizers to show off their introductions. So far, six varieties with the surname of Meidiland have been introduced by color—white, pink, scarlet, red, pearl (blush pink), and Alba (white, and a terrific ground cover).

Some diehard enthusiasts of Modern Roses complain that the blooms of landscape roses don't display the high-pointed centers associated with prissy Hybrid Teas, but most gardeners consider this a small price to pay for such a trouble-free rosebush.

I think these newcomers might have even changed my mother's mind.

OLD FORMS, NEW HABITS

In an attempt to arbitrate the two main camps of rosarians (those who refuse to grow any roses but Heirloom varieties and those devoted to Modern hybrids), rose breeders are introducing new cultivars that often unite the best of both worlds. Peter Beales, for instance, crossed 'Scharlachglut' (a Shrub rose from the House of Kordes) with 'Tuscany Superb' (a Gallica) to produce 'James Mason' in 1982. If you weren't aware of its heritage, you'd swear that 'James Mason' was pure Gallica, except for its bush, of course, which grows to be 5 feet wide and almost as tall. Otherwise, blossoms reveal a strong Gallica heritage. Alas, the bush is not everblooming, although it is profuse in early summer.

David Austin, perhaps the greatest rose arbitrator of all time, experienced the same disappointing results when he launched his hybridizing career with 'Constance Spry', the result of marrying 'Belle Isis' (a Gallica) with 'Dainty Maid' (a Floribunda). Although 'Constance Spry' looked precisely like what Austin had in mind, she bloomed only once each year. Austin's subsequent crosses, of course, brought him the roses of his dreams—varieties that look like Heirloom Roses, but, like Modern hybrids, bloom repeatedly.

Those identical hybridizing platforms are making their way to American shores. With roses reaching All-America Selection test gardens, for example, an increasing number of roses appear that resemble their distant once-blooming ancestors but bloom repeatedly, as do their Modern parents. I see this trend throughout all categories—Hybrid Teas, Grandifloras, Floribundas, and landscape roses. Presently, there's a Miniature rose among those being considered for recognition in 1996 that looks for all the world like an Antique mini, except that it blooms throughout summer.

DISEASE RESISTANCE

As already mentioned, roses on trial for All-America consideration are judged for 15 separate qualities. One is disease resistance, and it seems to carry more weight than any other.

When I first planted my test garden, I cared for its bushes the same way I do those in my cutting field, including spraying them no less often than every 10 days. Consequently, they never contracted diseases. When I judged the roses for the first time, they all scored the same where disease resistance was concerned. Since it was apparent that I was making no contribution in evaluating this element, I began spraying the test roses only half as often as I did my own. I soon learned that that was all I had to do in order to spot those varieties prone to mildew, rust, or blackspot.

Although it would appear that disease resistance should be an isolated quality, it's not. When a rosebush contracts diseases, everything about it is affected—the overall appearance of its foliage, the form and shape of its buds and open blossoms, and certainly its overall flowering effect.

Hybridizers are rising to the challenge, with the introduction of new varieties that are easily twice as able as their predecessors to ward off common

rose ailments. I predict that it will only get better.

EASIER PRUNING

Since I'm not enamored of Miniature roses, when I finally consented to grow them at all (to satisfy the buying public), I resolved not to give them the care at pruning time that I afford roses with larger blossoms. Not only did I refuse to cut each stem as though it grew on a Hybrid Tea rosebush, I cut them with hedge clippers, with no regard for the distance between my cuts and a budding eye.

I didn't admit to my ruthless ways at first, preferring instead only to agree with visitors who commented on how nice it was that individual varieties of my Miniature roses grew at the same height. Now I learn that other gardeners had the same idea long before it hit me.

Britain's Royal National Rose Society has been experimenting with unconventional pruning techniques for more than three years at their official test garden at St. Albans, and not merely with Miniatures. A test program is under way on Hybrid Tea and Floribunda roses (England doesn't embrace the Grandiflora category) that compares

'Carefree Wonder' is the second landscape rose to walk away with an All-America Rose crown. It's showy indeed, with shocking pink petals that have a creamy reverse. Like other rose varieties hybridized with the landscape in mind, 'Carefree Wonder' is resistive to diseases and generally well tempered.

traditional pruning methods with "rough methods" (all stems cut to the same horizontal height), using pruning shears and hedge trimmers. So far, results are a virtual toss-up, except that the rough method "seems to give better short-term results than traditional pruning."

In an article by Royal National Rose Society secretary Ken Grapes, published in the August 1992 issue of *The American Rose*, the British researchers point out that traditional pruning methods have been favored because Modern Roses were for years plagued with dieback, the tendency for unproperly cut stems to "die back" to the place where a proper cut should have been made. Now, they say, "rose breeding has come a long way and many modern varieties don't suffer badly from the effects of dieback because they are so much more vigorous." Further, their trials "showed that rough pruning and hedgetrimmer pruning caused no more dieback than traditional pruning."

Leaving themselves an obvious out, the British experimenters go on to allow that "it is possible that roses which are roughly pruned may become overcrowded in the center and therefore more prone to diseases. Traditional pruning encourages the development of open-centered bushes. It may therefore be necessary to alternate between rough or hedgetrimmer pruning and traditional pruning."

I agree wholeheartedly with the last statement. Although you may see me

Roses of the future are not only resistive to diseases, they're also wondrously colored, many in patterns no one has seen before. Another bonus is occasional fragrance that's stronger than any preceding, similarly colored rose.

with hedge clippers near my beds of Miniature roses, presently you'll never catch me with power trimmers near my Hybrid Teas, Floribundas, or Grandifloras. Someday? Who knows.

FRAGRANCE

While everyone associates fragrance with roses, something went amiss when Modern varieties began appearing in bold new colors. The general public was so excited by roses in shades they never thought possible that they didn't seem to mind if fragrance was missing.

"I'll just mix this scentless beauty with some of my powerfully perfumed old-timers," gardeners must have said at the time. Recently, however, the buying public has put its foot down. More specifically, they sniff before they buy.

Once again, hybridizers pay attention.

Modern white roses, for instance, have never been long on perfume. Some were scented, of course, but fragrance seemed to be an added plus to a well-formed, long-stemmed white rose. Recently, perfume has crept back to its rightful place among white and off-white Modern Roses. 'White Lightnin'', for example, has an unmistakable lemon scent to its heady perfume, and the increasingly popular pure white 'Margaret Merril' is deliciously scented. On an optimistic note for the future, there's a pure white Hybrid Tea in the trials for 1996 recognition that's more fragrant than any pure white rose I've ever smelled.

COLOR

Since genetic engineers assure us that a blue rose is just around the corner, I've been asking people what they'll think of such a find.

"Oh, I don't expect to like a blue rose," most folks say, shaking their heads. "It's unnatural."

Natural or not, any fool would trade his left toe for a blue rose—it's worth a potential fortune. Worldwide, $25 billion is spent on cut flowers annually, one fifth of that on roses. Fancy blossoms sell for up to $10 per stem. A blue rose is predicted to fetch $20.

What worries me is not the marketability of a blue rose but rather its precise color. Excited over synthesizing delphinidin (the pigment in petunias that turns their petals blue), scientists are eager to transfer the gene to roses, but I've never seen a truly blue petunia, only deep lavender or bluish purple. It seems to me that researchers should be fiddling with delphiniums, morning glories, or lobelia—flowers that are unarguably blue.

I worry, too, that the blue darling might not hold its color, since even the gene isolators point out that delphinidin can go either red or blue depending on the pH of the soil in which plants grow. Red flowers like to sink the roots of their plants in alkaline soil, whereas plants that bloom blue prefer acidic conditions. Roses, however, have a decided preference for neutral soil. Would you care to alter the pH of an entire rose bed just to satisfy one of its inhabitants? Neither would I.

I believe the "blue" rose that these researchers first unearth will be no more than "bluish." Still, that's not all bad. Such a rose could then be turned over to rose hybridizers who will improve on its color or, at least, its performance.

Remember that when 'Sterling Silver' was introduced in 1957, the Modern Rose world went nuts. Not only was a Modern, everblooming rose truly mauve, it was also intensely fragrant. Alas, it was a pitiful performer. Still, it supplied pollen for a host of mauve roses that followed, not the least of which is 'Angel Face'.

So, let's cheer the arrival of our first blue rose, then drum our fingers waiting for the real thing. It will happen.

VASE LIFE

What thrills me more than the prospect of a blue rose, even one the color of lapis (which the smart money is on), is the second goal of plantsmen obsessed with genetic engineering: to extend the vase life of cut flowers. These clever fellows say that blossoms wither and die because of ethylene, a compound that shortens the life of cut blossoms. To halt the premature effects of ethylene, they claim, antisense compounds must be employed. Originally developed for medical applications, antisense compounds have already been proved to effectively prolong the vase life of carnations. Although the task will be tougher for woody-stemmed flowers such as roses (compared to herbaceous, fleshy-stemmed plants such as carnations), I'm sure they can bring it off. After all, if science can turn rose blossoms blue, it can surely prolong their lives.

EPILOGUE

Thanks to a friend who directs the Royal Horticultural Society's headquarters at Wisley, just outside London, I had the great privilege of meeting England's esteemed rosarian Graham Stuart Thomas. My friend took three of us to Thomas's home and on a short tour of his small garden. I was rather tongue-tied over meeting Mr. Thomas, but not so shy as to keep from discovering what I was dying to know.

I wanted to ask straight out if he had a favorite rose, but how could I be so crass? I rehearsed a speech admitting how dumb a question it was and how I personally hated such a query, but it was awkward and I was certain I'd never unravel my feeble rationale in sequence.

Sure enough, when I seized the moment for popping the question, words came out predictably garbled. I flubbed to the point of finally blurting, "Do you have a favorite rose?" The moment those artlessly phrased words tumbled out of my mouth, I wanted to apologize, then quickly turn and leave.

Maybe because he's such a gentleman, or perhaps due to having been through such pedestrian questioning before, Mr. Thomas didn't flinch. Quite the contrary, he kindly said, "I'm not certain it's my favorite rose, but I can't imagine a garden without 'Reine des Violettes'," then led us to its bush.

I was shocked. 'Reine des Violettes'! I grew the famous Hybrid Perpetual and admired its heritage, but a candidate for favor? Never.

I'm certain Mr. Thomas would be equally shocked to learn that 'Color Magic' is my favorite rose. To each his own.

I had a similar experience with a visitor to my garden who took a fancy to the Gallica rose 'Cardinal Richelieu', which I think one of the ugliest varieties in all rosedom. I've never seen a blossom of Richelieu whose color looked real. Worse yet, blooms turn a disgusting shade of brown before dropping their petals.

I can't tell you now why I had that bush, unless it was out of misguided "good form," or perhaps because I wanted to photograph it. In any case, there it was in all its horrid murky purple glory.

"Oh, I think that's the prettiest rose I've ever seen," my visitor said when she spotted the Cardinal.

"It's yours," I responded in tempo. "Come back in December and we'll dig it up." She did.

I've seen people swoon over roses that made me want to avert my eyes. Similarly, I've noticed eyeballs roll heavenward when I carry on over a bloom of 'Bewitched', 'Madame Hardy', 'Sea Pearl', 'Sombreuil', 'Pristine', or another of my pets.

Actually, specific favoritism over roses doesn't bother me, but narrow-minded generalities make me crazy. For instance, I have no time for those gardeners who think it's chic to grow only Old garden roses. "Oh, I wouldn't *think* of growing modern roses," many of them say, "they are so garishly colored." Garish, my foot. On the other hand, I know some Modern Rose enthusiasts who refuse to admit any Heirloom Rose to their garden "because they don't bloom enough." Bull.

When it comes to roses, just as with food, decor, clothing, movies, or anything else, it's all a matter of taste. Still, I'll never forgive Gertrude Stein for that damnable phrase, "A rose is a rose, is a rose."

Gertrude was dead wrong.

GLOSSARY

ALBA roses developed from a natural cross between the Damask rose *R. damascena bifera* and *R. canina,* a species native to Europe. Alba roses were once called tree roses because they often grow taller than 6 feet; they are also extremely hardy and tolerant of considerable shade. Most Alba roses blossom white or near-white and carry a strong perfume.

ANTHER. The pollen-bearing part of the stamen.

BALANCED FERTILIZER contains a balance of all three essential elements—nitrogen (N), phosphorus (P), and potassium (K).

BALLING. The refusal of rose blossoms to open fully because petals are damp and stuck together.

BAREROOT roses are winter-dormant plants sold with no soil around them. Bareroot bushes are graded according to specific standards of number of canes of specific height.

BASAL BREAK. A major new growth emanating from rosebushes at or just above the bud union.

BLIND GROWTH develops foliage but no new flowers.

BOSS. A bunch of stamens in the center of a blossom.

BOURBON roses developed on the Île de Bourbon from a natural cross of *R. chinensis* and *R. damascena.* Because of their graceful vigor, Bourbon roses make fine climbers and grow well on fences; they are also the first family of

Old garden roses for whom precise parentage was recorded. Blossoms vary in color from pure white to deep red; most are powerfully fragrant. Although no subsequent bloom flush ever rivals the first, many Bourbon roses flower sporadically throughout summer and modestly in fall.

BREAK. Any new cane or lateral growth originating from a bud eye.

BUD. An immature flower.

BUDDED roses are varieties of roses that have been grafted onto rootstock.

BUD EYE. The "eye" on the node of a stem; the red or green spot from which all new rose growth originates.

BUD UNION. The bulbous landmark that develops after a hybrid rose is grafted onto rootstock.

BUDWOOD. Fresh woody growth from a specific variety, intended for budding onto rootstock.

BUSH roses are those bushes with upright, often rigid growth habits that are praised for their remontancy rather than for their contribution to the landscape.

BUTTON EYE. A dense collection of aborted modified leaves at the center of a flower that gives the impression of a (usually green) button.

CALYX. The protective cover over rosebuds that later divides into five sepals.

CANDELABRA. An especially large (some-

times unmanageable as cut flowers) cluster of blossoms on a strong stem (often from a basal break).

CANE. A major stem on a rose plant from which lateral stems grow.

CENTIFOLIA roses are the result of complicated hybridity between at least four distinct species roses. Although it is uncertain how the original *R. centifolia* came into being, its family was developed extensively by the Dutch during the seventeenth century. Bushes of Centifolia roses are often lanky, and blossoms are globular, softly colored, heavily petaled, and richly perfumed.

CHINA roses are distinguished among Old garden roses primarily because of their ability to blossom recurrently each year. Blossoms of China roses have whimsical naive charm, and the bushes on which they occur have airy growth habits and sparse foliage. Because China roses are diploid, their chromosome structure made it difficult to mate them with other roses of the late eighteenth century.

CLIMBERS are climbing roses that blossom repeatedly each year.

CONSULTING ROSARIAN. A person so devoted to roses that he or she is deemed qualified to offer advice. A good consulting rosarian is worth his or her price in gold; nitpickers give roses a bad name.

CULTIVAR. A *culti*vated *var*iety with unique characteristics.

DAMASK roses are believed to originate from a natural cross between an unidentified Gallica rose and *R. phoenicea*, a species. Damask roses are lofty growers (often to heights greater than 5 feet), and foliage is generally gray-green, elongated, and downy. Blossoms are usually clear pink and powerfully fragrant.

DEADHEADING. The removal of spent blossoms.

DECORATIVE BLOSSOMS. Those with informal, not showy, shape.

DIEBACK. The progressive dying back of rose wood. Classically, dieback occurs when any rose wood is cut at the wrong place, after which stems start to die in a downward direction until the spot is reached where a proper cut should have been made. Rose wood need not always die in a downward direction, however; there is also dieup.

DIPLOID. A plant with two sets of chromosomes.

DISBUDDING. The early removal of buds to ensure that mature blossoms reach their greatest stage of beauty. For roses that look best one-to-a-stem, disbudding requires the removal of one or two small side buds. For roses best grown as sprays, disbudding requires the removal of the centermost, largest bud.

DOUBLE roses have more than 21 petals per bloom.

ENGLISH ROSES are those hybridized by David Austin, a rose breeder in Albrighton, England, whose dream it was to unite the best qualities of Heirloom Roses (Old Rose form and fragrance) with those of their Modern offspring (disease resistance and remontancy). He has succeeded.

FLORIBUNDA roses are hardy, disease resistant, and free-flowering Modern Roses that blossom in clusters rather than one-to-a-stem. Although generally praised for their contribution to the landscape at large, many Floribun-das also produce blossoms as shapely as those of any Modern Rose.

FLUSH. An intense period of blooming.

GALLICA roses, highly developed between the mid-seventeenth and nineteenth centuries, are the oldest distinct family of garden roses. The majority of Gallica roses blossom in strong colors, although often with subtle combinations of colors or distinct stripes; almost all are fragrant.

GRANDIFLORA roses began in 1954 with the variety 'Queen Elizabeth', the result of a cross between 'Charlotte Armstrong' (a Hybrid Tea) and 'Floradora' (a Floribunda). Grandiflora roses occur in sprays, as do Floribundas, but individual blossoms should be formed similarly to the Hybrid Tea.

GROUND-COVER roses are those varieties that grow prostrate along the ground, either hugging it or matting to 2-foot heights.

HEIRLOOM ROSES are the same as Antique or Old garden roses—those introduced before 1867.

HYBRID roses result from mating two separate rose species or varieties.

HYBRID MUSK roses began when a German nurseryman mated the species *R. multiflora* and 'Rêve d'Or', a Noisette. Soon after, an English clergyman named Pemberton (and various members of his staff) improved the family. The majority of Hybrid Musk roses mature into 5- to 6-foot shrubs that bloom profusely in early summer and modestly in autumn. Hybrid Musk roses have little to do with the true Musk rose except for their vague lineage via Noisette roses and a fragrance that embraces a musky quality in an otherwise sophisticated bouquet.

HYBRID PERPETUAL roses were hybridized during the mid-nineteenth century, when rose shows became popular. At the risk of clumsy plants, Hybrid Perpetual roses were bred for the elegant appearance of their bud and partly opened blossoms—the types that won ribbons. Although thousands were introduced into commerce, only a fraction remain. Most varieties of Hybrid Perpetual roses repeat-flower each year, but nowhere near so often as their Modern offspring.

HYBRID TEA roses began with the introduction of 'La France' in 1867. Although there is wide variation in color and bloom form among today's Hybrid Teas, classically buds are tall, high-centered, and as shapely as possible. The "Hybrid" portion of the name refers to hybridizers' efforts to mix rose lineage and come up with something new. "Tea" refers to the fact that these roses are descended from the Tea rose, which originated in China. Also, the fragrance of Hybrid Teas is thought to be similar to that of tea leaves (more accurately, the wooden crate in which bags of tea were stored). Although many Hybrid Teas flower in clusters, most gardeners think of them as one-to-a-stem. All bloom throughout summer.

IMBRICATED PETALS are piled one on top of another. Rose blossoms with this many individual petals usually divide their bloom into quarters before they finish aging, at which point button eyes become conspicuous.

INFLORESCENCE. A cluster of one or more sprays of florets.

MINIATURE roses are diminutive versions of other rose varieties. Once, the plants of miniature roses were supposed to fit under a teacup. Now, "minis" (as they're called) grow on shrubs, too.

MODERN ROSES are hybrid roses, introduced to commerce after 1867.

MOSS roses resulted from a sport of a Centifolia rose. Although Moss roses appeared as early as the late seventeenth century, they weren't developed until the second half of the nineteenth century, when they were bred extensively from multiple parentage. The sizes of bushes on which Moss roses grow vary widely, as do the colors of blossoms. "Mossing" results from the formation of conspicuous glandular mosslike growth on stems, calyxes, sepals, and even foliage.

NODE. The point of attachment of leaves to stems.

NOISETTE roses were begun by John Champney, a rice farmer in South Carolina, probably from a cross between one of the original China stud rose and an unidentified Musk rose. Later the Noisette brothers improved the family by introducing Tea roses as parents. Eventually, Noisette roses became famous for freely producing fragrant, softly colored, silky blossoms, albeit on tender bushes. Most varieties of Noisettes are most famous as climbers rather than as shrubs.

OLD ROSE blossoms are those that are cupped or shaped like a rosette rather than with a high, pointed center. Old Roses are sometimes separated from Modern Roses by a date—1867—the year in which 'La France', the first Hybrid Tea rose, was hybridized. When speaking of Old Roses, the terms "Heirloom" and "Old garden rose" are often substituted.

OWN-ROOT roses are those grown from cuttings rather than budded onto rootstock.

PH. The number on a 14-point scale that indicates the relative acidity or alkalinity of a soil sample. A pH of 7.0 is neutral; higher numbers are for alkaline soil, lower for acidic. The ideal pH for roses is near 6.5 (slightly acidic).

PISTIL. The female organ of a flower, including the stigma, style, and ovary.

POLLEN PARENT. The male parent of a hybridized rose.

POLYANTHA roses originally resulted from a cross between the species *R. multiflora* and the China stud rose 'Old Blush'. Subsequent crosses produced roses with clusters of fragile blossoms on tough-growing, short bushes. Although Polyantha roses are resented for their lack of fragrance, they're praised for their trouble-free, free-blooming bushes.

PORTLAND roses emerged after the Duchess of Portland sent a rose imported from Italy that bloomed all summer to the hybridizing staff at Malmaison. French breeders developed a family that is characterized by upright, mid-height shrubs that produce dense foliage and shapely, short-stemmed blossoms.

RAMBLERS are climbing roses that bloom once each year.

REMONTANT. The ability to blossom continuously throughout a season. The term "remontancy" is used interchangeably with "repeat flowering," "recurrent flowering," and "perpetual flowering."

ROOTSTOCK. The rose variety onto which other rose varieties are budded. Hopefully, the rootstock remains underground, and only the hybrid budded above grows above ground.

RUGOSA roses are descendants from *R. rugosa*, a particularly hardy species rose that flourished in northern China, Korea, and Japan more than 3,000 years ago. Although recent Rugosa hybrids are modest growers, like their ancestor, most possess unusually sturdy growth habits and flourish in poor soil even when neglected. Some varieties require little or no pruning; many are intensely fragrant; most produce hefty crops of hips, often while shrubs are still in bloom.

SEEDLING roses grow from seeds harvested from a rose hip, whether naturally crossed or hybridized.

SEMIDOUBLE roses have between 10 and 20 petals per bloom.

SEPAL. One of five divisions of the calyx, resembling bracket-shaped, individual leaves that lend architectural support to the bloom held above them.

SHRUB roses differ from rosebushes in gracefulness. Whereas most Modern bushes are bred for their ability to repeat-flower, shrubs are for the garden at large. Shrub roses are not only easy to grow, many varieties also grow gracefully naturally. Although the majority of shrub roses in commerce bloom throughout summer, some blossom only once.

SINGLE roses have between 5 and 12 petals.

SPECIES roses are wild roses.

SPORT. A spontaneous rose mutation that results in new colors or growth habits of an existing variety with no assist from mankind. A rosebush with white blossoms, for instance, may suddenly bloom deep red along one stem. Or a rose that supposedly grows only as a shrub suddenly starts to climb.

STAMEN. The male organ of a flower, composed of the pollen-producing anther and filament.

STIGMA. The tip of the pistil.

SUCKER GROWTH grows from rootstock rather than from the hybrid budded above. Blossoms of rootstock are rarely pretty, although roses such as *R. chinensis* produce nice flowers. Sucker growth should be eliminated from plants as soon as it's indisputably recognized.

SYSTEMIC fertilizers, insecticides, and miticides are absorbed directly into plants through foliage or roots.

TEA roses originated from crosses of Bourbon and Noisette roses with two of the original stud roses from China. Although Tea roses' bushes lack vigor and hardiness, many gardeners believe that their lovely blossoms handily compensate for all such deterrents.

TETRAPLOID. A plant with four sets of chromosomes.

UPRIGHT rosebushes are those that grow sternly vertically.

SOURCES

UNITED STATES

Antique Rose Emporium
Rt. 5, Box 143
Brenham, TX 77833
409-936-9051
800-441-0002
Heirloom and Shrub roses.

Jackson & Perkins
1 Rose Lane
Medford, OR 97501-0701
800-292-4769
Wide selection of varieties growing on virus-free rootstock.

Edmund's Roses
6235 S.W. Kahle Rd.
Wilsonville, OR 97070
503-682-1476
Fax: 503-682-1275
Modern roses

Garden Valley Ranch Nursery
498 Pepper Rd.
Petaluma, CA 94952
707-795-0919
Fax: 707-792-0349
Wide selection.

Greenmantle Nursery
3010 Ettersburg Rd.
Garberville, CA 95440
707-986-7504
Heirloom roses.

High Country Rosarium
1717 Downing at Park Ave.
Denver, CO 80218
303-832-4026
Winter hardy roses.

Heirloom Old Garden Roses
24062 Riverside Dr. N.E.
St. Paul, OR 97137
503-538-1576
Own-root roses.

Lowe's Own Root Rose Nursery
6 Sheffield Rd.
Nashua, NH 03062
603-888-2214
Own-root roses.

NorEast Miniature Roses
P.O. Box 307
58 Hammond St.
Rowley, MA 01969
508-948-7964
800-426-6485
Fax: 508-948-5487
or
P.O. Box 473
Ontario, CA 91762
800-426-6485
714-984-2223
Fax: 714-986-9875

Roses of Yesterday and Today
802 Brown's Valley Rd.
Watsonville, CA 95076
408-724-2755
Fax: 408-724-1408
Heirloom roses.

Sequoia Nursery
2519 E. Noble Ave.
Visalia, CA 93277
209-732-0190
Minis and Ralph Moore varieties

Tiny Petals Nursery
489 Milnot Ave.
Chula Vista, CA 91910
619-422-0385
Miniature roses.

Wayside Gardens
1 Garden Lane
Hodges, SC 29695
800-845-1124
Generalists.

CANADA

Hortico, Inc.
Robson Road, RR 1
Waterdown
Ontario, Canada LOR 2H1
416-689-6984
Fax: 416-689-6566

Pickering Nurseries, Inc.
670 Kingston Rd., Hwy. 2
Pickering
Ontario, Canada L1V 1A6
416-839-2111

ENGLAND

David Austin Roses
Bowling Green Lane
Albrighton
Wolverhampton WV7 3HB
England

Peter Beales Roses
Attleborough
Norfolk NR17 1AY
England

AUSTRALIA

The Perfumed Garden Pty Ltd.
47 Rendelsham Avenue
Mt. Eliza, 3930
Australia

NEW ZEALAND

Trevor Griffiths & Sons Ltd.
No. 3 R.D.
Timaru
New Zealand

SOUTH AFRICA

Ludwigs Roses C.C.
P.O. Box 28165
Sunnyside
Pretoria 0132
South Africa

INDEX